The Process
of Composition

Second Edition _____

The Process of Composition

JOY M. REID
Colorado State University

PRENTICE HALL, Englewood Cliffs, New Jersey 07632

Library of Congress Cataloging-in-Publication Data

Reid, Joy M.
    The process of composition.

    Includes index.
        1. English language—Composition and exercises.
2. English language—Study and teaching—Foreign
speakers.   I. Title.
PE1413.R37 1987   808'.042   87-13938
ISBN 0-13-723065-6

Editorial/production supervision:
   Martha Masterson and Joseph O'Donnell, Jr.
Cover design: Karolina Harris
Manufacturing buyer: Margaret Rizzi

 ©1988, 1982 by Prentice-Hall, Inc.
A Division of Simon & Schuster
Englewood Cliffs, New Jersey 07632

Printed in the United States of America

10 9 8 7 6 5 4 3 2 1

ISBN 0-13-723065-6   01

Prentice-Hall International (UK) Limited, *London*
Prentice-Hall of Australia Pty. Limited, *Sydney*
Prentice-Hall Canada Inc., *Toronto*
Prentice-Hall Hispanoamericana, S.A., *Mexico*
Prentice-Hall of India Private Limited, *New Delhi*
Prentice-Hall of Japan, Inc., *Tokyo*
Prentice-Hall of Southeast Asia Pte. Ltd., *Singapore*
Editora Prentice-Hall do Brasil, Ltda., *Rio de Janeiro*

Contents

Preface   xi

1   The Fundamentals of Writing   1

Objectives of the Course 1
The Audience 2
Showing and Telling 3
General and Specific 6
The Paragraph 8
Subject and Topic 8
The Topic Sentence 9
Writing the Topic Sentence 11
The Point Paragraph 12
The Process of Writing a Paragraph 14

2   Developing and Supporting Ideas   17

Developing Ideas 17
Supporting Techniques 23
Methods of Development 30

3 Planning the Essay   42

Selecting a Topic   43
Abstract and Concrete Topics   44
Title of the Essay   45
Organizing a Topic   45
Prewriting   45
The Thesis Statement   48
Paragraph Relationships   51
Essay Outlining   52
Complete Body Paragraph Outlining   56
The Introduction   57
The Body   60
The Conclusion   60

4 Drafting and Revising the Essay   68

Coherence Devices   69
Transitions   70
Paragraph Hooks   75
Revision of Drafts   79
Peer Revision   82
Editing   82
Student Samples of the Essay   83

5 Persuasion and the Argumentation Essay   88

Introduction   88
Goals of Persuasion   89
Reliability of the Writer   90
Planning the Argumentative Essay   91
Generating Material   95
Logical Fallacies   99
Student Samples of Argumentative Essays   103

6 Summary and Analysis   109

Introduction   109
Writing a Summary   110
Planning an Analysis   113
Student Responses   118
Alternative Summary-Analysis Forms   123

7   Introduction to the Research Paper   128

Selecting a Topic   129
General Format of the Research Paper   133
Going to the Library   135
Identifying Descriptors   137
Library Etiquette   138
Field-Specific Formats for Research Papers   139

8   Library Research   143

Using the Card Catalog   144
Using Periodicals: Indexing and Abstracting Journals   146
Identifying and Locating Periodicals   154
Other Research Sources   156
Using Library Materials   161

9   Writing the Research Paper   165

Documentation   165
References   171
Twelve Common Problems (and Solutions) Encountered
   by Student Researchers   174
Student Samples   176

10   Grammatical Explanations and Exercises   195

Verb Problems   195
Sentence Structure and Punctuation Problems   200
Sentence Combining   211
Diction   214
Editing   220

Appendix   224

The Resume   224
Business Letter Writing   230

Index   233

Student Essays

Expository Essays

Childhood in War and Peace   65
  Eva Szymanska (Poland)
Reunion of Korean Kin   83
  Se Yeong Hamm (Korea)
Coffeehouses in Turkey   85
  Jamal Asaad (Saudi Arabia)

Argumentative Essays

The Effect of the U.S. Foreign Policy in Vietnam   103
  Van Tran (South Vietnam)
The Necessity of Korean Foreign Language Education
  for Korean-American Children   106
  Sung Sik Pak (Korea)

Analysis Essays

The Dangers of Television   118
  Harriet B. Fidler (U.S.)
Should a Woman Work Outside the Home?   124
  Mohammed Akade Osman (Sudan)

Preface: Second Edition

When Prentice Hall invited me to do a second edition of *The Process of Composition,* I was delighted. Like many textbook writers, I had begun to collect advice, suggestions, and additional materials even while the book was in press. Moreover, since the first edition was published, ESL composition has flowered; much research and many textbooks have expanded teachers' options and students' opportunities.

The major revisions in *The Process of Composition* reflect both native and non-native speaker composition research, as well as years of feedback from teachers and students. The changes involve function rather than form; the fundamentals of the book remain the same. Briefly, the revisions involved the following:

1. The first chapters have been shortened, principally because *The Process of Paragraph Writing* (Reid and Lindstrom, Prentice Hall, 1985) covers the paragraph in great detail.

2. The middle section has been expanded, primarily with student-generated exercises and samples that will assist teachers and students; thus, the essay becomes the major focus of the textbook. The chapter on Argumentation and the one on Response to Written Material have been reversed; students suggested that change.

3. The research paper section has been completely rewritten and refocused, the better to emphasize more specific research strategies for academic students; student samples of the various parts of a research paper have been annotated for easier teaching and learning.

4. The grammar/sentence structure section and the appendix remain essentially unchanged; the inside front and back covers contain important composing strategies and revision processes that will now be more easily accessible.

Otherwise, *The Process of Composition* remains the advanced level ESL writing text of the first edition, which was based on the following assumptions:

1. No composition book is perfect for every class and every teacher. Therefore, this book covers the fundamental techniques and methods of composition, yet the format allows the teacher to insert additional exercises and assignments that are both class-specific and provide for individual teacher emphasis. This flexibility should give the experienced teacher a focus for materials and the newer teacher a foundation on which to build.

2. Academic writing has specific formats that are *expected* by academic readers. Many ESL students (like many native speaker/writers) have little or no concept of these formats. These students need to learn acceptable forms of academic prose.

3. Composition students in general, and ESL students in particular, need to spend more time practicing writing than reading about theories of writing. To that end, this book presents material in a concise form, more outline than text, more workbook than textbook.

4. Advanced ESL students are pre-university adults who will be subject to the academic and cultural expectations of an American university. In order to function with professors and with U.S. students, ESL students in advanced writing must understand the importance of written English and the necessity of individual commitment to learning the skills. To reach this goal, this book requires students to select their own topics, that is, to write about what they know, and the assignments require the students to make the course personally relevant.

Overall Structure of the Course

The first weeks of the course review basic paragraph writing: writing for an audience, the qualities of a paragraph, selection of a topic, generation of ideas through a variety of prewriting strategies, supporting techniques, and methods of development.

In following weeks, the students apply what they have learned to the writing of essays; the paragraphs they have learned to write during the first weeks have the same structure as body paragraphs in essays. In addition, they incorporate and expand the process of paragraph writing: prewriting, rough-draft construction, revision, and the final draft. In this section, students concentrate on expository, argumentative, and analytic prose.

Finally, in a continuing spiral, the students finish the last weeks of the course by writing a research paper, either on a topic from their major fields or on a topic that interests them. During these weeks, they learn about library research: the *Readers' Guide,* indexing and abstracting journals, and other research and reference materials. They also apply their knowledge of writing essays in selecting, organizing, and writing the research paper, using citation techniques from their major fields.

In order to prepare the students for university writing, *The Process of Composition* is organized so that the most basic processes in writing—selection, the topic sentence, supporting techniques, and methods of development—are presented three times in the major sections of the book: the paragraph, the essay, and the research paper. This spiraling technique enables the students to practice the basic processes again and again in increasingly complex contexts and thereby avoids the motivation problems involved in simple repetition. For additional reinforcement in these processes, the students are required to *revise* each assignment. In some cases, the students are asked not only to revise but also to lengthen and to rewrite assignments. In each assignment, the basic processes are stressed, so the students have sufficient opportunity to produce and polish the format.

Some sections of *The Process of Composition* are optional; short modules on such skills as writing resumes and business letters, doing sentence combining, and even learning to use basic reference materials can be used or not, depending on the needs of the students and the priorities of the teacher. These options offer the teacher flexibility in planning the course and structuring individual projects or assignments.

Concentration in the course is on academic writing skills. While the techniques used in description and narration (physical detail, illustration, personal experience) are fundamental to all good writing, they are presented in *The Process of Composition* as supporting techniques for exposition and argumentation, the rhetorical modes most often used in university writing. Students are assigned expository paragraphs and essays (explaining topics of their choice to a specific audience), argumentative essays (persuading an audience that an opinion about a controversy is valid), and summary/response essays (evaluating written material for an audience).

Because the course is based on academic writing, it is based on principles of composition rather than on grammatical structures. Naturally, ESL students, even at the advanced level, continue to have grammatical weaknesses. *The Process of Composition* deals with grammar problems that are specifically related to writing: punctuation, sentence structure, verb-tense agreement, prepositions, and so forth. But because the book concentrates on the process of writing, grammatical explanations and exercises focus only on those problems that are directly related to the *production* of written English. These explanations are in a separate section so that they can be used individually as class needs become evident. The grammar section, then, can often be presented as part of the *revising* process.

In order to produce students who can function in a university class, controlled writing as such is not used in *The Process of Composition;* however, the students are taught to write according to a nearly mathematical set of rules, to write in a very specific format, according to a formula. Each paragraph begins with a topic sentence; the four to eight sentences that follow are supporting sentences that explain, define, clarify, or illustrate the topic sentence. Both the introduction and the conclusion have specific forms and several techniques from which the students must choose. While this prescriptive, even arbitrary, formula may seem artificial and unnatural to the ESL students at first, the overall structure of the paragraph or essay teaches the students a method of writing that is acceptable to the majority of university professors. If, later in their university careers, the ESL students submit a paper that is not mechanically perfect, which has second language errors not familiar to the professor, at least the format will be understandable, and the student will have a better chance of communicating.

The ultimate goal of such an approach is that the students will finish the advanced ESL class in writing with knowledge of the format of most university assignments and with the confidence that they can *construct* an essay (a critique, a report of research, a term paper) if they know the necessary material. The analogy is with word roots and affixes in vocabulary building: If the students can see some logic in the formation of the language, their confidence in being able to produce the language increases.

Finally, in keeping with the philosophy of having students read as little as possible, the writing samples in *The Process of Composition* are short, limited in number, and consist of student writing by both native and ESL speakers. The samples are about topics that students consider relevant and are written in language that students can understand. Moreover, they are viable: The students have models they are *able* to imitate.

Finally, I write textbooks for students and teacher's manuals for teachers. The teacher's manual for *The Process of Composition* includes a suggested syllabus, techniques for teaching, additional exercises, explanations and answers to exercises, and suggestions for approaching the material. For a *free* copy of the Teacher's Manual, write Prentice Hall, Englewood Cliffs, New Jersey 07632.

Acknowledgments

My thanks to my colleagues Peggy Lindstrom, Katie Knox, and Leslie Noone for their suggestions; to former TAs Maryann O'Brien (now administrating the Language and Culture Program at the University of Houston), Jim Griswold (now a geologist in New Hampshire), Linda Stratton (now teaching in the Peace Corps in Mali), Mark Mancosky (now working in Vail), Judy Solanki (now teaching at Lewis and Clark), and Dave Tyler (now teaching in Kuwait); to Tony Lueck, Betty Hacker, Jan Gilligan, Evelyn Haynes, and Barbara

Burns for their assistance with the library module; to Martha Pennington (University of Hawaii), Margie Swindler (University of Missouri), Ilona Leki (University of Tennessee), Lin Grissith (Glendale Community College), and Mark Sawyer (International University of Japan) for their careful reviews of manuscript and textbook; to Pam Kirshen and Brenda White, Andy Roney and Ben Greensfelder of Prentice Hall for their encouragement; to the many students whose written work I have used; and especially to Steve, Shelley, and Michael, who persevered.

J.M.R.

The Process
of Composition

1

The Fundamentals of Writing

Objectives of the Course

This is a course in essay writing. That implies that you must master certain skills that will enable you to write competent university essays. You must understand and be able to produce the techniques by which academic writers communicate to academic audiences. At the end of the course, you will be able to demonstrate a command of the following skills:

1. Prewriting: think before writing
    A. Understand the assignment
    B. Choose a subject that you are interested in
    C. Narrow the subject so that it can be adequately covered within the limits of the assignment
    D. Collect ideas
    E. Consider the audience
2. Organization: write straightforward prose
    A. Begin and end the paper clearly
    B. Write a thesis statement of opinion and/or intent
    C. Move smoothly from one paragraph to another
3. Development: support ideas
    A. Use specific details to explain general ideas
    B. Use facts, examples, physical description, and personal experience to develop ideas

4. Revision: look again, change and strengthen
   A. Reconsider the needs of the audience
   B. Reconsider the purpose(s) of the paper
5. Grammar and mechanics
   A. Use language with precision
   B. Avoid common errors of grammar and sentence structure
   C. Strengthen writing through editing

The Audience

Two essential rules for this course are

1. Write about what you know.
2. Always write for an audience.

The audience is an essential concept for all writers. Writers choose their subjects and their methods of presenting material (diction, sentence structure, organization) according to who will read the finished product.

In order to communicate successfully, to write essays that have interest and value, you must decide

A. Who you are: a student? a son or daughter? an expert?
B. Who your audience is: classmates? parents? the admissions officer?

Your decisions about who you are and who your audience is will determine

A. What you write: what does your audience know? what are the interests, the needs, and the expectations of your audience? what does your audience *not* know? what might your audience want to know? what do you know that you can communicate to your audience?
B. How you write: will you use short sentences and simple language? will you use sophisticated concepts and terms? will you use charts or photographs?

Audience Expectations

Suppose you went to a movie titled *First Love.* You sat in the theater expecting . . . two young people, beautiful scenery, romantic music. Instead, during the first three minutes of the film, you saw five brutal murders, unspeakable violence, and terror. How would you feel? Confused? Angry? Would you leave the theater? Or ask for your money back?

Suppose you took a trip to Hawaii; you expected . . . sunny weather, warm temperatures, a peaceful ocean. Instead, a hurricane occurred; the weather was rainy, windy, and cold for your entire trip. How would you feel? Disappointed? Frustrated? Would you leave Hawaii before your vacation was finished?

Suppose you bought a book for a beginning biology course at your university. You began to read the first chapter, expecting ... basic concepts, clear explanations, and simple language. Instead, the pages contain terms and diagrams that a graduate student in biology would have difficulty understanding. How would you feel? Puzzled? Resentful? Would you drop the course?

All audiences have expectations. U.S. professors also have expectations; when they make writing assignments (essays, laboratory reports, research papers), they *expect* their students to write in very specific ways. If a student does not fulfill the expectations of the professor, the results could be confusion, frustration (and a lower grade on the paper!).

Many native speakers of English are familiar with the expectations of U.S. professors. One of your major objectives in this class will be to discover those expectations and to learn how to fulfill them.

_____ EXERCISE 1A _____

1. Write a paragraph about "How I Spent Last Saturday." Think about your audience. Your selection of ideas will be different if you write:
   A. a letter to your grandmother
   B. a memo to your advisor
   C. a note to your best friend
2. Write a paragraph describing a tree for the following three audiences:
   A. an elementary school child
   B. your class
   C. a professor of botany
3. You have been gambling in Las Vegas and have lost all the money you were going to use to go to the university this semester. Write a letter to two of the people listed below. The goal of this letter is to obtain the money necessary for school. NOTE: Truth need not be a part of this letter.
   A. the political leader of your country
   B. the university financial aid officer
   C. your rich grandfather
   D. the head of the CIA

Showing and Telling

In the paragraphs below, students wrote about their mothers. The information in these paragraphs demonstrates the differences between

SHOWING	TELLING
(Demonstrating)	(Asserting)

Simply telling your reader what you want to communicate may be easy, but it is rarely very interesting or even very believable. In order to *support* your statements, you will need to use specific details and examples. In other words, showing your reader that what you have presented is valid will make your essay more interesting and more believable.

Read the sample paragraphs. Which sentences in each paragraph simply *tell* about the mother? Which sentences *show*—that is, which sentences contain specific details and examples about the mother? In addition, which sentences discuss the mother? Do some sentences tell about the writer instead?

It started nineteen years ago when she brought me into the world. Maw gave me the best care any child could have gotten. She has taught me more than any teacher in school and is overflowing with love. Always understanding and easy to communicate with and there when needed. She's the best: my "Maw."

Mom is a gray-haired lady of about 72 years. She is very sweet when she wants to be and very difficult when she puts her mind to it. I had to teach her how to drive at the age of 50, and the only safe place to teach her was in a wheat field. She is a determined lady; for example, when I was teaching her to drive she backed up the car until it boiled, but she did learn how to back. She has more trouble now keeping her stories in correct order and true. I love my mother more as I grow older. I realize some of the things she had to go through to raise me.

An essay on my mother you said, and I began thinking what to write. I just realized that it's possible that I don't truly know my mother, or at least not as well as I'd thought. She's about an inch shorter than I am and we look very much alike. Both of us have a spreading hip problem. My mom's always there. She's easy to talk to and I like hearing her opinions. I really admire her because she went back to school a few years ago and now is teaching in an elementary school. She really loves her job and the children. She also has plenty of time to keep up just about everything else that she did before working. Now that my brothers and sisters and I are older and more on our own I'm very glad that my mother's the way she is. She has accepted the fact that we have lives of our own, and she is going on living hers. My father has also benefited from this. They really make a good team.

My mom can handle just about anything that life can throw at her. Usually she's the most excitable person in our house. I just can't imagine what it would be like without her. Except that I would feel as though some great knowledge had been torn from my own self.

My mother was born in the Federal Republic of Germany in 1918. She grew up in the Bavarian Alps and lived there until her family moved to the city of Marlsruhe which lies near the Black Forest, along the Rhine River. Just prior to World War II, my mother married my father and I came along in 1939. In 1945, after the war and after my father had been killed in action, my mother met and married my stepfather and travelled with him to the United States to live with him and me in California where she still resides.

The following paragraphs were written by students in response to an assignment to write a paragraph about their names. The students tried to *show,* by using factual information, details, and examples, what their names meant. Are there specific details in the paragraphs? What makes each paragraph interesting? What details are *memorable?*

My complete name is Lili Margarite Chan Gonzalez. My first name, Lili, was the name of a ballet dancer. She was my grandfather's fiancée. They never got married because one night after her show she was killed with a knife in the street where she used to live. In my country most of my friends call me Lilian because they say that Lili is a diminutive of Lilian. My second name is the name of a flower and also the name of a saint. In the Catholic religion, our second name must have a Catholic meaning. Chan, my third name, is a Chinese name. I really don't know anything about it. My real last name is Gonzalez, and it is a very common Spanish name.

Lili Gonzalez
(Brazil)

My full name is Adel Addeb Ali Hassan Ali Ebram O'hide Salamah Faraq Al-Hadad. These ten names are my name plus my father's and my grandfather's from my father's side. It is a custom in Arabia that every child has to be called by his father's side. My family name is supposed to be Al-Hadad, but for some reason my sixth grandfather was famous, so his sons and grandsons took his name to be a family name. All of these names are Arabian. As it is everywhere, one name has been repeated, maybe because it was common during that time.

Of course, I just use three of these names at school, and in most of my daily life I just like to be called by my first name, Adel. Besides that point, we have another habit of calling the child Mohammed when he is born for the first seven days. So actually I would have twenty names if we add Mohammed before each of my other names, as it is common to do back home. I remember all of these names because it is believed that we should be proud of our grandfathers.

Adel Salamah
(Saudi Arabia)

My name is Sin Sing Chiu, Henry. Anyone who looks at my first and second name will be puzzled by the meanings that they convey in the English language. The two words seem to indicate that I have committed so many crimes that I have come to "sing" them out. However, Sin Sing have completely different meanings in the Chinese language. In my family, every male generation is assigned a definite first name; mine happened to be Sin, which means "kind" in Chinese. The second name is given by my grandfather. He thinks that kindness should be widespread over the lands and seas. It is for this reason that I have received the name Sing which means "voice." Chiu is my last name, and I am proud of it, because it is one of the names of the dynasties in China, and it includes a very large family. We even have generation books dated back to our great-great-great grandfathers. My English name, Henry, was chosen by my brother; it is for convenience that I have adopted this name. Since my Chinese name is not very easy to say, I can be remembered by my English name.

Henry Chiu
(Hong Kong)

_____ EXERCISE 1B _____

1. *Write a paragraph about your name. Use the process for paragraph writing on pp. 14–15.*
2. *Exchange paragraphs with a classmate. Use the checklist on p. 16 to analyze your classmate's paragraph.*

General and Specific

In writing a paragraph you will need to know the difference between a general idea and a specific detail. Between the two, many levels may exist. In the examples below, each word is more specific than the word above it. That is, each of the subsets is *subordinate* to the word above it. You indicate this sub-ordination by *indenting* the word.

solar system
  planets
    earth
      North America
        United States
          Colorado
            Fort Collins
              Colorado State University
                a classroom

essay
  paragraph
    sentence
      word
        syllable
          letter

tree
  trunk
    branch
      twig
        leaf

In the examples below, each general word is followed by several more specific words. All of the more specific words are equally specific; that is, each is on the same level of generality. This means that each of the more specific words is a *coordinate* of the word before it. Notice that a more specific word can become a general word.

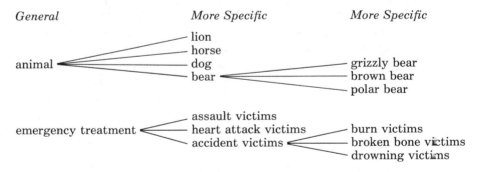

General   *More Specific*   *More Specific*

animal — lion, horse, dog, bear — grizzly bear, brown bear, polar bear

emergency treatment — assault victims, heart attack victims, accident victims — burn victims, broken bone victims, drowning victims

In the examples below, each general sentence is made more specific.

1. *General:* Airlines transport people all over the world.
   Specific: United Airlines has daily flights from Denver to New York City and London.
2. *General:* Foreign students often have adjustment problems in the United States.
   Specific: Morella has trouble understanding her American roommate.

Choose two of the following general words. Write a general sentence about each word, and then write a more specific sentence about each word.

1. fish
2. hospital
3. transportation
4. movies
5. flowers

Make specific statements from the general statements below.

1. People who play sports sometimes get hurt.
2. National parks are crowded during the summer months.
3. Learning a second language is difficult.
4. Gardening can be fun.

The Paragraph

A paragraph is a series of sentences that develop <u>one idea</u>. In U.S. academic prose, that idea is usually stated in a general form in one sentence, called the <u>topic sentence</u>. That sentence tells your audience what to expect in the paragraph. The rest of the sentences in the paragraph provide the reader with specific explanation or proof (evidence, support) of the general topic sentence. The supporting sentences help the reader understand more clearly what the writer means; they show that the topic sentence is valid.

Of course, a reader does not have to agree with your topic sentence. But if your paragraph is complete, the information should show the reader that your point of view is worthwhile and clear.

Subject and Topic

SUBJECT: A general area of interest

    A. Sports
    B. World Travel
    C. Education

TOPIC: A subject that has been narrowed so that it can be covered thoroughly. How narrow a topic is depends on the assignment.

Narrowing a subject to a topic can be compared to a wide-angle camera lens that zooms in to focus on a single small flower. By *focusing* your attention on a small part of the subject, you can narrow the subject to a restricted area that you can cover in depth rather than superficially. In the examples below, the subjects have been narrowed.

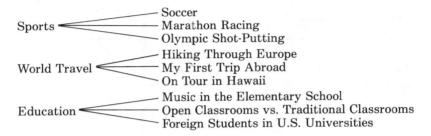

Sports
— Soccer
— Marathon Racing
— Olympic Shot-Putting

World Travel
— Hiking Through Europe
— My First Trip Abroad
— On Tour in Hawaii

Education
— Music in the Elementary School
— Open Classrooms vs. Traditional Classrooms
— Foreign Students in U.S. Universities

Further narrowing of a topic can make the resulting paragraph even more interesting to the audience because a narrow topic forces the writer to be *more specific*, to *show* by example, fact, physical description, and personal experience rather than simply to *tell*.

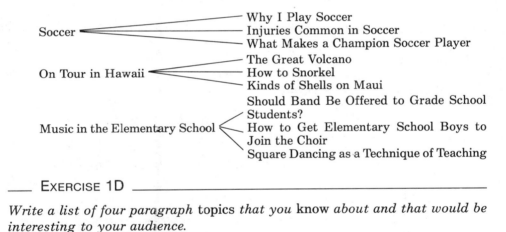

Soccer
— Why I Play Soccer
— Injuries Common in Soccer
— What Makes a Champion Soccer Player

On Tour in Hawaii
— The Great Volcano
— How to Snorkel
— Kinds of Shells on Maui

Music in the Elementary School
— Should Band Be Offered to Grade School Students?
— How to Get Elementary School Boys to Join the Choir
— Square Dancing as a Technique of Teaching

___ EXERCISE 1D _____

Write a list of four paragraph topics that you know about and that would be interesting to your audience.

The Topic Sentence

For every topic, you can write several different paragraphs. Each of these paragraphs will have a *topic sentence* that will

    A. Introduce the topic in the paragraph
    B. Be the most *general* sentence in the paragraph
    C. Be the most *important* sentence in the paragraph
    D. Contain *controlling ideas* that the following sentences in the paragraph will

1. explain
2. define   } that is, the sentence
3. clarify   will *support* or *prove*
4. illustrate   } the topic sentence

Note: A controlling idea is a word or phrase that the reader can ask questions about: How? Why? In what ways? What does that mean?

In the sentences below, the controlling ideas are circled, and the questions a reader could ask follow that topic sentence:

1. It is very (difficult) to be (alone) in a (foreign country.)

    Why? In what ways?

2. There are several (unusual superstitions) in my (country) about (death.)

    What are they? Why are they unusual?

3. The most (serious problem in higher education) in Venezuela is the (growing number of students) who (fail courses several times.)

    Why is the problem so serious? How many students fail? What exactly makes this situation a problem?

4. Most (people) have the (wrong idea) about the (definition of statistics.)

    What is the wrong idea? What is the right definition?

___ EXERCISE 1E _____

In the topic sentences below, circle the controlling ideas. Then write specific questions that the paragraph following each topic sentence might answer.

1. There are differences in shape, color, and taste between the two most popular varieties of dates in Saudi Arabia.

    Questions: _____

2. One of the most recent technical advances in the use of water is the development of hydroelectric power.

    Questions: _____

3. The creativity of the preschool child can be developed with special activities.

    Questions: _____

4. Violence in the sport of hockey is destroying the quality of the game.

    Questions: _____

Writing the Topic Sentence

1. A topic sentence *cannot* be a simple statement of fact because in a fact there are no *controlling ideas* that need *development.* Examples of facts that are *not* topic sentences:

    A. *You can buy these socks at K-Mart for $1.98.*
    B. *We celebrate Christmas on December 25.*

2. Weaker topic sentences are often simple personal opinion; the controlling idea in "I like" or "I think" is difficult to support. Examples of simple statements of opinion that are weak topic sentences:

    A. *I can't help liking this book.*
    B. *I like dogs better than cats.*
    C. *It is my opinion that smoking causes cancer.*

3. A successful topic sentence usually contains an *opinion* that will be proved or supported in the paragraph, or a *statement of intent* that the writer will explain in detail in the paragraph. Examples of topic sentences that have an opinion or a statement of intent:

    A. *Snakes make <u>better</u> pets than dogs or cats.*
    B. *Smoking <u>can cause</u> genetic defects in an unborn child.*
    C. *Marathon racing is <u>good</u> for the soul as well as for the body.*
    D. *To see Europe on a <u>mere</u> $10 a day, try hiking.*
    E. *Building a room that utilizes passive solar energy <u>can reduce</u> heating costs.*

____ EXERCISE 1F _____

Choose three of the following subjects. Narrow each to a topic you could write a paragraph about. Then write a topic sentence for each topic.

computers	censorship	advertising	agriculture
horses	electronics	nuclear power	jewelry
botany	newspapers	adult education	dormitories
skiing	sports cars	revolution	space travel

The Point Paragraph

Each paragraph you write will contain a topic sentence and four to eight sentences that will *support* the topic sentence. These supporting sentences will be more specific than the topic sentence. Notice that the more specific ideas are indented. A diagram of a balanced, detailed paragraph looks like this:

TOPIC SENTENCE (CONTROLLING IDEAS)
   A POINT NUMBER ONE
     1
     2 } SPECIFIC DETAILS
   B POINT NUMBER TWO
     1
     2 } SPECIFIC DETAILS
   C POINT NUMBER THREE
     1
     2 } SPECIFIC DETAILS
CONCLUDING SENTENCE

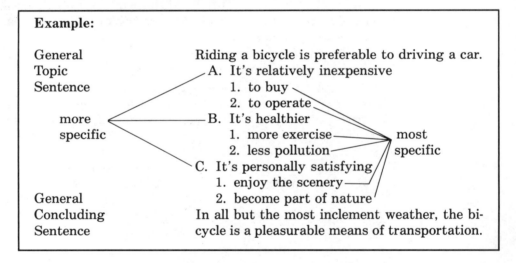

Example:

General Topic Sentence — Riding a bicycle is preferable to driving a car.
more specific
A. It's relatively inexpensive
   1. to buy
   2. to operate
B. It's healthier
   1. more exercise — most specific
   2. less pollution
C. It's personally satisfying
   1. enjoy the scenery
   2. become part of nature
General Concluding Sentence — In all but the most inclement weather, the bicycle is a pleasurable means of transportation.

Resulting paragraph:

Riding a bicycle is preferable to driving a car. First of all, a bicycle is relatively inexpensive to buy and to maintain. While a car may cost thousands of dollars to buy and hundreds of dollars annually, a good bicycle will cost only a hundred dollars or so, and its annual maintenance cost is very small. Biking is also healthier; not only does the biker get more physical exercise than the driver, but bicycles are nonpolluting. The consequence is a person with strong legs and a strong heart whose bicycle helps keep the environment clean. Finally, bicycling is, unlike driving, personally satisfying. Instead of being a robot inside a machine, the biker pedals along, enjoying the scenery, becoming a part of nature. In all but the most inclement weather, the bicycle is a pleasurable means of transportation.

Michele Eastman
(U.S.)

____ EXERCISE 1G ____

Read the two paragraphs below. Then outline each paragraph according to the format for the point paragraph outline given on page 12.

1. *Write the topic sentence of each paragraph. Circle the controlling ideas in each topic sentence.*
2. *List the two to four main points given in each paragraph.*
3. *Under each main point, list the specific details used to support each point.*

In the minds of many people, the octopus is considered an animal of hell, a devil-fish; however, for me this strange creature has amazing powers. First, the octopus has excellent, humanlike eyesight; the eyes, like those of vertebrates, have lids, irises, crystalline lenses, and retinas. When a predator appears, the orange-brown eyes, which are mobile and so can be turned in different directions, flash in the sea like the sun in the sky. Similarly amazing is the octopus's facility for changing shape. Generally its favorite hiding place is a small cavity in a rock; the octopus, usually a round marine animal, can make itself entirely flat like an envelope or it can stretch itself like India rubber in order to enter the small crevice. This remarkable animal can also transform itself by changing color: white, black, and even red! The agents for these color changes are the chromatophores, the color cells; the octopus has two different kinds of cells, one for the dark colors and another for the light ones. Why does the octopus have all these transforming abilities? Because he has lost the protective shell of his ancestors and must therefore have alternative ways to survive in the sea.

Annick Burkhalter
(Switzerland)

It is hard for foreign student wives to be able to make many American friends since most of their husbands go to school full time while they have to stay at home taking care of the children and the house. This situation makes it almost impossible for them to go out often and meet people. Furthermore, most of the foreign wives don't speak English at all when they first come here, and this keeps them from having a conversation with an English speaker. Finally, foreign students usually live in student housing, and generally the Americans who live there go to school. In many cases, even if only the husband is going to school, the American wife will be working. Consequently, the American couple does not have time to socialize, and the foreign student wives have very few American friends.

Carmen Ortiz
(Venezuela)

The Process of Writing a Paragraph

1. Choose a subject that you know about.
   Example: Studying Abroad

2. Identify your audience
   Example: Classmates

3. Narrow your subject to a topic that will interest your audience.
   Examples: Advantages and Disadvantages of Being a University Student in the United States

   $\vee$

   Problems of Living Alone While Studying at a University in the United States

   $\vee$

   Most Serious Problem of Living Alone While Studying at a University in the United States

4. Collect some ideas about your topic.
   Examples: Having to clean the apartment
   No one to wake me up in the morning
   Having to shop and cook for myself
   Missing classes because I don't keep a regular schedule
   Spending my money too quickly
   Having to do the laundry
   Loneliness
   Don't get my studying completed—no one to discipline me

5. List details about some of your ideas that will interest your audience.
   Examples: waking up: late for class, never time for breakfast
   housework: wastes time, looks nice when finished
   loneliness: homesick, no American friends

6. Limit the ideas to the most important ones you want to communicate.

   Example: housework ⎫
         or   ⎬ choose one → housework
     loneliness ⎭

7. State the main idea of the paragraph in your topic sentence.

   Example: Since I began (living in an apartment) and going to school, (my biggest problem) has been (the housework.)
              controlling ideas

8. The Point Paragraph

   Since becoming a student at a university in the United States, the most serious problem of living alone has been my housework.
   - A. Cleaning the apartment
     1. Takes away from my studies
     2. Makes the apartment look nice
   - B. Shopping for food
     1. Don't know the English names
     2. Spend time asking for help
   - C. Cooking my food
     1. Food uncooked or overcooked
     2. Sometimes made incorrectly
   - D. Doing my laundry
     1. Far away—wastes time
     2. Instructions are complicated
     3. Have to sit with the women

   If I did not have to do these jobs, I would have many more hours to concentrate on my studies.

9. Write the paragraph, using the details you have listed.

Since I began living in an apartment and going to school, my biggest problem has been the housework. Cleaning the apartment is not too bad; although it takes time away from my studies, at least when I finish the apartment looks nice. Shopping for my food is more difficult because I don't know the English names of many foods, and often I have to spend extra time asking for help. Cooking my food is a bigger problem. I have never had to cook before, and usually the results are discouraging. Sometimes the food is burned, sometimes it is not cooked enough, and sometimes I have not measured correctly, so the food tastes terrible. The worst problem is doing my laundry. The laundromat is far from my apartment, and I waste much valuable time. I also have trouble with the complicated instructions, so occasionally I end up with pink socks or a shirt that is too small. Mostly I am embarrassed as I sit in the laundromat with all the women, and so I wait until all my clothes are dirty before I do this horrible task. If I did not have to do these jobs, I would have many more hours to concentrate on my studies.

Jeong-Shwu Liu
(Taiwan)

_____ EXERCISE 1H _____

1. Use the subject "*The Advantages and Disadvantages of Being a University Student in the United States.*" *Follow the steps given in the process above to decide on a topic, narrow the topic for your audience, and develop ideas for your topic. Then make a point paragraph outline and write the paragraph.*

2. *Exchange paragraphs with a classmate. Use the checklist below to analyze the paragraph.*

REVISION CHECKLIST

A. *Is the paragraph about* <u>one idea?</u> *What is that idea?*
B. *Underline the topic sentence. Circle the controlling ideas.*
C. *What questions do you expect will be answered in the paragraph?*
D. *Does the paragraph communicate successfully?*
E. *What is the best part of the paragraph? Why?*

2

Developing
and Supporting Ideas

The sentences that you select to support the topic sentence of your paragraph depend on

the audience;
the purpose of the paragraph.

As you write a paragraph, you should ask yourself:

1. Which technique would best support my topic sentence?
2. Which technique would best convince my audience that my topic sentence is valid?

Developing Ideas

Most student writers agree that *telling* is easier than *showing*. Developing detail to explain and support an idea is often a time-consuming task. Fortunately, there are several strategies that student writers have found successful in generating details.

Look at the paragraphs below. Each student writer has used a different planning and generating strategy to write a successful paragraph.

Topic { Generally, there are many words that mean "to eat" in Thai culture but one should know how to use them correctly.

Body {

To eat →
- SA-WOEL — King's family
- { RUP-PRA-TARN
  RUP-TARN — General and polite
  TARN
- CHANT } — Monk
- KIN → — General

—The word sa-woel is a particular one for the monarch's family only.
—If you want to serve some meal to the monks, you're supposed to say *chant,* a meal which is designated for the monks.
—In general one will use *rup-pra-tarn* or *rup-tarn* or *tarn* for everyone. These words mean to eat in terms of politeness.
—If you want to talk with anybody who is close to you and easy, you also can use the word *kin.*

However, there are a lot more local words to mean "to eat" which is dependent on each section of the country.

TO EAT

Generally there are several words that mean "to eat" in Thai culture, but one should know how to use them correctly. Thailand is one of a few countries in the world that has a monarch system. To show our respect to the king's family, we always use some special words when we want to discuss them. For instance, the word *SA-WOEL* is a particular one that means "to eat" for royalty. In terms of Buddhism, we also have lots of words for the monks. The word *CHANT* means "to eat" for them. We will only use it if we want to invite the monks to have a meal. In addition, the Thais will say *RUB-PRA-TARN* or *RUB-TARN* or *TARN* which are polite ways of saying "to eat." We also use the word *KIN* to ask anyone to eat who is close to us, such as our family or friends. There are a lot more local words that mean "to eat" that depend on the part of the country.

Chakan Theerasatiankul
(Thailand)

We have several discrimin(ate) slang terms for a sir
get married until in her late 20's in Japanese. In Japar
creasing, and the marriageable age is going to be high;
women still try to get married (until) 25 years old; other·
by the discriminate words. First, "old Miss" is the most widespro
is a title used before the name of an unmarried woman, but in Japanese it me
a young unmarried woman, hence, a single woman who is not young is called
"old Miss." Second, (urenokori) is also a discrimin(ate) word for unmarried woman. The original meaning is the unsold thing like a woman who is left on the
shelf. Finally, Christmas cake" is a metaphor for a woman who can't get married
until her late 20's [because] near the Christmas thousands of Christmas cakes
are displayed in the stores, but they are never sold out and become old and go
staple.

SLANG TERMS FOR A SINGLE WOMAN

We have several discriminatory slang terms in Japanese for a woman who
doesn't get married until her late twenties. In Japan, the number of career wom-
en is increasing and the marriageable age is getting older; however, many women
still try to get married before they are twenty-five years old. Otherwise, they are
often hurt by embarrassing labels. First, an older unmarried woman may be called
an "old miss," the most widespread slang word. Every Japanese person knows
that noun. "Miss" is a title used before the name of an unmarried woman in
English, but in Japanese it means a *young* unmarried woman, so a single woman
who is not young is called an "old miss." Another discriminatory word is *urenokori*. The original meaning is "an unsold thing," and it means a woman who
has been left on the shelf. Finally, the term "Christmas cake" has the same meaning. Like the leftover Christmas cakes that grow old and stale after the Christmas season has passed, the older single woman is labeled in this derogatory
manner. In Japan, getting married is more important for a woman than having
a job and being independent, so many discriminatory words for an unmarried
woman exist.

Kaori Tomisawa
(Japan)

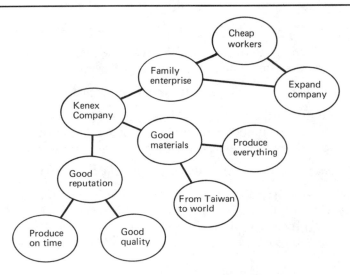

THE KENEX COMPANY

There are three reasons that the Kenex Tennis Company is so successful in Taiwan. First, the company was started as a family enterprise. The family all worked, so they saved a lot of money in salaries. That money allowed them to expand the company rapidly. Second, the Kenex Company buys good raw materials, so the products—tennis shoes, tennis balls, tennis racquets—are high quality. That makes their products marketable all over the world because the company has a good reputation. They produce on time, and they deliver their products quickly and efficiently. For these reasons, I believe that the Kenex Company will grow even bigger and better in the future.

Mickey Chyu Kwang-Jim
(Taiwan (R.O.C.))

Generating Strategy #4: **OUTLINING**

HOW I PREPARED TO COME TO THE U.S.

In a refugee camp—wrote letters to countries

A. Immigration interview
    1. difficult to complete history
        (a) very young
        (b) couldn't remember
    2. frightened

    B. Waiting
    C. Immigration called
        1. found parents for me
        2. arranged my trip
    D. Worrying
        1. about my English
        2. about my new family
Arrived—nice family

HOW I PREPARED TO COME TO THE U.S.

In 1980, I spent two years in a refugee camp in Thailand, and I decided to write letters to all the countries in the world, asking them if they would accept me into their country. Finally, the Immigration Office of the United States interviewed me. That test was very difficult for me because I had to complete a history about my parents, my family, and my relatives. Since I was very young, I didn't remember very much about my relatives and my family. After my interview, I waited for a response. I knew that the Immigration Office would decide whether or not I should come to the U.S. I waited for about four months; then they called my name, and they made a photograph for my passport. I was so excited about the trip, but during that time I was worried, too, because I didn't speak English, and I wondered who my new parents would be. I didn't prepare anything for my trip because I didn't know I was going to go to the U.S. until the last minute. When I arrived, my new parents made me feel welcome in their home. They are very friendly and happy all the time.

Farid Soeu
(Cambodia)

Generating Strategy #5: TREEING

TELEVISION ADVERTISEMENTS IN INDONESIA AND IN THE U.S.

Although television advertisements in both Indonesia and the United States have the same goal (to attract people to buy products), there are many differences between advertisements in the two countries. In Indonesia, the government has the authority to control the items advertised, and they also control the time those advertisements are presented. Generally, the items advertised are for the basic needs of the people, such as food, clothing, and housing, or for their well-being, such as medical treatment, transportation, and family planning. These ads are presented in half-hour periods. For example, food items are advertised at 6:30 P.M., just before the national news, while advertisements for family plan-

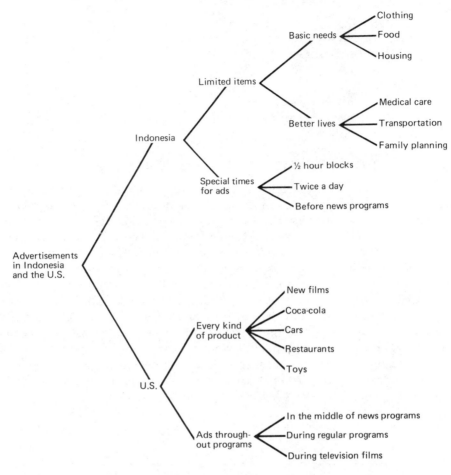

ning are broadcast from 8:30 to 9 P.M., just before the international news. In contrast, U.S. advertisements are not controlled by the government, and the advertisements are broadcast throughout the 24-hour programming day. Every kind of product is advertised, from restaurants to automobiles, and from vacation places to new films. These advertisements occur for about twenty minutes of every hour, but they usually appear for two or three minutes every ten minutes. In the middle of a news program, for example, we can see a two-minute advertisement for dishwashing detergent or Coca-Cola; during a television film, we can see advertisements for vitamins or children's toys. In conclusion, the differences between advertisements in the United States and in Indonesia are probably due to the government control of advertisements in Indonesia.

I. R. Sutadi
(Indonesia)

SUBJECT: *Automobile Accidents (causes/effects)*

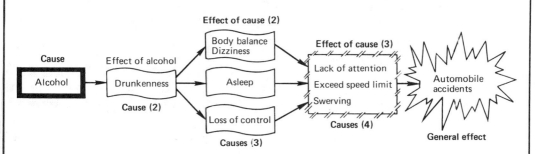

AUTOMOBILE ACCIDENTS

The majority of automobile accidents result from alcohol. A person who has drunk too much beer gets into a strange state called drunkenness. This state is marked either by an unpleasant feeling of loss of balance, or by falling asleep. Either of these problems is dangerous for drivers. On the road, a drunk driver is too dizzy to pay attention to traffic signs, and his lack of control may lead him to run a Stop sign, exceed the speed limit, or swerve his car. As a result, he may either hit another car or a person. It is very likely that he will crash his car, and often he will kill or injure himself and others. Therefore, the government has established stricter laws against drunk drivers.

Komba Elukessu
(Nigeria)

____ EXERCISE 2A _____

Look at the topics you selected for Exercise 1E. Choose one of those topics. Using one of the generating strategies demonstrated above, develop some ideas and details for your topic.

Supporting Techniques

There are several general purposes for writing:

> to explain or educate
> to entertain or amuse
> to persuade or convince

After you have identified your audience and your purpose for writing, you will decide on the supporting techniques you will use to achieve your purpose. Usually your decision will be based on the details you have generated:

Have you outlined *facts?*
Have you brainstormed from *personal experience?*
Have you made clusters of *examples?*
Have you listed details of *physical description?*

Remember: you can use more than one supporting technique in your paragraph. You might, for example, use a <u>physical description</u> of a <u>personal experience</u>, or you might use <u>facts</u> in an <u>example</u>.

Facts

The following paragraphs are developed by facts: numbers, statistics, and other pieces of information that can easily be verified.

Based on the Recommended Daily Allowances set by the National Food and Nutrition Board, the basic fast-food meal in America provides adequate protein. The meals from McDonald's, Burger Chef, and Wendy's—hamburger, french fries, and milkshake—provide more than two-thirds of the 56 grams of protein recommended per day for an adult male: 38 to 45 grams. However, half of a ten-inch pizza from Pizza Hut was the protein champion. When ordered with cheese, sausage, mushrooms, pepperoni, onions, and green peppers, it provides 72 grams of protein and also contains less fat than any of the other meals. The least amount of protein is in a fish sandwich, fries, and cola meal from Arthur Treacher's Fish and Chips, but its 22 grams are still adequate.

Jay Johnson
(U.S.)

During the ten-year period from 1968 to 1978, the economy of Korea grew by an impressive annual growth rate. This remarkable progress, often referred to as the "Miracle of the Han River," has been achieved despite the country's lack of natural resources and the worldwide oil crisis of 1973–1974. To put it concretely, GNP (Gross National Product) increased by ten times, and per capita income rose from $100 in the first year to $1200 last year. Korea's export growth during the same period especially aroused the attention of both developed and developing nations. For example, Korea shipped only $50 million worth of goods to foreign markets in 1968, but by 1978 the exports increased 300 times to $15 billion. In fact, Korea is now one of the biggest exporters in the world and the world's top exporter of consumer electronic products, textile garments, plywood, footwear, cement, and ships.

Jooh Lee
(Korea)

—— EXERCISE 2B ——

1. Underline the topic sentences in the paragraphs above and circle the controlling ideas.
2. What are the *facts* given in the paragraphs?
3. Are the paragraphs complete? Is the information in each of the paragraphs sufficient for the reader to understand the topic sentence and to think that the topic sentence is valid?
4. Choose one paragraph and make a point outline for it.

Note: Using *facts* to support a topic sentence requires that the writer be certain that the facts are accurate and relevant; using an authoritative source for your facts can make your support more believable to your reader. In the paragraphs above, what authoritative sources are mentioned?

Physical Description

The five senses—sight, hearing, smell, taste, and touch—offer writers a source of detail about the world around them.

1. Sight: shape—round, square, flat
            color—red, blue, green
            light—bright, dark
2. Sound: quality—clear or muffled, loud or soft
3. Smell: quality—sharp, sweet, clean, fresh
            effect—suffocating, intoxicating
4. Taste: quality—bitter, flat, sweet, sour
5. Touch: texture—smooth, rough, sharp, dull
            temperature—hot, cold, lukewarm
            weight—heavy, light

Writers can also compare one sense with another to communicate impressions to the reader.

1. Sight: The fat lady looked exactly like a beach ball in that multi-colored cape.
2. Sound: As we sat in the house trailer, we thought the heavy rain sounded like a thousand ping-pong balls as it fell on the tin roof.
3. Smell: In the humid summer the dirty apartment smelled like a dead goat.
4. Taste: The strange fruit tasted like a sour cucumber.
5. Touch: The kitten licked my hand; her tongue felt like sandpaper.

___ EXERCISE 2C _____

Read the paragraphs below. Underline the topic sentence in each paragraph. Circle the words or phrases of physical description.

Once I went hiking with a group from my school to the mountains near Riyadh. Before we started the hike, the sunlight was shining brightly. When we went into the woods it was quite dark like the sun was no longer in the sky. We felt that we were walking in hallways because the trees were so big and tall that they prevented sunlight from coming through. It was absolutely quiet and silent like a sad and grim night. In the distance we heard some birds cackling and some turkeys gobbling as if they didn't want us to be in this place. Also small brooks were bubbling here and there. Although the weather was extremely hot, the water of the brooks was almost too cold to touch. After hiking four miles, we became exceedingly tired. We felt that we had accomplished a great journey.

Shams Othman
(Saudi Arabia)

MY FAVORITE PLACE

The best place for me to forget all my worries is under a palm tree at dusk. When I am worried about a problem or just want to be alone, I will go to the beach around six in the afternoon and sit in the shade of a palm tree. The sand is a little hard to sit on, but this does not bother me. As the wind blows like a whistle, and the waves become softer as they reach the shore, the air will have a slight smell of the sea. The pelicans pass by in groups of seven before they disappear behind the horizon. Others float on the water, hoping to catch a fish before leaving. As time passes, there is an immense silence; the sun begins to descend, and the sky changes from tones of dark blue to canary yellow and finally to deep orange. As the sun slips below the horizon, I leave behind my worries.

Luana Pereira
(Venezuela)

Note: Using *physical description* to support a topic sentence requires that writers be precise in their choice of words. Using the right word to describe or explain a point will affect your readers' responses as well as their understanding. Successful written communication is based on word choice. A general or vague term will often confuse rather than clarify the point. To practice *precision in diction*, and to expand your vocabulary

1. Use a dictionary to check the exact denotation, i.e., the meaning of the word you want to use.
2. Use a *thesaurus* (a dictionary of synonyms) that not only gives the synonyms of words, but also gives information concerning the different *shades* of meaning.

___ EXERCISE 2D _____

Examine each of the following sets of words. Decide whether the synonyms have a positive or negative connotation. Which words have masculine or feminine connotations? Which words are formal? Which are colloquial?

A. Intelligent: clever, smart, shrewd, ingenious, knowing
B. Love: admire, cherish, approve, idolize, respect
C. Distasteful: repugnant, repellent, abhorrent, obnoxious
D. Pale: pallid, ashen, wan

What connotations (associative responses) do these words hold for you?

A. red
B. Mary
C. politician
D. New York City
E. capitalist

Supporting a topic sentence by the use of examples often makes a general statement understandable on a more concrete level.

How many examples are enough? In the first paragraph below, a single typical example, with many details, is sufficient. In the second paragraph, several examples with fewer details support the topic sentence effectively.

The assumption that children of divorced parents prefer to remain with their mother, and indeed that the mother wants them, may sometimes be false. For instance, one divorced man exhausted the courts, the lawyers, his finances, and himself while attempting to regain custody of his four children. The mother had been an alcoholic and had shown little interest in the children's welfare even prior to the divorce, yet it was not until the children reached their teens that their custody was reconsidered. The drug and truancy problems of these youngsters were brought to the attention of the juvenile judge, who discovered that they had been unhappy at home for some time. Their love for their mother had long since disappeared, and they asked to be placed with their father, so after seven years the custody error was rectified. Undoubtedly, there are many similar cases which have not been resolved. While the child custody laws seem fair in theory, they are not always fair in practice.

Roberta Scott
(U.S.)

Agrarian reform in Venezuela has had positive and negative effects on agriculture. For example, some farmers have obtained loans from the government which they have invested in their land. Many of these farmers have bought machines to work on their land. They have cultivated the land very fast. Therefore, they have already obtained benefit from their land, and Venezuela has too. But many farmers have not spent the loan money on their land. Instead, they have bought houses or cars, and the majority have used this money to go to the capital because they want to live there. The result is that many farms are abandoned, and nobody wants to cultivate them.

Morella Andrade
(Venezuela)

___ EXERCISE 2E _____

Choose one of the topic sentences you wrote for Exercise 1F (p. 11). Use one of the strategies demonstrated earlier in this chapter to develop the topic sentence. Make a point paragraph outline. Then write the paragraph.

_____

Personal Experience

Sometimes the most effective way to develop a paragraph is an illustrative story. By telling the reader a brief story of an actual incident that supports the general statement, you strengthen and support the topic sentence. In the paragraphs below, the writers use personal experiences to support their topic sentences.

The reason I don't drink whiskey very often is because I had a bad experience with it. Eight months ago, I went drinking with my friends after a graduation ceremony at my university in Japan. The day was our last day as students. Everyone was aware that we wouldn't be able to meet each other after this day, so everybody was going to enjoy this night drinking liquor. While reminiscing about our university times, I drank considerable whiskey. When I started to go home with some friends, I became aware that I had drunk too much. I don't remember anything about getting home. On the following day, my friends said that I fell from the train platform when I was walking at the edge of it. At just that time, a train was coming to that platform, so my friends tried to help me, but they couldn't help because they were also drunk. I asked why I was living now. Their response was that the train came to the opposite side of the platform. I swore not to drink too much after I heard this story.

Hiro Yabuki
(Japan)

Why don't I like plays? When I was only twelve years old there was a play shown about the Algerian revolution during French Colonialism. That was a time in my country's history when the French stayed in Algeria for 130 years. The play was written about a true story and was written by a French reporter who lived with the French army in Algeria. The play was about what the French did with the Algerian people until the liberation. In the middle of the play, we saw two French soldiers coming out of a tavern. They went into the street, really drunk. Suddenly, they met an Algerian woman who was pregnant. One of them said, "I bet she has a baby boy." The other said, "No, I swear it is a girl." Then, after an argument, they bet some francs and followed the woman. They caught her, and one of them took a dagger and pushed it into her belly. How cruel it was! I really could not stand the sight, and went out of the theatre, swearing not to see any more plays in my life.

Rhoma Mohamed
(Algeria)

> **Note:** When using personal experience, writers must decide how much detail is necessary. Analyzing the *unity* of the paragraph is often the key. Only those details that relate directly to the topic sentence are essential. In the paragraph above, for example, what the writer wore to the play, who else attended the play, or who the actors were would not be necessary to support the topic sentence.

___ EXERCISE 2F ___

Choose a subject, narrow it to a topic, and write a paragraph using personal experience to support your topic sentence. Generate ideas for your paragraph by using one of the strategies demonstrated earlier in this chapter. Make a point paragraph outline. Then write the paragraph.

Methods of Development

Another decision that student writers must make is how to present their ideas. In academic writing, several methods of development are commonly used to present written material:

Process   Comparison-Contrast
Extended Definition Cause-Effect
Classification

Choosing to use one method of development depends on:

an analysis of your audience
the purpose of your paragraph
the material you have (facts, examples, physical description, and/or personal experience)

Process: "How to ... "

Topics for process paragraphs range from the scientific laboratory report (How We Did This Experiment) to recipes (How to Bake Bread) to humor (How to Fall Off A Ski Lift).

Usually process paragraphs are organized chronologically (in *time*): first step, then second step, and so forth. As a result, the reader is able to follow clearly the process being described. Precision in diction and logical progression from one step to another are necessary for successful process paragraphs.

HOW I PREPARE FOR A CANOE TRIP

It is not only the canoe trip itself which pleases me; I also like the preparation for the canoe trip. First, I enjoy shopping for the food. When I go away for the whole weekend, I buy quite a lot of fresh groceries instead of canned ones because I like cooking in a real sense. I buy dairy goods, eggs, meat, vegetables, and potatoes. Next, I enjoy packing the tent, which I usually set up to dry and air during the week previous to the excursion. Although I have gone through this particular routine many, many times, the simple taking down, folding, and packing of the equipment always fills me with hopes and expectations. Finally, checking the marine chart, which I generally do the night before I leave, thrills me. Looking over the chart for alternative water roads and camping places almost enables me to make the trip in my mind ahead of time. The chart shows the archipelago outside Stockholm, a vast area with thousands of small islands and straits. It really takes some planning to choose a route for a weekend trip. Despite the fact that I have paddled in this Baltic archipelago for many years, I have so far succeeded in selecting different routes each time.

Tommy Hansen
(Sweden)

BECOMING AN ACUPUNCTURIST

A very rigid system of examinations, which consists of two parts, is used to accredit acupuncturists in China. The first part is a day-long oral scrutiny of a student's knowledge by his professors. Each student is questioned on his familiarity with the principles of acupuncture, diagnostic techniques, and the classic texts. The professors require near-perfection in the answers. A single error often means failure. On the second day, if the student passes the oral examination, he demonstrates his ability with the needles of acupuncture on a life-sized wooden statue of a man which is covered with wax and filled with water. Tiny holes have been drilled through the wood at approximately 165 acupuncture points on the body. There are no markings on the figure and the holes are invisible under the wax. The examiner poses a situation to the student. The student then names a point on the body for the treatment of a specific situation. If it is the correct location, he is asked to demonstrate how to insert the needles. The student chooses the right kind of needle and pushes it through the wax, using the proper technique. If he is right, water streams from the hole. If he is wrong, he never becomes an acupuncturist.

Kelly Cobb
(U.S.)

1. Is the chronological organization in each paragraph clear?
2. Are the specific details in each paragraph helpful in following the process that is examined?
3. What techniques of support are used in each of the paragraphs?
4. Is every step of each process clear for the reader? Does a step need to be added in either of the paragraphs? Does a step need to be left out because it is too obvious or because it is irrelevant?

Extended Definition: "The meaning of . . . "

Formal definition: Term = class + distinguishing detail

$$\downarrow \qquad \downarrow \qquad\qquad \downarrow$$

A triangle is a plane figure with three sides.

Simple (formal) definitions of concrete words are often short and complete. Such words as apple, pencil, and dictionary can be defined in a single sentence. However, the more abstract a word is, the more difficult it is to define it simply. Words such as knowledge, love, and democracy require extended definitions. A paragraph of extended definition uses techniques of support (facts, example, physical detail, and personal experience) to more fully explain words.

Read the following paragraphs. Notice that in each case an abstract word or term is defined by using supportive techniques.

HAPPINESS

Happiness means different things to different people. For example, some people believe that if they have much money or many things, they will be happy. They believe that if they are wealthy, they will be able to do everything they want, and so they will be happy. On the other hand, some people believe that money is not the only happiness. These people value their religion, or their intelligence, or their health; these make them happy. For me, happiness is closely tied to my family. I am happy if my wife and my children live in harmony. When all members of my family share good and sad times, and when my children communicate with each other and work together, I am happy. Although the definition of happiness depends on each individual, my "wealth" of happiness is in my family.

Bonar Siregar
(Indonesia)

KACHINA DOLLS

A kachina doll is a small, carved, wooden, humanlike representation of the supernatural beings worshiped by the Hopi Indians. Kachinas are not gods: as their name denotes, *ka* for respect and *china* for spirit, they are respected spirits of the dead, of mineral, plant, bird, animal, and human entities. Kachinas are not gods, but rather they are intermediaries or messengers to the gods. In the polytheistic Hopi society, all plants and animals, as well as some inanimate things, have spirits which the Hopi visualize in human form. When a Hopi goes to gather yucca roots to use as shampoo, he prays to the spirit of the first plant he finds and passes it by, gathering the second one. When he goes hunting, he prays to the spirit of the game and apologizes for having to take its life. Thus the spirits of men, animals, and plants are the kachinas most often carved into kachina dolls.

LaDean McConahay
(U.S.)

___ EXERCISE 2H ___

1. *Write a paragraph of extended definition using one of the following words. Generate details, using one of the strategies demonstrated earlier in this chapter. Make a point paragraph outline for your paragraph; then write the paragraph. Label in the margins the techniques of support you used to support your topic sentence.*

   A. prejudice
   B. diplomacy
   C. normal
   D. patience

2. *Exchange paragraphs with a classmate. Using the checklist on p. 16, analyze that paragraph.*

Comparison-Contrast:
"X is like Y" OR "X is different from Y."

Comparison-contrast is a method of development that will essentially compare (show likeness) or contrast (show difference). The purpose of comparison is to show how persons, places, and things that are usually considered very different are alike in some ways. The opposite is true of contrast: the paragraph is written to show how persons, places, and things that are often considered very much alike are different in some ways.

> **Note:** The word *comparison* is sometimes used to mean both comparison and contrast. Check with the instructor who is giving the assignment to be certain.

There are two ways to organize comparison-contrast paragraphs. Your decision about which to use will depend on your purpose, your audience, and your available material.

Plan A

Discuss first one subject, then the other:

1. All of subject A, point by point
2. All of subject B, point by point, so that it parallels the points about A

Plan B

Discuss one part of both subjects, then another part of both subjects:

1. Part one of subjects A and B
2. Part two of subjects A and B

Special concerns of comparison-contrast paragraphs

A. Be clear and distinct in your own mind about the *purpose* for which the comparison-contrast is being done. Are you trying to explain, entertain, or persuade?
B. Establish the basis upon which two things are compared-contrasted. For example:
   1. One is preferable to the other.
   2. What happened in one case may happen in another.
   3. While both are different, both are acceptable (such as customs or solutions to the problem).

Read the comparison-contrast below and then do the exercises that follow.

Comparison

Raising houseplants involves nearly as much care and knowledge as raising children. First, both plants and children are sensitive to their environments. For example, a plant will grow faster and be much healthier if it is raised in an environment of tender, loving care. The same is true for a child, who will be happier and healthier if his parents love and nurture him. Similarly, proper care of

---

houseplants requires a basic knowledge of plants on the part of the owner. He must know, for example, which of his plants need direct sunlight and which need to be kept in shady places, and how much water each plant requires for the best growth and appearance. Parents, too, must have a basic knowledge of their children's needs in order to provide what is necessary for the best physical and mental development. Finally, the owner of houseplants must be willing to provide the best possible care for his plants. A child needs time and energy from his parents, too, to play with him, to talk to him, and to care for him. Generally speaking, happy, healthy plants and children are the result of extra time, knowledge, and energy.

Arden Boyer-Stephens
(U.S.)

Comparison and Contrast

TWO VISITS TO PARIS

Even though the cityscape of Paris has not changed during the past decade, my enjoyment of my first visit to Paris ten years ago was a hundred percent greater than that of my recent visit last summer. In 1977, I visited Paris as a member of a high school tour group. I met new friends on the airplane, and they provided me with security for my first trip abroad. However, my next visit to Paris was a solitary, lonely trip; I traveled alone and had to protect myself all the time. In 1977, I had friends to talk with and share the new sensational atmosphere; we spent a night at a five-star hotel and talked all night about our adventures, and we often stopped at a café for a cup of coffee and a piece of cake. In contrast, in 1987, I had to share a room with strangers, so I had no one to talk with. Moreover, wherever I went was no longer exciting. I visited many of the same places, but I could not express my feelings to anybody. I saw many people sitting in cafés, and I even stopped at several that I remember, but even a cold glass of beer no longer looked fascinating to me. I finally realized that my friends in 1977 had made Paris lively and memorable for me.

Shinei Tsukamo
(Japan)

Contrast

Unlike the United States farmer, who harvests rice by using machines, Indonesian farmers use human power. Generally American farmers use ploughs, combines, and harvesters to get their grain from field to market. Men drive the expensive machines which pick, separate, and bind the grain. These men are paid good salaries for their work. In contrast, most Indonesian harvesters are women. Their equipment consists of a single tool called "anai-anai," a small blade attached to a bamboo stick. The women cut the stems of the rice handful by handful and put the bundles into a basket which they carry on their backs. As soon as the basket is full, the harvester goes to the owner. The wages depend on how many bundles they cut, but normally they get one bundle of every eight.

Endah Frey
(Indonesia)

___ EXERCISE 2I ___

1. Underline the topic sentence in each paragraph and circle the controlling ideas.
2. What do you *expect* each paragraph to be about? What questions do you expect will be answered in each paragraph?
3. What techniques of support are used to support each topic sentence?
4. What form of organization does each paragraph have?

___ EXERCISE 2J ___

Choose one of the subjects below, or choose your own topic, and write a paragraph using the following process:

1. Narrow the subject to a topic.
2. Make two lists: one of comparison, one of contrast.
3. Generate details for each list.
4. Decide which lists would be the most interesting material for your audience.
5. Organize the material according to Plan A or Plan B.
6. Write a topic sentence that indicates the *reason* for writing the paragraph.
7. Write either a comparison or a contrast paragraph.
8. Label in the margin the techniques of support you used in the paragraph.

SUBJECTS

sports	ways of walking
jobs	living in the dormitory
buildings	types of food

Classification: "Kinds of . . . "

Classification paragraphs divide persons, places, things, and ideas into groups according to a common basis. A single subject can be classified in various ways, according to various "classes:"

College Students

according to
class standing
$\begin{cases} \text{freshman} \\ \text{sophomore} \\ \text{junior} \\ \text{senior} \end{cases}$
according to
major fields
$\begin{cases} \text{engineering} \\ \text{agriculture} \\ \text{chemistry} \\ \text{sociology} \end{cases}$

according to
religion
$\begin{cases} \text{Protestant} \\ \text{Catholic} \\ \text{Muslim} \\ \text{Jewish} \end{cases}$

In university writing you will most often be asked to classify scientific topics, such as chemical elements, insects, or historical causes of war. The same rules for classification apply in these cases.

A successful classification occurs when

1. the classes are arranged according to a logical method.
2. the classes are relatively complete.
3. the classes do not overlap.
4. the classes have a ruling principle: "according to."

Read the paragraphs below. Notice the techniques of support—use of examples in the first paragraph, and facts and physical description in the second paragraph—that are used to *explain* the classes.

Since I began to study English, I have noticed three kinds of persistent errors in my speech; I think these errors are also the most common mistakes made by Spanish-speaking students. The first is that I speak sentences which are similar to Spanish. For instance, I will say, "I have bought *a blouse nice*" instead of *a nice blouse*. Another mistake is that I often translate directly from Spanish, forgetting the characteristic idiomatic expressions in English like "getting along with." Some vocabulary words can't be translated literally: "silverware," for example, is a common name in English for eating utensils which aren't necessarily made of silver. My final mistake in spoken English is the grammatical problem of verb endings: I will often say "She *do* the shopping" instead of *does* or "It is possible *solve* your problems" instead of *to solve*. If I can correct these three problems in my English, I think Americans will be able to understand me much better.

Esther Gencel
(Peru)

RICE

In my native language, there are six words for rice. We use different words for different types of rice or for different situations. For example, *padi* refers to the rice seed. If the rice is planted in the field, we call it *padi sawah,* and if it is planted on a hill, we call it *padi huma.* In my country, farmers who live in the higher regions of the country produce *padi huma,* while those who live in the lower elevations produce *padi sawah.* We can differentiate these two by their color: *padi sawah* is gold while *padi huma* is reddish brown. Moreover, *padi sawah* needs more water to grow than padi huma. Both *padi huma* and *padi sawah* only refer to the rice grain. We call uncooked rice *beras,* and the cooked rice *nasi.* For example, my mother tells me to cook the *beras* so that we can have *nasi* for dinner tonight. *Pulut* is another name for *nasi* or uncooked rice; the difference between these two is that *pulut* is more starchy compared to *nasi,* and it is naturally sweeter when cooked. Having more than one word for rice in our language indirectly reflects our culture, because in Malaysia rice is our staple food. We have rice everyday, and maybe that is the reason why we have so many words for rice.

Zainah Muhamed
(Malaysia)

___ EXERCISE 2K _____

Choose two of the subjects below and classify examples of these subjects. Narrow the subjects to topics that would be suitable for discussion in a paragraph. Follow the formula: According to _____, _____ fall into three (four, five) categories: _____, _____, _____ .

automobiles	food
pilots	television
music	communication

Cause-Effect:
"Why ... happened," OR "The effects of ... "

Cause-effect paragraphs investigate why things are as they are, or why something happened, or the effects of an event or a situation.
Kinds of Causes:

1. Immediate: the causes the writer first encounters
2. Underlying: the causes that took place before the immediate cause.

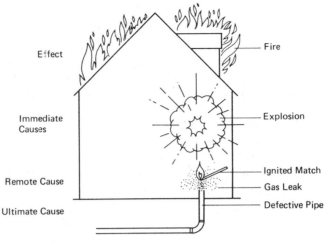

Effect

Fire

Immediate
Causes

Explosion

Remote Cause

Ignited Match

Gas Leak

Ultimate Cause

Defective Pipe

FIG. 2-1

In more complex explanations of cause-effect, an effect can sometimes become a cause. For example, a fire may have been caused by a match being lit in a house where there was a gas leak. The gas leak may have resulted from a defective gas pipe, which in turn was installed incorrectly several years ago. Thus cause and effect form a chain of events. (See Figure 2–1.)

Form of the *cause* (or *reason*) paragraph:

1. Begin with a statement of the effect.
2. Explain the immediate causes of (or reasons for) that effect.
3. Explain the underlying causes (or reasons) that led to that effect.
4. Conclude with what has caused the effect.

Form of the *effect* paragraph:

1. Begin with a statement of the cause.
2. Discuss the immediate (or short-term) effects of the cause.
3. Explain the long-term effects of that cause.
4. Conclude with a statement of the direct relationship between the cause and the effects.

Read the paragraphs below. Underline the *causes* in the first paragraph and the *effects* in the second.

Causes

There are many reasons why I have been unhappy since I have come to the U.S. First, the weather in the winter is so cold, and I am frequently sick during that season. Also, because I don't own a car, transportation is very difficult. In order to go to the market or the doctor, I must take a taxi or call a friend. Another reason I am not happy is that I am very lonely. I miss my family terribly, and my English is not good enough to make American friends. The most important problem I have is that my government has not sent money to me from my country. Although I think that the money will come soon, I am still very worried. Consequently, I am very unhappy.

Zhilla Djankook
(Iran)

Effects

THE EFFECTS OF APARTMENT LIFE

My decision to live in an apartment during my first year of college had several negative effects. First, I lived with three girls from my country, so I did not improve my English because I spoke Malay most of the time. Moreover, we took exactly the same classes, so I did not have a chance to meet or study with my other classmates. Instead, I tended to spend more time studying with my roommates. Furthermore, since I did not have many American friends, I did not learn very much about American culture; I did not celebrate Halloween or Thanksgiving or Christmas. Finally, I did not share experiences with people. I did not attend parties or go skiing or even spend leisure time in the Student Center. So although my life during my first year of college was secure and pleasant, if I could change one thing about my first year in college, I would choose to live in the dormitory; I think my life would have been more interesting and fun.

Norlela Othman
(Malaysia)

___ Exercise 2L _____

1. *Choose one of the topics below (or choose a topic of your own). Use the process for writing a paragraph on pp. 13–14 to plan a paragraph. Generate ideas for your paragraph by using one of the strategies demonstrated earlier in this chapter.*

Cause(s) of:	*Effect(s) of:*
headaches	student fatigue
automobile accidents	living in a dormitory
the success (or the failure)	American food on international students
of a sports team	studying for the TOEFL

2. *Exchange paragraphs with a classmate. Use the checklist on p. 16 to analyze the paragraph.*

____ EXERCISE 2M _____

1. *Write five separate paragraphs on the single topic of ESCAPE. Choose five of the titles below. Follow the process for writing paragraphs on pp. 13–14. Generate material for these paragraphs by using several of the strategies demonstrated earlier in this chapter.*

ESCAPE:	How to Escape	Two Similar Escapes
	Definition of Escape	Two Different Escapes
	Kinds of Escapes	Causes of An Escape
		Effects of An Escape

2. *Exchange paragraphs with a classmate. Use the checklist on p. 16 to analyze the paragraphs. Also:*
   A. *Identify the audience for the paragraphs.*
   B. *Identify the techniques of support used in each paragraph.*

ng the Essay

Many academic writing assignments require that you *explain* ideas, opinions, or processes. These assignments are often approximately 500 words long (2 double-spaced typewritten pages). Such an essay is a series of paragraphs about one subject (see the schematic representation in Figure 3–1).

The essay has:

1. **A beginning:** Called the <u>introduction</u>, this paragraph is the first in the essay.
2. **A thesis sentence:** Generally located at the end of the introduction, this sentence is the most general, most important sentence in the essay. It contains controlling ideas that limit and direct the rest of the essay.
3. **A middle:** Called the <u>body</u> of the essay, these paragraphs explain, define, clarify, and illustrate the thesis sentence. Each body paragraph consists of a topic sentence and several supporting sentences. The number of body paragraphs depends on the length and complexity of the assignment.
4. **An end:** Called the <u>conclusion</u>, this paragraph completes the essay.

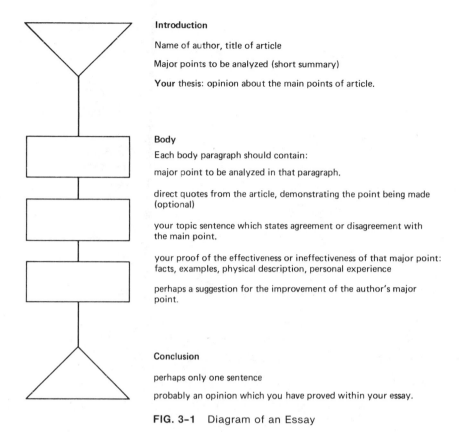

Introduction

Name of author, title of article

Major points to be analyzed (short summary)

Your thesis: opinion about the main points of article.

Body

Each body paragraph should contain:

major point to be analyzed in that paragraph.

direct quotes from the article, demonstrating the point being made (optional)

your topic sentence which states agreement or disagreement with the main point.

your proof of the effectiveness or ineffectiveness of that major point: facts, examples, physical description, personal experience

perhaps a suggestion for the improvement of the author's major point.

Conclusion

perhaps only one sentence

probably an opinion which you have proved within your essay.

FIG. 3-1 Diagram of an Essay

Selecting a Topic

Often the subject for an academic assignment is chosen for the student by the professor. However, the student frequently must narrow the subject to a topic. Selecting a topic for an essay is similar to choosing a topic to write about in a paragraph. The same process applies:

1. Write about what you know.
2. Identify your audience.
3. Decide on the purpose of the essay.
4. Select a topic that will interest your audience.

Some topics are too broad to be covered in a single essay. These topics need to be narrowed. As you begin to narrow your topic, decide what methods of development you could use to present your topic to your audience. Several methods of development are possible for each topic.

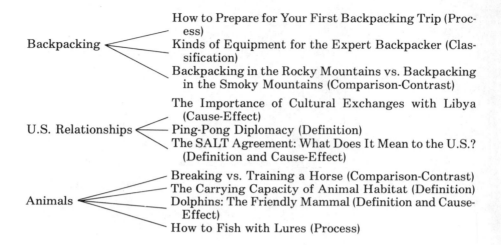

Backpacking
- How to Prepare for Your First Backpacking Trip (Process)
- Kinds of Equipment for the Expert Backpacker (Classification)
- Backpacking in the Rocky Mountains vs. Backpacking in the Smoky Mountains (Comparison-Contrast)

U.S. Relationships
- The Importance of Cultural Exchanges with Libya (Cause-Effect)
- Ping-Pong Diplomacy (Definition)
- The SALT Agreement: What Does It Mean to the U.S.? (Definition and Cause-Effect)

Animals
- Breaking vs. Training a Horse (Comparison-Contrast)
- The Carrying Capacity of Animal Habitat (Definition)
- Dolphins: The Friendly Mammal (Definition and Cause-Effect)
- How to Fish with Lures (Process)

Abstract and Concrete Topics

The more *abstract* your topic is, the more difficult it is to support, and the more difficult it is to keep your audience's interest. For that reason, abstract topics are usually not as successful as *concrete* topics.

Examples of abstract topics that are difficult to support include:

1. Patriotism: The Greatest Virtue (Definition and Cause-Effect)
2. How to Judge Bad Art (Process)
3. Relationships: Love and Hate (Definition? Classification?)

Examples of concrete topics that are often more successful include:

1. Four Types of Waitresses (Classification)
2. How to Install a Roof Vent in a Van (Process)
3. Getting Married vs. Staying Single (Comparison-Contrast)
4. Should the Olympics Be Reorganized? (Cause-Effect)

—— EXERCISE 3A ——————————————

Choose four of the subjects below. Narrow each to a topic. Use the strategy of "treeing" (—<) to discover different ways to present your material. Then decide what the principal methods of development would be for each topic.

elementary school art	pinball machines
air pollution	tape decks
exercise	dancing
neighbors	traffic
pet owners	forest fires

Title of the Essay

Often the selection of a topic will function as the title for your essay. The purposes of titles are:

1. To attract the reader
2. To give the reader an idea of what the essay is about
3. To provide focus for the essay

Titles should be clear, concise, and precise. The title is a *phrase*, not a sentence, and all extra words should be excluded. Other rules for titles include:

1. Use no quotation marks
2. Center on the top of the first page
3. Either capitalize *all* the letters in the title or capitalize the first letter of all the important words (small words like "in" and "a" need not be capitalized)

Examples:
THE KORAN AS A BASIS OF LIFE
THE ENERGY CRISIS } (all capitals)

Three Chess Champions
Social Problems in Egypt's Rural Areas } (each major word capitalized)

Organizing a Topic

1. The body paragraphs in an essay can all be organized according to a single method of development, or the body paragraphs can be developed using two or more separate methods.
2. Each of these methods of development will be supported with one or more supporting techniques: facts, examples, physical details, or personal experience.
3. In deciding what methods of development and supporting techniques to use, keep in mind

The 3 A's:

A. The intended audience   Audience
B. The purpose of the essay   } Assignment
C. The material you have to present   Available material

Prewriting

Once you have decided on a topic for your essay, asking yourself questions often helps to plan the ideas and the structure of the essay. Questions to ask to gain information about a topic include

WHO: am I writing about? A person, a group of people?

WHAT: am I writing about? An event, a problem, a belief, a process, or a comparison?

WHEN: am I writing about? A contemporary person, event, or situation? The past? The future?

WHY: am I writing about a person, place, event, problem, or belief? Why did the event occur? Why did the problem arise?

WHERE: are the people? Where did the event take place? Where does the problem exist?

HOW: is the person involved? How did the event or situation begin? What are the results? What will be the results? Can the results be changed? Do I want them changed?

As you begin to plan your essay, you may begin with a general subject and then narrow to more specific details (see Figure 3-2). Asking questions about the general subject may lead you to an interesting topic.

Another way to begin essay planning is to begin with a single idea (perhaps a fact) and then, by asking questions, discover the topic you would like to communicate to your audience (see Figure 3-3).

Another form of prewriting is *brainstorming:* the process of writing as many thoughts as you have as quickly as you can. In this process, there is no formal organization. Only after you have finished brainstorming will you go back and *select* and *organize* the material. Brainstorming can be a functional part of essay writing both because it permits you to see immediately how much you do know about a topic (and how much you *don't* know), and because it allows you to organize, on paper, the material you have.

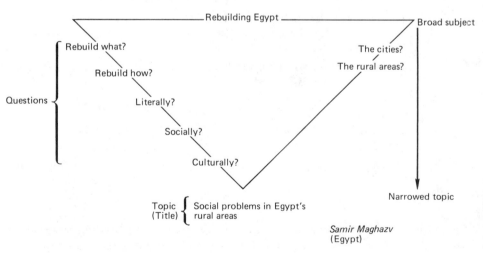

FIG. 3-2

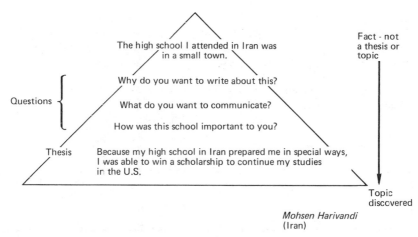

The high school I attended in Iran was in a small town.

Questions
- Why do you want to write about this?
- What do you want to communicate?
- How was this school important to you?

Fact - not a thesis or topic

Thesis: Because my high school in Iran prepared me in special ways, I was able to win a scholarship to continue my studies in the U.S.

Topic discovered

Mohsen Harivandi
(Iran)

FIG. 3–3

Brainstorming

FORESTS AND WATER RESOURCES

Forests have a function of preserving the water resources, and for this reason the headwater forests have been treated carefully. An opinion: "the existance of a forest is a negative factors rather than a contributive factor to the efficient use of water"—attracts public attention these days, this opinion does not seem to be well-grounded (from the administrative point of view). As farmers know from experience, forests improve the use of water by stabilizing ~~and extending~~ the diescharge. In order to meet the increasing demand for water and securing more water resources, the forest investmane has to be exapnded.

loss of water by the transpiration of trees (30% to 60% of the total amount of precipitation) → no function of preserving water resources → forest investment in the form of the public enterprise is reasonable.

opposite opinion

However, water shortages occur ever two to three years—seasonal unbalance, annual instability of the precipitation has to be compensated. Forests stabilize the discharge by storing the water supplied by the rainfall and making it flow gradually.

Forests prevent soil from flowing into the reservoir of a dam and maintain the function of dams and keep the efficiency of water utilization.

> 20–40 year old conifer plantations consume 6.0–8.0×10^4 m³/ha of water every year—more than 97% of which is due to the transpiration of trees in the spring and summer seasons.

more facts needed

Many cities suffer water shortages every summer in Japan. Only the water consumption of the trees is stressed.

T. Goto
(Japan)

_____ EXERCISE 3B _____

Choose one of the topics you narrowed in Exercise 3A (or choose a topic of your own). Use the chosen topic as a title for an essay of approximately five hundred words. Generate ideas for your essay, using one of the strategies demonstrated in Chapter 2. Use the following questions as you develop ideas:

1. What questions must (might) you answer about your topic?
2. What information do you already have about your topic?
3. What additional information will you need to complete your essay?

The Thesis Statement

Each essay you write will contain a thesis statement. This statement is usually one sentence that gives the purpose of the essay.

1. The thesis is the strongest, clearest statement in the essay.
2. The thesis should come at the beginning of the essay, usually at the end of the introductory paragraph.
3. The thesis sentence must not be a simple statement of fact that requires no elaboration. A simple statement of fact has no possibilities for development.

   Example: *Mrs. Brown, my neighbor, has four cats and three dogs.* (not a thesis)

4. The thesis will probably not be expressed as a question, for a question contains no attitude or opinion. The answer to the question is the thesis statement.

5. The thesis will contain <u>controlling ideas</u> that will be used in the ι sentences of the body paragraphs of the essay.

Example: *A (successful soccer coach) has (four qualities).* > (controlling ideas circled)

6. The thesis may be a <u>statement</u> of <u>opinion</u> that you will explain and prove in the body paragraph of the essay.

Example: *My neighbor, Mrs. Brown, owns four cats;*

these (animals) present a (serious health hazard) in our > (statement of opinion)
(neighborhood.)

7. The thesis may be a <u>statement</u> of <u>intent</u> that you will explain and illustrate in the body paragraphs of the essay.

Example: *This essay will show (how corn is planted) and* > (statement of intent)
(why this method of planting is successful.)

A successful thesis statement results from <u>selection, qualification,</u> and <u>specificity</u>. For example, if you were assigned to write a 500–word expository essay—an essay that *explained* something—you might choose the Koran as your subject. In order to reach a valid thesis for the essay, you might go through the following process:

1. *The Koran is wonderful.* (The controlling idea is simply a judgment, and cannot be supported.)
2. **The Koran is the perfect book for everyone.** (Still too much generalization and judgment.)
3. *The Koran is one of the best religious books in the world.* (Somewhat qualified, but still too general: *best* and *worst* are hard words to support.)
4. *The Koran is one of the most important religious books in the world.* (Better: more qualified, more objective in language, but an additional controlling idea would direct the essay more clearly.)

The (Koran) is one of the (most important religious books) in the > (controlling ideas circled)
(world,) it is the basis for the (life-style of millions) of people. (Reasonable, specific opinion that can be supported in an essay.)

_____ EXERCISE 3C _____

Below are student samples of thesis statements, followed by the theoretical organization for the remainder of each essay. Circle the controlling ideas in each thesis statement. Can you see how each of these essays could be developed? Would you use different methods of development? Would your techniques of support differ?

Essay A

atement of Intent:

*vador, uneven distribution of wealth, overpopulation, and politcal cor-
ire the major problems.*

Audience: professor of a political science class

Purpose: to explain the major problems in El Salvador

Methods of Development: extended definition, cause-effect

Techniques of Support: facts, examples

Alfredo Chorro
(El Salvador)

Essay B

Thesis Statement of Intent:

*The reasons I came to the U.S. to study soil science were to educate myself and
then to return to Libya to apply my education.*

Audience: classmates

Purpose: to explain the reasons for studying in the U.S.

Methods of development: classification, cause-effect

Techniques of support: personal experience, examples

Mohammed Yacob
(Libya)

Essay C

Thesis statement of opinion and intent:

Michelangelo's three famous sculptures—the Pieta, David, *and* Moses—*demonstrate his artistic genius throughout his life.*

Audience: professor of an art history class

Purpose: to explain the opinion about Michelangelo's sculpture

Methods of development: comparison-contrast, cause-effect

Techniques of support: physical description, examples

Sergio des los Santos
(Mexico)

Paragraph Relationships

In academic essays, the thesis statement is directly related to the topic sentences in the body paragraphs. Each topic sentence relates to and deals with one or more of the controlling ideas in the thesis. Each set of supporting sentences that follows a topic sentence relates directly to that topic sentence. In this way, the essay will be as unified, and as complete, as the paragraphs you wrote during the first part of the course. (See Fig. 3-4).

The following is a student sample of paragraph relationships.

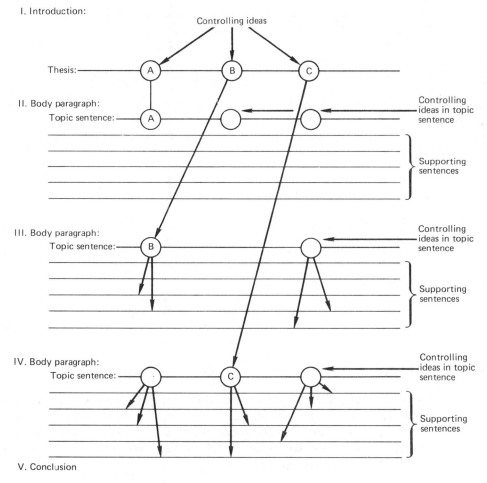

FIG. 3-4 Diagram of Paragraph Relationships within an Essay

MICHELANGELO'S GENIUS

Thesis Statement of Intent: The greatest sculptural works of Michelangelo—the *Pietà, David,* and *Moses*—demonstrate his lifelong artistic genius.

Body Paragraph Topic Sentence: The *Pietà* demonstrates Michelangelo's early artistic genius.
    A. How?
    B. In what ways?

Body Paragraph Topic Sentence: Michelangelo's sculpture *David* shows his genius in middle life.
    A. How?
    B. In what ways?
    C. How does it compare/contrast with the *Pietà?*

Body Paragraph Topic Sentence: Finally, the statue of *Moses* makes clear that Michelangelo's creative energies were still significant in old age.
    A. How?
    B. In what ways?
    C. How does it compare/contrast with the *Pietà* and *David?*

Concluding Sentence: Michelangelo's long life was filled with art; his sculptures show his lifelong artistry.

___ EXERCISE 3D ___

Use the topic you developed ideas for in Exercise 3B. Write a thesis statement (of opinion or intent) for your essay. Then write topic sentences for the body paragraphs of your essay.

Essay Outlining

Student writers sometimes have difficulty organizing the material they have gathered for an essay. One way to order your ideas is to outline your essay.

Usually an essay outline consists of words and phrases; sometimes it consists of complete sentences. While writing your outline for an essay, try to keep the words and phrases *parallel.*

Topic: Marriage Preparation in Somalia

Thesis Statement of Intent: Preparation for marriage in Somalia consists of very important tasks such as working hard to earn money, collecting contributions of livestock, getting money from relatives, and preparing items for the home.

Body Paragraph Topic Sentence: A man who intends to marry has the responsibility to have money.
  A. must work to collect money
      1. working in villages and towns (poor man)
      2. selling part of livestock (rich man)
      3. become a businessman
          (a) selling cigarettes
          (b) selling clothes
  B. must conserve money

Body Paragraph Topic Sentence: Collection of livestock and money is another preparation for marriage.
  A. collect from his family
      1. amount of contribution: one to four heads
      2. contribution is a tradition
  B. collect from friends

Body Paragraph Topic Sentence: The woman who wishes to marry spends her time making items for the house.
  A. items such as mats, wooden posts, and water containers
  B. collaborates with family members, relatives, and friends

Concluding Sentence: Preparing for marriage is a long and tedious task in Somalia, but it is essential for the establishment of a new family.

Jamal Al-Bahdon
(Somalia)

Below is an outline that states the thesis sentence and the topic sentence in each body paragraph. The controlling ideas are circled.

  I. **Thesis:** (Rural areas in Egypt) have (three serious problems): (poverty,)(lack of education), and (poor medical care.)

Audience: professor of an agricultural economics class

Purpose: to explain the most serious problems in rural Egypt

II.   Topic Sentence: (Poverty) is the overriding factor in (Egypt's rural areas.)

Method of development: extended definition

Techniques of support: facts, examples, physical description

III.   Topic Sentence: As a result of this poverty, the (people) in the rural areas are (rarely educated); almost no one goes to school past the age of twelve.

Method of development: cause-effect

Techniques of support: facts, examples

IV.   Topic Sentence: Because the people are so poor and so poorly educated, (medical care), even when it is available, (is unused.)

Method of development: cause-effect

Techniques of support: facts, examples, physical description

V.   **Conclusion**

Samir Maghazy
(Egypt)

_____ EXERCISE 3E _____

Below are examples of the simplest form of outlining: the first sentence is the thesis statement of each essay, and the following sentences are the topic sentences of the body paragraphs. Each of the essays will be about 500 words. Each will have an introductory paragraph, with the thesis statement at the end; each will have three body paragraphs and a concluding paragraph.

For each paragraph outline:

1.   identify the audience
2.   identify the purpose
3.   Circle the controlling ideas in
   (a)   the thesis statement
   (b)   the topic sentences
4.   What techniques of support could be used in each body paragraph?
5.   What methods of development could be used in each body paragraph?

HOW IRANIANS CELEBRATE THE NEW YEAR

I. <u>THESIS</u>: We Iranians have many traditional customs for celebrating the first days of the new year.
II. First of all, many days before our new year, we do a lot of shopping.
III. During the first day of the new year, families go to visit each other.
IV. Another custom is the visit of a special person whom we call "Amu-Now-Ruz;" he acts very much like Santa Claus.
V. At the end of this very long day, families are happy and relaxed.

THE CONTROLLER AS THE FOUNDATION IN A SUCCESSFUL COMPANY

I. <u>THESIS</u>: No matter what the size of the company, a competent controller in charge of the financial management is necessary.
II. The controller is in charge of a variety of financial information concerning the company, and he must have complete and immediate knowledge of this information.
III. An efficient and successful controller has a good work plan and a good team to work with.
IV. A relationship of mutual respect between the finance department and other departments in the company is essential for a successful controller.
V. The value of a good controller to a corporation is immeasurable; he is the foundation of the company's success.

Marie Pecina
(Mexico)

EDUCATION IN THE U.A.E.: PAST AND PRESENT

I. <u>THESIS</u>: Since the United Arab Emirates became known to the world in 1971, there has been a marked change in the country's general education.
II. Before the establishment of the U.A.E., the education system in the Trucial Coast Emirates was in a low state.
III. Today, schooling is available throughout the country.
IV. Adult education also plays an important role in the U.A.E.
V. The University of the U.A.E. is the latest achievement in the educational sector.

VI. Because of the changes in the education system in the U.A.E., the country is now ready to step into the industrialized world.

Arif Besker
(United Arab Emirates)

Complete Body Paragraph Outlining

The development of single paragraphs that you studied in Chapter 2 was good practice for the development of body paragraphs in an essay. Each body paragraph will contain a topic sentence and supporting sentences.

In the same way you used the *point paragraph* to develop paragraphs in Chapter 2, the body paragraphs of an essay can be completely outlined. An outline of an essay of approximately 500 words might look like the following:

I. Introduction (leading to the thesis)   (40–60 words)

II. Body Paragraph: On this line a phrase indicating the topic sentence
    A.
    B. ———————————————— supporting details for the
    C.   topic sentence
        1.
        2.   supporting details for C
    D.

III. Body Paragraph: Phrase indicating the topic sentence
    A.
        1.
        2.
        3.

                                          each body paragraph will be 4–8 sentences, 100–125
    B.   words
    C.
    D.
        1.
        2.

IV. Body Paragraph: Phrase indicating the topic sentence
    A.
    B.
        1.
        2.

C.
    1.
    2.
    3.

V. Conclusion   (40–60 words)

Note: Academic essays usually contain an introduction, several body paragraphs, and a conclusion. The introduction and conclusion are generally *shorter* than the body paragraphs because they do not have many sentences of supportive detail. The body paragraphs are longer and are usually of approximately equal length. A very short body paragraph shows a lack of balance and often indicates a lack of organization.

The length of the parts of the essay depends on the overall length. An essay of 700 to 900 words, for example, will probably have six to nine paragraphs (an introduction, four to seven body paragraphs, and a conclusion). A research paper of 2,500 words would have more paragraphs, and each paragraph would be relatively longer.

___ EXERCISE 3F _____

Use the topic that you have been working with in this chapter. Make a complete essay outline of the material you have collected. Make point paragraphs for each of the body paragraphs in the essay.

The Introduction

THE
INTRODUCTION

The general statement(s) with which you begin your introduction should make your audience interested in your topic, and should lead logically to your statement of thesis:

The purpose of the introduction is to introduce the topic to your audience and to state the purpose of your essay in the thesis statement. The introduction:

1. often opens with a general statement about the topic.
2. gives the reader general information about the topic that is needed to understand the essay.
3. narrows from that general information to the thesis statement of opinion or intent.

Example: If you were writing an essay about the Koran, and you had already written your thesis, you might choose a controlling idea (or ideas) from that thesis and construct an introductory statement for your essay:

Thesis: *The Koran is one of the most important religious books in the world: it is the basis for the life-style of millions of people.*

Controlling ideas: *religion (faith), book, life-style, Koran (Islam), world*

Any of the following sentences could begin this essay; each announces *generally* the topic of the essay, and each could be interesting for the audience.

1. Of all the *religions* in the *world* today, Islam ranks second in numbers; the *Koran,* the Holy Book of Islam, is the basis of the Islamic spiritual community.

2. Eight words in Arabic from the *Koran* summarize the central belief of the *world*'s 750 million people who practice the Muslim *religion:* "There is no god but God, and Mohammed is the Messenger of God."

3. Just as the Bible is the foundation of Christianity, so the *Koran* is the touchstone of Islam, the *religion* of 750 million Muslims *worldwide*.

4. Islam is the world's youngest universal *faith,* and the second largest, with 750 million adherents, to about 985 million for Christianity.

Whichever sentence you choose to begin your introduction, the other sentences in the introduction would add general information (two to three sentences) that would lead the audience to your thesis statement. Notice that the sentences in your introduction *relate* directly to the thesis statement.

Avoid the following problems in introductions:

1. The *apology, complaint,* or *personal dilemma:* weakens the essay because it distracts the reader.

I have now walked three times completely around the campus in a serious effort to come up with a suitable topic for this paper. When I noticed a pedestrian getting run over by a bicycle, I knew that that would make a good topic for my discussion. Although I couldn't care less about the welfare of the two people involved, I went over nevertheless (I hope I never have to do it again) and asked if I could be of any assistance. Thank God they said no.

Even though I don't know very much about glycosis, I decided to write what I can.

2. The *panoramic beginning:* impossible to narrow to a thesis without a break in unity.

Since the beginning of time, man has been intimately concerned with the process of life; we are all more or less involved with the same topic.

War is a topic that has been handled admirably by poets throughout the course of history and man's conscious destruction of his fellow man.

Examples of good introductions:

Vitamin D Deficiency

interesting sentence

background information

thesis statement of intent

Every schoolboy knows that vitamin D is the sunshine vitamin, and that vitamin D is essential for good health. Until the twentieth century, however, little was known about this important vitamin, and people who lived in temperate climates tended to suffer every winter from the lack of vitamin D. Even today, although knowledge about vitamin D has been available for more than fifty years, many people still suffer from vitamin D deficiencies. This essay will describe the chemical makeup of vitamin D, the group of diseases called rickets that afflict people who are deficient in this vitamin, and solutions to avoid such deficiencies.

Saleh Saeed
(United Arab Emirates)

Small Town Relationships in El Salvador

background information

thesis statement of opinion

Almost all of the small towns in El Salvador are similar in their geography and general appearance. In addition, many of the people who live in these towns have a special lifestyle. In contrast to life in larger cities, people in small towns share many things and all kinds of experiences. This unusual sharing contributes to a familial relationship among neighbors.

Rita Saravia
(El Salvador)

____ EXERCISE 3G _____

Write an introduction for the essay you have been working on. Be sure that your information

1. interests your audience;
2. gives necessary background information about the topic of your essay;
3. leads to your thesis statement (of opinion or of intent) at the end of the introduction.

The Body

THE BODY

The paragraphs you have been studying in the first section of this book have the overall structure of the body paragraphs of an essay:

The goal of each body paragraph is to state a topic sentence that is directly related to the thesis, and to support that topic sentence.

1. Each makes a point, a solid point that is enlarged into a block of support.
2. One point is made in each paragraph, and each paragraph is approximately 125 to 150 words (four to eight sentences).
3. Each paragraph is a self-contained, fully developed unit. Like the essay itself, every paragraph has three parts: the beginning, the middle, and the end.
   A. Beginning: Topic sentence that is directly connected to the thesis
   B. Middle: Several sentences that explain and illustrate the topic sentence
   C. End: A conclusion that draws together the point made in the paragraph

—— EXERCISE 3H ————————————————————

Write the body paragraphs for your essay. Use the process for paragraph writing on pp. 13-14. Make sure that

1. each topic sentence relates directly to the thesis statement;
2. each topic sentence has controlling ideas;
3. the supporting sentences in each body paragraph relate directly to the topic sentence.

The Conclusion

THE CONCLUSION

The conclusion borrows from everything that has gone before, summarizing without repeating exactly, suggesting, predicting. In so doing, it gives the essay its final shape, and gives writers a single last chance to show that their theses are valid.

To write a strong, graceful conclusion

1. Look at your thesis and make sure the conclusion is integrally connected.
2. Begin your conclusion with a narrow statement that connects your concluding paragraph with the last body paragraph.
3. From this point, begin to broaden toward your final sentence. Notice that the structure of the conclusion is the opposite from the introduction.
4. Use *ideas* from the body paragraphs to conclude—controlling ideas, for example—but do not simply recopy topic sentences.
5. The conclusion may also contain a *prediction* based on material in the essay, a *solution* to a problem stated in the essay, or a *recommendation.*

Examples of Successful Conclusions

Women's Liberation in Japan

summary { To conclude, the role of women in Japan used to be to take care of their families; women were not educated, so they did not have jobs. However, after the women's education system was improved, Japanese women became part of the job force in my country. Nowadays, many women have jobs, but there are still problems with low salaries and limited opportunities. Fortunately, these problems are being

prediction { solved, so in the future there will be no difference between men's and women's jobs.

Sumiko Ishii
(Japan)

The TOEFL Examination: Why?

summary { In conclusion, it is not fair to deny a student university admission because he or she has not passed the TOEFL test, especially if that student has studied English in the United States for a semester. One question comes to mind: What is the purpose or the aim of the university? The TOEFL examination was created to measure the language proficiency of students *not* in the U.S. who were applying to U.S. universities. When that university receives the foreign applications, it will be able to know from their TOEFL score if they are able to study in English. However, if the student applies in person, and if that person has the

solution { recommendations of the intensive English language program, the reason for the TOEFL is gone. In these cases, the TOEFL test is not necessary.

Saleem Ghoulom
(United Arab Emirates)

Avoid these problems in your conclusions:

1. Too much summary: if your essay is short (500 words), your reader will probably remember most of the main points. It is necessary only to refer to these points briefly. Of course, in a very long essay, or in a research paper, more summary will be necessary.

2. Any completely *new idea:* if a new idea occurs in the conclusion, the reader may turn the page, expecting clarification and proof of the idea. If the idea is important enough to be included in the summary, include it earlier in the essay as well.

___ EXERCISE 31 _____

Write a conclusion for your essay. Be sure to summarize the main ideas of your essay briefly. Then write either a prediction or a solution.

Read each of the following introductions and conclusions. Then do the exercises that follow.

I

background
information
{ Although the Watershed Management Division in Thailand was established eighty-four years ago, watershed management has not progressed as it should have. That is because there are three major

thesis
statement
of opinion
{ problems: the invasion of watershed areas by the populace, the lack of research by the scientists, and the deficiencies of budget and personnel by the government in Thailand.

***

summary
{   To conclude, we can see that none of the problems is easy to solve and that each is related to the others. Because of the money shortage, the scientists cannot do proper research, so we cannot expand our work. The lack of data from research results in our not being able to demonstrate our work to get enough money from the

solution
{ government. The best solution is to choose a particular area and work on the problems that exist there, gathering data and solving problems; then we can present these data to the government to make them see how very important the Watershed Management Division is.

Arthorn Boonsaner
(Thailand)

---

1. Underline the thesis sentence in the introduction above and circle the controlling ideas.
2. Based on the thesis, what will each of the topic sentences in this essay be concerned with?
3. What concluding techniques are used in the conclusion?
4. Who is the audience for this essay?

II

background information
{

One obstacle that most foreign speakers find when they come to the United States to study at the university level is the TOEFL examination. Before permitting a foreign student to enroll, universities demand that they have a high score on the TOEFL exam.

thesis statement of opinion
{

Although the TOEFL has been devised to measure the students' English skills, it is not the best way to judge because of the nervousness of the students taking the test, and the luck involved in passing or failing the test.

***

summary
{

I am just another student who plans to study in the U.S. and who wishes the people in charge of the TOEFL examination could find a better system of testing the English skills of foreign speakers. Perhaps a series of tests over a period of time would reduce the anxiety of students whose university admission now rests on a single day of testing. Certainly the test takers should be permitted short breaks between sections of the test in order to relax their minds. Finally, the TOEFL should be better standardized so that it reflects more clearly a student's English proficiency.

solution
{

Malula Moncada
(Nicaragua)

---

1. How does the author interest the reader in the introduction?
2. Based on the introduction and conclusion, what techniques of support will probably be used in the body paragraphs: facts, examples, physical description, or personal experience? How do you know?
3. This conclusion begins with an apologetic tone; should the writer eliminate that apology?
4. What concluding techniques are used?

---

introductory material	There is an important discussion in Saudi Arabia about the Saudi students in the U.S., and about their progress in their studies. Some support sending students abroad to study and others
thesis sentence	object. But it has been proved that the progress that graduate students have made is much better than what ungraduates have made.

***

summary	In conclusion, there is no reasonable need to send hundreds of undergraduate students yearly to study in the western countries. But there is an actual need to help graduate students to study
concluding opinion	in the well-known universities all over the world in order to give them a chance to know about the updated information in their fields.

Mahmoud Shadli
(Saudi Arabia)

___ EXERCISE 3L ___

1. Is the thesis in the introduction above a statement of opinion or a statement of intent?
2. Circle the controlling ideas in the thesis statement.
3. Based on this introduction and conclusion, what methods of development might be used in the body paragraphs of the essay?
4. Based on this introduction and conclusion, what questions will probably be answered in the body paragraphs of the essay?

___ EXERCISE 3M PEER EVALUATION EXERCISE ___

1. *Exchange essays with a classmate. Read your classmate's essay. Answer the questions below:*

PEER EVALUATION

1. Does the introduction begin with general information related to the thesis?
2. Is the thesis statement:
   A. a statement of opinion?
   B. a statement of intent?
   C. both opinion and intent?

3. Circle the controlling ideas in the thesis stateme
ling ideas also in the topic sentences in the body
say?
4. What methods of development are used in each l
the answer in the margin.
5. What techniques of support are used in each b
line the best details.
6. Does the conclusion contain a prediction, a so
dation?
7. At the end of the essay:
   A. write comments to your classmate
      (1) The best part of the essay is . . .
      (2) Questions I still have are . . .

2. *Give the essay back to your classmate. Look at your essay. Read your*
classmate's comments. Discuss the comments and the questions with your
classmate.

Childhood in War and Peace

title

background information

> Historical events change children's lifestyles. Some children lead carefree lives while others have no childhood at all. For example, my mother spent her childhood when there was a war in my country, Poland, but I did not spend my childhood

thesis statement of opinion

> during wartime. Therefore, my mother's childhood and mine were the opposite; our schooling and our activities after school show the dramatic differences in our lives.

controlling ideas

topic sentence

> My mother and I began to study when we were seven years old, but we studied in different ways. I began to study

at a school close to my home. According to a law in my country, all children between the ages of seven and fifteen have to study eight years in school. On my first day of school, I had many books, notebooks, and colored pencils in my backpack, all of them bought for me by my parents. My backpack was heavy, but I was very proud of my "luggage;" all the people who saw me knew that I was a student! I liked school because there were many children. When I had breaks between my classes, I played with my classmates or I went to my favorite place, the big library. I was very excited by the books on the shelves, and I knew I could look at them and read them. For me, a little girl, it was an inspiring experience. I liked to study, and the fact that I was studying in my na-

techniques of support: personal experience, physical description, examples

tive language was not dangerous for me and my family. Why did I say "dangerous"? Because when my mother began to study, studying in Polish could have been the cause of severe punishment for her and her family.

When my mother was seven years old, her father, who was a professor, told her: "You are a big girl now. You should know how to read and write in Polish and also how to count. I will start teaching you how to do that. But remember—you cannot talk about it to anybody who is not a member of our family." On my mother's first day of school, she did not have special books, notebooks, and colored pencils. She wrote on pieces of paper that my grandfather burned after she finished her work. She also did not have library books, so she tried to read the newspapers that my grandfather kept at home. It was necessary for my mother to begin studying this way because my country was occupied by the Germans. No Polish could exist at that time. Studying something in Polish was illegal, and people who did it could be killed. My mother's "class" was small; it had only eight students, children from my mother's neighborhood, and only one teacher, my grandfather. They studied while risking their lives.

topic sentence

Not only were (my mother's) and my schooling (different,) but also our (activities after school.) When I returned home

controlling ideas

after school, dinner was usually ready and waiting for me. Sometimes I helped my mother and father when they were cooking. That was very nice, because while we were cooking, we talked about many things. After dinner, I did my homework, and when I finished, I went to swim in the school swimming pool, or I went to the public library in my city, and I read books. I could do these hobbies because I did not have to work. I only helped my mother take care of our home, but this activity was quite pleasant. During the weekends, I went with my parents to the sea, and I played with them and with other children. Sometimes we went to the movie theater or to a museum. That was the way I spent my free time.

techniques of support: personal experience, physical description, examples

method of development: comparison-contrast

In contrast, my mother and her relatives lived near a German weapons factory, and they had to work at that factory. The work was very hard, too hard for children, but children were treated in the same way as adults during the war. Working and illegal studying were difficult for my mother, so she did not have much time for playing. Moreover, she knew that it could be very dangerous to play outdoors because there were many German soldiers who sometimes shot at Polish children for fun. My mother could not go with her parents to a movie theater or to a library because these places were closed during the war. In fact, she seldom saw her parents together because they worked on different shifts in the German factory. Instead, she took care of her younger brother and cooked dinner for the family. Her time was filled with work, either at home or at the German factory.

summary

Although my mother and I lived in the same country, she was a child thirty years before me when there was war in the world. Consequently, my mother learned too much about life as a little girl. As a child, I did not have to work hard, and I also did not have much responsibility. My child-

recommendation

hood was peaceful and safe. Both my mother and I agree that all children should live as I did because childhood is usually the only time in life when people can be carefree and can live without problems.

Eva Szysmanska
(Poland)

4

Drafting and Revising the Essay

Most professional writers would agree that writing and rewriting DRAFTS is the basis for most successful authors. Academic writing is no different; student writers must be prepared to write a draft, revise it, and then write another draft. This process may occur several times: drafting and revising, drafting and revising, until an essay (or a technical report, or a research paper) is ready for the audience.

The strategies for drafting an essay for a first-year composition class, an argumentative paper for a speech class, or a master's thesis have the same general objectives:

1. an introduction that
   A. appeals to the needs and interests of the audience.
   B. gives background information about the topic.
   C. has a strong, clear thesis statement (of opinion and/or intent) that gives the main idea of the essay.
2. body paragraphs that
   A. have topic sentences that relate to the thesis statement and that contain controlling ideas.
   B. contain supporting sentences that explain, define, and/or illustrate the controlling ideas by using facts, examples, physical description, and/or personal experience.
   C. present material that uses appropriate methods of development.

3. a conclusion that
   A. summarizes the main idea(s) in the essay.
   B. emphasizes the important points.
   C. offers a prediction, a solution, or a recommendation.

___ EXERCISE 4A _____

Choose one of the subjects below (or choose a topic of your own) for an essay that will explain *something. The essay will be 500–700 words long. Using one of the generation strategies demonstrated in Chapter 2, develop some ideas for your essay.*

Subjects

Transportation in My Country
How to Study for the TOEFL Examination
3 (4, 5, 6) Words for _____ in My Language
American Slang Words
Why I Am Majoring in _____

Coherence Devices

A well-organized essay is the basis for coherence (an essay that "sticks to-gether"). An essay with a clear thesis statement, a carefully identified audi-ence and purpose, and body paragraphs that support the topic sentences will have a sense of logic that makes the essay easy to read and understand.

However, there are additional *coherence devices* that will make your es-say smoother and more sophisticated. The smooth flow of ideas *within a para-graph* may be achieved by using one or more of the following:

1. The use of pronouns: when a sentence depends on the sentence before it for a pronoun referent, the two sentences "stick together."

   Example: English *is considered an international language.* It *is spo-ken by more than 260 million people all over the world.*

2. The repetition of key words and phrases: repeating words within a paragraph, particularly the controlling ideas in the topic sentence, will make your paragraph seem smoother.

   Example: Pollution *of our environment has occurred for centuries, but it has become a significant* health problem *only within the last century. Atmospheric* pollution *contributes to respiratory* disease*, and to lung* cancer *in particular. Other* health problems *directly re-*

lated to air (pollutants) *include heart* disease, *eye irritation, and severe allergies.*

Repeating the *exact* word is only one form of this coherence technique. Using a synonym for one of the controlling ideas (for example, using "disease" for "health problem") is also a coherence device.

3. Transitional words and phrases: these words generally have very little specific meaning in English, but they indicate the relationship of one idea to another.

Transitions

Transitions in English, sometimes called connectors, have different grammatical uses. The list below indicates how transitional words or phrases are usually used:

1. Introductory words: (most common; notice comma)
    <u>At first</u>, we did not understand.
    <u>Similarly</u>, Carol's hair was curly.
    <u>Furthermore</u>, we need to study.

2. Subordinate Conjunctions: (note sentence structure)*
    We went <u>because</u> we were excited.
    <u>When</u> Ali arrived, the party was over.
    <u>Although</u> we were late, we were still happy.

3. Coordinate Conjunctions: (note sentence structure)*
    Maria likes pizza, <u>and</u> Jose does too.
    They are going to the mountains, <u>so</u> they are taking warm clothing.
    Siti and Saffiyah write very well, <u>but</u> their friend does not.

Below is a list of some of the transitions available to the writer. These transitions are arranged according to how the writer might use them.

1. To signal relationship in time, use **chronological transitions** (see process paragraphs in Chapter 2).

Introductory Words		*Subordinate Conjunctions*	
presently,	the next day,	before . . .	during . . .
at length,	soon afterward,	after . . .	when . . .
afterward,	by that time,	since . . .	while . . .
meanwhile,	at that moment,		
next,	from then on,		
first,	within an hour,		
soon,	at last,		
later,	earlier,		
second,	then		

---

*For a more complete discussion of connectors and sentence structures, see Chapter 10.

2. To signal relationship in space, use **spatial transitions** (see physical description paragraphs in Chapter 2).

Introductory Words

a little farther on,	next to X,
in the next room,	at the center of the circle,
at that altitude,	across the way,
between those cities,	about a foot to the left,
beyond this point,	just to the right,

3. To signal that what follows is similar to what precedes, use **comparison transitions** (see comparison paragraphs in Chapter 2).

Introductory Words

likewise,	once again,
similarly,	in much the same way,
at the same time,	once more,
in like manner,	compared to X,

4. To signal a contradiction or contrast, use **contrast transitions** (see contrast paragraph, Chapter 2).

Introductory Words		*Subordinate Conjunctions*	*Coordinate Conjunctions*
however,	nevertheless,	although . . .	, but
conversely,	on the other hand,	even though . . .	, yet
even so,	in spite of this/that,	whereas . . .	
unlike X,	on the contrary,		
nonetheless,	in contrast,		
instead,			

5. To signal that what follows is an **illustration** or an **example**, use **middle paragraph transistions** (see example paragraphs in Chapter 2).

Introductory Words

for example,	for instance,
frequently,	specifically,
similarly,	in particular,
in general,	to illustrate,
in order to X,	that is,
generally,	occasionally,
usually,	especially,

6. To signal that what follows is a result of what precedes, use **cause-effect transitions** (see cause-effect paragraphs, Chapter 2).

Introductory Words		Subordinate Conjunctions	Coordinate Conjunctions
therefore,	as a result,	since ...	, so
consequently,	as a consequence,	because ...	, and that is why
finally,	for this reason,		, and so
thus,	on the whole,		
then,	in other words,		
due to X,	accordingly,		

7. To signal that what follows is **additional** or supplementary, use **middle paragraph transitions** (see classification paragraphs in Chapter 2).

Introductory Words		Coordinate Conjunction
in fact,	furthermore,	, and
then, too,	moreover,	
again,	in addition,	
first,	besides that,	
naturally,	for that matter,	
surely,	of course,	
indeed,	to be sure,	
in fact,	as a matter of fact,	
to repeat,	in other words,	
besides,	as noted earlier,	

8. For concession, use counterargument transitions (see the argumentative essays in Chapter 5).

Introductory Words		Subordinate Conjunctions	Other
of course,	after all,	although ...	although X may be true,
certainly,	to be sure,	even though ...	

9. To signal that what follows is a summary, use **conclusion transitions** (see introduction and conclusion exercises, Chapter 4).

Introductory Words	
therefore,	in a word,
in short,	in conclusion,
on the whole,	in summary,
to summarize,	finally,
in brief,	
to conclude,	

—— EXERCISE 4A ————————————————————————

Put appropriate transitions in the paragraphs below. Use the transitions listed at the end of each paragraph; use each transitional word or phrase only once. Notice that some of the blanks in each paragraph will use introductory words

(_____,), some will use subordinate conjunctions (_____ . . .), and others will use coordinate conjunctions (, _____).

I

Shopping at K-Mart enriches my vocabulary. _____ I don't like spending money, I like shopping _____ it gives me a chance to practice my English. K-Mart is the best place to practice. It is a large store, _____ there are many customer assistants who speak English fluently. I look for many items in many parts of the store, _____ in each area I find a different customer assistant who is eager to help me practice English. _____, I am careful to read the section names; _____, I also read the information on the packages of the items I wish to buy. _____, everytime I shop at K-Mart, I leave the store with some new words that increase my English vocabulary.

Hamad Omar
(Saudi Arabia)

Transitions: although   because
                , and   , so
                in addition,   in conclusion,
                moreover,

II

MY DRIVING TEST

I had many difficulties during my first driving test. _____, when my instructor wanted me to drive on a road where I had never driven, I was very nervous and worried. _____, I drove very slowly and cautiously. Unfortunately, that caused the engine to stall in the middle of the road. I panicked and tried to start the engine, _____ no matter how hard I tried, the engine would not start. _____, my instructor had to start the engine for me. _____, just a minute later, I was very embarrassed _____ the engine stalled a second time. My instructor became impatient; he started the engine again. _____ the engine stalled a third time, I could feel the anger of my instructor. I tried to prepare myself for the scolding. _____, the cars behind me were so angry that they honked for quite a long time. _____, my instructor gave up and took over my place to drive. _____ this incident did not cause any accidents, it was such a terrible and embarrassing incident in my life.

Ngai Peng Ng
(Singapore)

Transitions:	, but	instead,
	first,	although
	therefore,	as a result,
	finally,	, so
	then	because

III

There are three words in the Malay language that represent a person who cures diseases with traditional treatments: *bomoh, dukun,* and *pawang.* The meanings of those words depend on the status of the healer in his society. _____, *bomoh* is a person who is in charge of a small village. _____ he got the knowledge about healing from his ancestors, _____ sometimes he cannot treat his patient _____ he has limited experience. *Dukun* is a person who specializes mainly in massaging broken legs or arms. He is often a famous person _____ many people prefer to see him rather than pay for expensive treatment in a hospital. _____, *pawang* is a high ranking person in society; he is very experienced, _____ he works for the Sultan at the palace. All of these men use a spiritual approach and nonchemical medicines to treat their patients; _____, each is responsible for a different part of society.

Nor Halim Hassan
(Malaysia)

Transitions:	since	, so
	however,	for example,
	because	, but
	finally,	usually

___ EXERCISE 4B _____

The following paragraphs contain many coherence devices.
  A. *Underline the transitional words and phrases*
  B. *Underline with wavy lines the repeated words and phrases*
  C. *Put pronouns in parentheses*

One way that K-Mart makes so much money is with the blue light. Drawing shoppers like flies to garbage cans, the f͏ specials" unload all types of slow-moving merchandise. Wheth a snowstorm, Halloween costumes in November, or day-ol sandwiches, the blue light disposes of this merchandise, whic devour like hungry dogs. Because they are caught up in the e͏ of the moment, many shoppers take advantage of these specials to buy screwdriver that they may never use or that blouse which doesn't quite fit. In addition, by purchasing the cheapest, most poorly constructed items, these shoppers assure K-Mart that they will return in a month to buy replacements. The blue-light specials are one sure way that K-Mart extracts $100 annually from every square foot of selling space in its stores.

Peter Cunningham
(U.S.)

If the University of Spain decided to use a "selective system" as a base for its enrollment, both the students and the university would benefit. Under the present open enrollment policy, anyone who chooses can begin university work; consequently, many students leave their studies after two or three years, and only a few students finish their degrees. For example, in the most popular fields like medicine and civil engineering, thousands of students begin each year, yet only 25% complete their work. As a result, the students become frustrated because they have to spend additional time finding another field to study or finding a job. The university also suffers because education costs money, and the money used for these students is lost when they do not finish. A selective examination would distinguish between students who have the aptitude and the desire to do university work and those who do not.

Pilar Sanchez-Monge
(Spain)

Paragraph Hooks*

A paragraph hook uses the coherence device of repetition. The writer repeats one or more words from one paragraph in the first sentence of the next paragraph. The "echo" of the words helps to "HOOK" the paragraph together.

The Lively Art of Writing, Lucile Vaughan Payne (New York: Mentor, 1965)

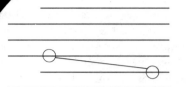

(repeated words)

Read the introduction about censorship below. Then study the different kinds of paragraph hooks available to the writer.

CENSORSHIP IN JAPAN

introduction
background
information

Nowadays in Japan, many books and magazines are published, and we can see a new movie in different theatres every week. Moreover, hundreds of movies and publications are imported from America and from European countries. Unfortunately, all artistic works, both domestic and foreign, are censored by the government. *Opponents* of this *government practice* say that *censorship* should be an *individual activity*, not the duty of the government.

thesis
statement

controlling ideas

Mari Kanada
(Japan)

---

1. The last word of Mari Kanada's first paragraph above can be "hooked" into the first sentence of the second paragraph and is used to introduce another idea:

   The constitution of the Japanese (government) guarantees our nation the right of freedom in artistic expression.

2. Another word (or words) in the first paragraph is hooked into the first sentence of the next paragraph:

   The (Censorship) Bureau is very strict in its definition of "obscene," and so many works that are considered (art) by other countries are banned in Japan.

3. A word (or words) from a sentence in the middle of the first paragraph is hooked into the first sentence of the next paragraph; a hook from the last sentence is used as well:

   Selection of what (movies) to see or what (books) to read is an (individual) adult activity in most free societies.

4. Idea hook: Instead of repeating an exact word or phrase, an idea (or ideas) in the first paragraph is referred to by using a synonym for the idea in the first sentence of the second paragraph:

In a democratic society, the (people) should have the right to choose what forms of (entertainment) they want to enjoy.

5. A combination of transitions and paragraph hooks is often the most effective means of linking paragraphs:

(The fact is) that the constitution of the Japanese (government) guarantees our nation the right of freedom in artistic expression.

(Because) the Censorship Bureau is very strict in its definition of "obscene," many of the works that are considered (art) by other countries are banned in Japan.

In most free societies, (however,) selection of what (movies) to see or what books to read is an individual adult activity.

In a (democratic society,) the (people) should have the right to choose what forms of (entertainment) they want to enjoy.

___ EXERCISE 4C _____

Read the paragraphs below. Circle the paragraph hooks and join them as in the sample paragraph. Then underline the transitions in the paragraphs.

In 1889, when the British occupied the Sudan, their first aim was to find land for planting cotton because many textile industries in England at that time needed cotton. After a serious study by the English agricultural experts, the Gezira area was chosen for the establishment of an agricultural project. The choice was excellent; even today, although there are now other agricultural schemes in the Sudan, still the (Gezira Project) is the most (successful) one.

The main reason for the (success) of the (Gezira Project) is its soil. The clay allows the construction of canals which do not require expensive concrete. *In addition* to that, the Gezira area slopes downwards towards the north and west. *This* makes the siting of the canal system relatively easy. *Furthermore,* a slight ridge runs from Hag village to Masid village along the eastern edge of the project. The main canal from the dam at Sennartown follows the line of the ridge; *consequently,* this gives good irrigation over the whole area.

Hashim El-Hassan
(Sudan)

. . . The cross-cultural classroom was a great help to me because it was a way to extend my experience beyond the campus, and it made me share my experience and knowledge of my culture with American students.

The first time I heard about the cross-cultural classroom was when Mrs. Griswold from the Foreign Student Office told me about the possibility of going to an American school and speaking to the students about my country. She told me that the goal of the program was to help children understand that people from foreign countries were not strange beings. I liked the idea, so I signed up with three other people. One was from India, another was from Mexico, the third was from Sweden, and I represented Saudi Arabia. We went to Washington Junior High School to speak to a seventh grade class. There were twenty-one students in the class who were about thirteen years old. The other three foreign students spoke first, and by the time it was my turn to present my information I was no longer nervous.

During my presentation I told the students about the main cities in Saudi Arabia and pointed out the places on a map. I tried to explain how the Moslem religion prevents people of other religions from entering the two holy cities, Mecca and Medina . . .

Mohammed Al-Sayed
(Saudi Arabia)

When I came to the U.S., I was aware of the life-style and customs of the American people, but in spite of my willingness, I have not been able to adapt to them. Some features of the American people I don't like are their indifference to what is happening in the world, their strange behavior between couples, and their hurry to try to live as much as possible in a short time.

My personal experiences have shown me that American students do not care to be informed about the world situation. Their talk is always about themselves and their city. For instance, if you ask an American student what he thinks of the political regime in Ecuador, he will only change the conversation to what he was doing over the weekend. Many of these students do not even know where foreign countries are. For example, a friend of mine met an American girl, and she asked him where he was from. He said, "Colombia," and she responded, "Oh, and how is life in Africa?"

Alberto Hermosillo
(Mexico)

For many centuries the Javanese culture has been influenced by Animism and Hinduism. Even though new religions are growing among the people—Moslem, Catholic, and Protestant religions—many people feel that traditional ceremonies are an obligation of being a Javanese. If they don't fulfill their obligation, they believe bad luck will come to them or to their family. When my fiancé and I decided to marry, my family encouraged us to have a traditional Javanese wedding ceremony, and we agreed.

Because a traditional Javanese wedding is so complicated, it needs plenty of time for preparation. First we had to decide how many people would be invited from outside of the housing complex: my friends from work, my husband's friends, my parents' friends from church and other communities. People from the housing complex are automatically invited. Then, because June is a popular month for weddings, we had difficulty finding a rental hall which would hold eight hundred people. . . .

Endah Frey
(Indonesia)

Revision of Drafts

RE means <u>again</u>. Re-vision means to "look again." The processes of revising are filled with "re-" words:

reread
reflect
reconsider
respond
rewrite

Revision takes place throughout the writing process. As the author thinks, plans, develops ideas, and writes, questions continually need answering:

How can I make this more interesting for my audience?
How can I fulfill the purpose of this assignment?

Is this enough detail? Too much?
What word should I use here?
Is this example related to my topic?
Have I defined this clearly?

When a writer completes a draft, the next logical step is to <u>reread</u> the draft several times; each rereading will focus on specific <u>reconsiderations</u>:

Focus on the Audience:

Who is the audience? What are their interests, experiences, education, prejudices?

What does the audience know about your topic? Not know? What would they be interested in learning?

What is your relationship to the audience?
    A. expert to novice?
    B. more experienced to less experienced?
    C. classmate to classmate?
    D. student to professor?

What is the audience's attitude toward your topic?
    A. passionately interested?
    B. hostile?
    C. ignorant, but willing to learn?
    D. mildly interested?
    E. professionally interested?

How does your essay communicate successfully with your audience?

    A. Does your introduction
          engage the reader's interest?
          give the plan for the essay clearly?
    B. Do your body paragraphs
          consider the experiences and needs of the audience?
          focus on the main points of the essay?
          present adequate information about the topic?
          give the quantity and quality of detail necessary to support the ideas in the essay?
    C. Does your conclusion
          leave the reader with a clear idea of the importance of the essay?
          impress the reader with the main ideas of the essay?

Focus on the Purpose:

What is the purpose of your essay?
    A. to explain X?
    B. to educate X?

C. to teach X how to do something?
D. to share your experience?
E. to give information?
F. to fulfill an assignment?
G. to entertain or amuse?
H. to persuade?
I. to solve a problem?
J. to report a discovery?
K. ?????????????????????

What do you want to emphasize in your essay?

A. the problem?
B. the solution?
C. the evidence?
D. what the reader can do?
E. the situation?
F. your expertise?
G. your opinion?
H. standards for evaluation?
I. ?????????????????????

Focus on Communication

How does your essay communicate your purpose successfully?
A. Does your introduction
  give adequate background about the topic?
  state a thesis of opinion and/or intent that gives direction to the essay?
B. Do your body paragraphs
  have topic sentences that are directly related to the thesis statement?
  give information: facts, examples, physical description, and/or personal experience?
  give details that explain, define, and/or illustrate the controlling ideas in the topic sentences?
  use methods of development that allow the information to be communicated?
  contain coherence devices that make the information flow smoothly?
C. Does your conclusion
  end emphatically, with focus on the main ideas?
  end effectively, perhaps with a prediction, a solution, or a recommendation?

Reread the draft to the essay on which you have been working. Use the check-list above to reconsider the essay.

What should be changed? How?
What should be added? Or eliminated? Why?
What should be simplified? Or elaborated?
What should be kept? How do you know?

Peer Revision

Often, your classmates can help by responding to your essay. Below is a check-list that student readers can use to help each other.

Peer Revision Checklist

1. Who do you think the audience is for this essay?
2. What is the purpose of this essay?
3. Underline the thesis statement and the topic sentences in the essay. Circle the controlling ideas in each.
4. What is the best part of the essay?
5. What questions could you ask the author?
   A. Are there places where more information is needed?
   B. Are there places that you find confusing?
   C. Are there details that do not contribute to the main ideas in the essay?
   D. Are there examples that do not relate to the thesis statement?
   E. Is there information that the audience will already know?

Of course, the most important part of peer revision is the writer's reconsideration of the reader's views. You should look carefully at the marks made by your peer, and you should listen carefully to any questions your reader may have. As you revise, remember that <u>you</u> have the final decision about changes; not every suggestion from your classmates will be useful.

Editing

After you have revised your essay, but *before* you turn in your final, completed draft, be sure to proofread your essay for grammar and sentence structure errors. Errors in grammar and sentence structure distract the reader and lessen your authority as a writer. Reread your essay slowly, perhaps aloud (so you can *hear* as well as *see* the errors), concentrating particularly on:

sentence structure   punctuation
vocabulary   verb tense
spelling   agreement

Student Samples of the Essay

Complete Outline

REUNION OF KOREAN KIN

I. Introduction

facts, cause-effect

    A. Separation of Korean kin between South Korea and North Korea since the Korean War

    B. Movement of Korean kin toward reunion in South Korea

thesis statement of opinion and intent

    C. Many (Korean people) eagerly (desire) the (reunion) of their (divided families).

II. Body Paragraph #1 (Explanation of background information)

controlling ideas

Topic Sentence: The (Korean War) was the main cause of the (division) of Korean (families).

facts, physical description

    A. North Korea attacked South Korea in 1950.
        1. The South Korean army scarcely had any weapons.
        2. The South Korean army was forced to retreat

    B. South Korea asked for help from the United Nations
        1. The U.S. urged intervention by the U.N.
        2. U.S. forces land on the Korean Peninsula.

    C. The South Korean–United Nations army purshed the North Korean army to the boundary between North Korea and China.

    D. China intervenes in the Korean War.
        1. The South Korean–United Nations army retreated to the present boundary.

paragraph hook

        2. The (war) ends in 1953.

III. Body Paragraph #2 (Explanation of the problem)

Topic Sentence: Many Korean (families) were (divided) by the (war).

facts, samples

    A. The North Korean army took some of the famous South Koreans.
        1. The North Korean government used these famous people as propaganda for communism.
        2. The government utilized the captured scientists to develop their military industry.

B. Some people escaped from North Korea, leaving their families there.

C. Other people tried to escape with their entire families, but they lost one another during the escape.

paragraph hook

D. The situation today, of (divided families) who wish to see each other, has made many people miserable.

  1. People in the south pray to God and hold ceremonies for their kin.

  2. People in the north have not been able to express their grief.

IV. Body Paragraph #3 (Explanation of the solution to the problem)

controlling ideas

Topic Sentence: The (movement) (to reunite) these (divided families) has begun in South Korea.

fact, example, physical description

A. Television and radio stations broadcast the faces and the names of family members.

B. The Korean Red Cross has been helping families reunite since September 1985.

C. The results have been meetings that were deeply emotional.

  1. One group of North Koreans came to Seoul to meet their divided families.

    (a) An old woman met her son.

    (b) An old man was brought with his son from the North.

  2. One group of South Koreans went to Pyeongyang in North Korea to visit their families.

V. Conclusion

summary

A. About ten million of Korea's 65 million people have been separated from their families since the war.

  1. Until last year, the isolation was total.

  2. No letters, no phone calls, or visits or news of any kind were allowed.

B. Now the isolation and grief are beginning to be overcome.

recommendation

  1. Much more work must be done to allow all the divided kin to reunite.

prediction

  2. Eventually, this will perhaps lead to the reunification of North and South Korea.

Se Yeong Hamm
(Korea)

Audience: Classmates who do not know about this problem.
Purpose: To explain the problem and the solution of Korea's divided families.

COFFEEHOUSES IN TURKEY

relation of introductory material to thesis

Perhaps there are many places in Turkey which would amaze foreigners, but undoubtedly visiting the coffeehouses is one of the most interesting cultural experiences. These prominent parts of Turkish society are very different from the coffeehouses in the western world. In spite of the fact that most of them consist of only one room, a small world exists there which reflects the different aspects of Turkish life. Coffeehouses in Turkey are really extraordinary places because of their historical importance, their functions, and their customers.

introductory material

thesis sentence: statement of opinion

background material

Even before the Turkish republic was established, the **coffeehouses** existed. They were called "Kiraothane," which means "readinghouses," because they were meant to be places where the educated **people** could go to read their newspapers while having their tea or coffee and smoking the Hubly-bubly—a special instrument used for a special tobacco found in Asia. In past times, only the wealthy **people** were educated, and they were the only **customers**. As time went on, however, a lot of **coffeehouses** were opened, and various kinds of **people** began to visit them. The purpose of the **coffeehouse** changed; the Arabic name disappeared, and they began to be called "Kahuehane"—"coffeehouse."

topic sentence

repetition of key words

Today almost every neighborhood has a coffeehouse; typically it is very simply decorated, but it has a special atmosphere. In the single room are a lot of chairs and tables. A bar is usually situated in one of the corners where the tea and coffee is made, soft drinks are kept, and the Hubly-bublies are prepared.

topic sentence

In most (coffeehouses) a big mirror hangs on one of the

technique
of support:
*physical
description*

walls, and in some of them a pool table is put in the middle of the room. Frequently a very old-fashioned radio on the bar plays continually in the smoke-filled room.

paragraph
hook

    Although (coffeehouses) are comfortable and

transitions

leisurely places, THEY also have some very strict rules. *For example,* women are not allowed inside because these places are for men only. *Naturally, if* a woman goes into a coffeehouse, SHE will lose the respect of men

technique
of support:
examples

use of
pronouns as
coherence
devices

there. *In addition,* boys under 18 years cannot enter because it is illegal: *as a matter of fact,* THEY cannot enter any place in Turkey where gambling is held. *Curiously enough,* customers in the coffeehouses play all kinds of card games except poker, which is forbidden because it is counted as serious gambling; *however,* most of the card games are very similar to poker and are usually played for money. A final restriction in coffeehouses is the prohibition of alcohol; IT is against the law and against religious principles to serve alcohol in

method of
development:
classification
("kinds of"
rules)

(coffeehouses).

paragraph
hook

    Nowadays (coffeehouses) are shared by all kinds

topic
sentence

of people who come to spend free time, meet friends, and have a quick cup of coffee or tea in the morning to begin a new day or in the evening before returning home. These coffeehouses are often the only places where different kinds of people come close and meet each other. *Thus,* one must not be surprised to notice that while two young men play cards at one table, two retired lawyers at the next discuss politics. It is *also* possible to see an aged doctor playing cards with three young university students while several taxi drivers watch the game as they wait for their customers. *Furthermore,* it is not unusual to see a clerk having a cup of coffee before work at one table while a bank manager does the same at another.

method of
development:
classification
("kinds of"
people)

transitions

Because of the camaraderie which exists in the neighborhood coffeehouses, most men in Turkey go there frequently. Some people think that the coffeehouses are unhealthy because of the smoke while others think they are bad because of the gambling. However, they remain a popular and important part of Turkish life.

summary

direct relation to thesis

Jamal Asaad
(Saudi Arabia)

5

Persuasion and the Argumentation Essay

Introduction

Persuasion is an activity we practice every day: convincing a younger brother to share a toy, persuading a shopkeeper to lower a price, convincing a friend to go to the movies. <u>Written</u> persuasion is sometimes more difficult because the reader does not see your facial expression, hear your voice, or experience your presence. For this reason, writing persuasive essays demands careful planning, analysis of your audience, and sufficient evidence to <u>prove</u> to your reader that your opinion is valid: that is, your opinion is worthwhile and should be considered.

___ EXERCISE 5A ___

Read the persuasive paragraph below. Notice that the student writer has clearly identified his audience (classmates who are tired of the winter climate) and the purpose of the paragraph (to persuade them to come to his country). How does this writer persuade his classmates? What supporting techniques does he use?

After a long, harsh winter in Iowa, wouldn't you like to get away from the snow and go to the beach? If you have the time, I know the place. I am talking about the best stretches of white sand beach in the whole of Southeast Asia. I know you have experienced beaches in the U.S., but the beaches near my home are more awesome than Fort Lauderdale and Malibu combined. Just picture this: white hot sand, so white that you need to wear sunglasses to guard against the glare, and so hot that your bare feet will jump. The temperature is always in the nineties, but the cool breeze from the sea will keep you comfortable. I know you love to surf, and that you hate crowded beaches. This beach gets the best waves in the world for surfing; you will be amazed at how tall the waves get. Best of all, you will be the only person surfing because the Vietnamese don't surf. Of course, there will be just a few beautiful girls to watch you, and they will be excited with your achievements. One last thing: it is cheap to come to my country, and while you are there you will stay with my family, so you will have no expenses. Just imagine yourself, surfing along the endless beach under the hot sun, and come to Vietnam!

Binh Tran
(Vietnam)

Goals of Persuasion:

1. To present an opinion to the reader
2. To explain, clarify, and illustrate that opinion
3. To *persuade* the reader that your opinion is valid
   A. to move the reader to action
   B. to convince the reader that the opinion is correct
      or, for a hostile audience,
   C. to persuade the reader that your opinion is at least worth considering
4. Opinions, then, must be supported by *EVIDENCE:* facts, examples, physical description, and/or personal experience.

How much proof is necessary? That depends on your audience.

1. If your readers will be friends and relatives who will accept your opinions because they like you, you will not need much evidence to persuade them.
2. If your readers will be people who agree with your opinion, you will not need much evidence, and you will not need to include *any* opposing view. Of course, then you will be writing *propaganda:* one-sided persuasion for people who agree with you.
3. If your audience will contain people who might not agree with your opinion, then the strength and validity of your evidence must be significant.

Kinds of evidence available to the writers:

1. personal observation
2. experiences of the writer
3. knowledge of the writer
4. interviews with authorities on the topic
5. research materials

―― Exercise 4B ―――――――――――――――――――――――――――――――

Choose a controversial subject that you know about and are interested in. Use a controversy from the list below, or one in your major field, or another you know about and are interested in. Begin collecting ideas for a 700–900 word essay.

Subjects
Should university students live in the dormitory or in an apartment off-campus?
Physical education classes (or freshman composition classes) should (or should not) be required by the university.
Should undergraduate international students study abroad?
The TOEFL examination should (or should not) be required for international students applying for university admission.

Reliability of the Writer

In order to strengthen your opinion, you must be an authority about your topic. Your reader should ask questions about the reliability of the author:

1. Is the author a well-known figure in the field?
   A. Johnny Carson about humor
   B. a famous biochemist about new research in that field
2. Does the author present any personal qualifications somewhere in the essay?
   A. biodata ("life information") at the bottom of the first page of an academic article
   B. references to qualifications in the introduction
3. Is the author an authority in an unrelated field? If so, the author's evidence may not be valid.
   A. a pediatrician writing about politics
   B. a movie star advertising aspirin
4. Does the author's opinion reflect a political, philosophical, or religious opinion? If so, the author's evidence may not be objective or complete.
   A. the President of Israel discussing Middle East policy
   B. the Pope discussing birth control

5. How recently was the evidence published? If the evidence is too old, new evidence may have superseded it.

___ EXERCISE 5C ___

To strengthen the essay you are planning, you need to show your reader that you are an authority about your topic. For your essay, write 50 words that describe how important, how well-known, how well-educated you are about your topic. This "biodata" will appear at the end of your completed essay and will show your audience that you are an authoritative author. NOTE: Truth need not be a part of this biodata (but, of course, biodata used for academic writing must be factual).

Examples:

<u>(name)</u> is the chair of the Department of _____ at Harvard University. He has published six books on the subject of <u>(your topic)</u>.

<u>(name)</u> is Professor Emeritus at Stanford University. She won the Nobel Prize for _____ in 1975 and has published widely on <u>(your topic)</u>.

<u>(name)</u> is a doctor of veterinary medicine who directs the National Animal Health Program in Washington, D.C. His publications include several books and many articles about <u>(your topic)</u>.

Planning the Argumentative Essay

1. Decide upon a topic.

   Example: The disadvantages of American food for the foreign student
2. Make a list of arguments. Since every controversy (argument) has two sides, you should be aware of both sides.

   Example:

   American food is:
   1. quick   1. tasteless
   2. easy to fix   2. not fresh
                      3. too starchy
                      4. too sweet

> **Note:** The side of the argument that is your opinion will often be longer, because that is what you want to emphasize.

3. Based on the information you have, decide on a tentative thesis.

Example: For the foreign student, American food is a problem: it is tasteless and not very nutritious.

Note: A controversy *must* have two sides; that is, the argument must be able to be answered both "yes" and "no" by different members of the audience. To test your topic, try the "although-because" sentence (see below). If your topic has two sides, this sentence will give the basic plan for your essay. You may use this test sentence as your thesis statement, or you may form another thesis.

Example:
Although American food is quick and easy to prepare, it is not as good as food from my country *because* it is tasteless, not often fresh, and has too much sugar and starch to be truly nutritious.

---

4. Select a suitable number of strong arguments, the strongest you have on your list. The number of arguments will depend on the essay assignment, the audience, and the available information.

5. Organize your arguments in order of importance and strength. Consider your audience: is each of your arguments interesting, valuable, and valid for that audience? Arranging the arguments from least to most important may help build your argument.

6. Use supporting material to prove that each of your arguments is *strong, viable,* and *correct.* Supporting techniques in argumentation are the same as they are in any other essay: facts, examples, physical description, and personal experience.

7. Select methods of development that will present your arguments in the strongest possible way for your reader. Methods of development include definition, comparison-contrast, process, classification, and cause-effect.

8. Many students stop right there. But intelligent readers won't. They see arguments on the other side, called "counterarguments." If the writer does not show an awareness of the counterarguments, readers might think either that the writer has not explored the subject thoroughly, or that the writer is presenting one-sided propaganda, afraid to admit the counterarguments. So the *writer* must look at the other side too.

9. Anticipating opposition, use one of the following transitions to introduce the counterargument:

Opponents of this position argue that . . .
Another argument against X is . . .
Critics of this position point out that . . .

It may be objected that . . .
Several questions come to mind:
At this point, one may wonder . . .
Certain objections must, of course, be considered . . .

Example: Of course there are some advantages to American food. First, and perhaps most important for the student, American food is generally quick and easy to prepare.

10. Now you, the writer, must refute that counterargument. It is real; it won't go away from your reader's mind. You must deal with major objections to your position, either by disproving them or by conceding their truth but showing that they are not as strong or valid as your arguments. Your refutation must do one of the following:

   a. correct your opponent's facts: the counterargument is UNTRUE/INCORRECT

   b. deny that the counterargument is related to the topic: IRRELEVANT

   c. compromise: although the counterargument is true, it is not enough to overcome your arguments: INSUFFICIENT

Example: But although American food is fast and quite easy to fix, sitting down to a dinner that tastes like cardboard and is not much more nutritious makes eating not very worthwhile.

Technique: insufficient

____ EXERCISE 5D _____

The audience for your argumentative essay is **hostile**. *Think about a mean, unpleasant, crotchety old man. He doesn't like you, and he doesn't like your topic. In fact, he doesn't like any topic. As you begin to generate material for your essay, think about this man. As you list the "pros" and the "cons" for your essay, consider:*

Will he accept your proof?

Is the evidence you are giving strong and valid?

What comments could this man make about your evidence?

The goal of your argumentative essay will be to force this nasty man to admit that your opinion has some merit. He may still not agree with your opinion, but he will have to recognize that your evidence is valid.

Possible Overall Structures for the Argumentative Essay

Below are three basic plans for argumentative essays. Notice that in each plan, one or more of the body paragraphs can be OPTIONAL (that is, you will *choose* either to use or *not* to use that paragraph). For your argumentative essay, the assignment (700–900 words) determines that your essay will have four to six body paragraphs. Longer assignments, of course, would require more body paragraphs.

Plan A

    I.   Introduction (+ thesis statement of intent)
    II.   Background paragraph about topic (OPTIONAL: depends on assignment, audience, and available material)
    III.   Pro argument #1 (weakest argument that supports your opinion)
    IV.   Pro argument #2 (stronger argument that supports your opinion)
    V.   Pro argument #3 (strongest argument that supports your opinion)
    VI.   Con (Counterarguments and your refutation)
    VII.   Solution to the problem (OPTIONAL: depends on the assignment, your audience, and the available material)
    VIII.   Conclusion (summary + solution, prediction, or recommendation)

Plan B

    I.   Introduction (+ thesis statement of intent)
    II.   Background paragraph about your topic (OPTIONAL: depends on the assignment, your audience, and the available material)
    III.   Con (Counterarguments + your refutation)
    IV.   Pro argument #1 (the weakest argument that supports your opinion)
    V.   Pro argument #2 (stronger argument that supports your opinion)
    VI.   Pro argument #3 (strongest arguments that supports your opinion)
    VII.   Solution to the problem (OPTIONAL: depends on the assignment, your audience, and the available material)
    VIII.   Conclusion (summary + solution, prediction, or recommendation)

Plan C

    I.   Introduction (+ thesis statement of intent)
    II.   Background paragraph about your topic (OPTIONAL: depends on the assignment, your audience, and the available material)
    III.   Counterargument #1 + Pro argument to refute it
    IV.   Counterargument #2 + Pro argument to refute it
    V.   Counterargument #3 + Pro argument to refute it
    VI.   Counterargument #4 + Pro argument to refute it (OPTIONAL: depends on available material)
    VII.   Solution to the problem (OPTIONAL: depends on the assignment, your audience, and the available material)
    VIII.   Conclusion (summary + solution, prediction, or recommendation)

Note: Your decision on which plan to use for your argumentative essay will depend on the material. For example, if you have parallel and equal numbers of pro and con arguments, you might choose Plan C. If, however, you have only one or two counterarguments, you will choose Plan A or Plan B. In addition, you must consider the audience. If you think that putting the counterarguments first and then building the pro arguments will result in a stronger positive reaction from the audience, then you should choose Plan B. If, instead, you believe that putting your counterarguments near the end of the paper would be more successful, then you should choose Plan A.

Generating Material

___ Exercise 5E _____

Below are three plans by student writers for three argumentative essays. Study each plan. Then make a similar plan for your argumentative essay.

I
Solar Energy: The Energy of the Future

Pro	Con
source (the sun) is free	costly to build a solar energy system
plentiful and inexhaustible	low efficiency compared to fossil fuels
safe, nonpolluting	
needs only simple technology	

Audience: classmates
Purpose: to educate and persuade the audience about the coming importance of solar energy
Techniques of support: facts, examples, physical description
Argumentative thesis: Although solar energy systems are initially costly and presently have relatively low efficiency, we need to develop solar energy because the source is free, inexhaustible, safe, and needs only simple technology.

Outline (Plan A)

    I.   Introduction: explanation of energy problem
   II.   Background paragraph: about sources of energy
  III.   Pro #1: resource of the sun is free, plentiful, and inexhaustible
   IV.   Pro #2: safe and nonpolluting
    V.   Pro #3: simple technology

(Techique:
counterargument
is insufficient)

VI. Con: cost and efficiency questions (short- vs. long-term costs and efficiency; initial investment high, but eventually much less expensive; research will increase efficiency).

VII. Conclusion: brief summary plus the solution to the energy problems (solar energy) and a recommendation to pursue research in solar energy technology.

Ragab Moheisen
(Egypt)

II
Insufficient Public Transportation

Pro	Con
only 4 short routes with one bus for each route	nice, helpful bus drivers
runs only 6 A.M. to 6 P.M.	free fare for university students
buses only come once an hour	
schedules usually not followed	

Audience: Director of Public Transportation
Purpose: to change and expand the bus system
Techniques of Support: facts, examples, personal experiences
Argumentative Thesis: Although this town has a team of nice, devoted bus drivers, and the bus fare for students is free, this city needs to expand and change its public transportation in order to better serve the citizens.

Outline (Plan B)

I. Introduction: statement of the controversy + thesis statement of opinion

(Techique:
Counterargument
is irrelevant)

II. Con: nice drivers and free fare for university students (true but not related)

III. Pro #1: limited service makes it difficult to go anywhere: 4 short routes and only 1 bus for each route

IV. Pro #2: limited time poses many problems (6 A.M. to 6 P.M.)

V. Pro #3: limited schedules (buses only come once an hour) and schedules are not always followed

VI. Solution: to establish fares for students and to raise fares for everyone in order to improve service in three areas: more buses, more routes, and better schedules

VII. Conclusion: a summary with emphasis on the solution and a prediction (if improvements are not made)

Angela Henao
(Mexico)

III
Should We Cut Trees Or Not?

Pro	Con
timber an indispensable material for modern life	harmful to the environment
	causes erosion and landslides
forests are renewable	need to preserve forests naturally
selective cutting and reforestation solves problems	destroys natural resources
	forests destroyed, ugly
appropriate management allows total forest land to remain stable	
harvesting trees is healthy for the forest; actually increases productivity	

Audience: general public

Purpose: to explain the controversy and to persuade the audience that harvesting trees can be environmentally sound

Techniques of Support: facts, examples

Argumentative thesis: <u>Although</u> preservationists believe that cutting trees harms the environment and destroys valuable natural resources, conservationists and forest managers believe that selective harvesting is actually good for forests and for people <u>because</u> it increases productivity and provides jobs and timber.

Outline (Plan C)

I. Introduction: basic controversy explained + thesis statement of opinion

(Technique: C-A is untrue)

II. Con #1 + Pro: forests destroyed (not with good management; reforestation makes forests renewable)

(Technique: C-A is insufficient)

III. Con #2 + Pro: causes erosion and landslides (knowledgeable forest management harvests carefully; selective cutting prevents)

IV. Con #3 + Pro: destroys natural resources (timber an indispensable material for modern life; forest industry provides jobs)

(Technique: C-A is untrue)

V. Con #4 + Pro: harmful to the environment (good management actually helpful to forest; increases productivity)

VI. Conclusion: compromise with recommendations: there should be limitations and standards for harvesting trees; must have appropriate forest management so that everyone benefits.

Shinsuke Yamazaki
(Japan)

___ EXERCISE 5F ___

Evidence that supports opinion is so important that without adequate evidence, an argumentative essay does not communicate successfully. Read the essay below. The lines at the end of each body paragraph have been added to indicate where evidence for the author's opinions should be written. What kinds of evidence could the author use? Think of some specific details that would support and strengthen each body paragraph.

Should the U.S. Get Out of El Salvador?

thesis
statement

For fifty years the Salvadoran people have been victims of the military governments that have abolished democracy. Once again, the military forces have taken over the power with the support of the U.S. Although the Salvadoran government (a military government) today says that the military aid received from the U.S. is necessary to maintain the democracy, the majority of Salvadorans say that this military aid has been used against them.

support
needed

The U.S. says that the military aid sent to El Salvador is to provide resistance against the Communists trying to get into that country. However, if the U.S. would stay out of El Salvador, the Communists would not feel it necessary to support the guerrillas. _____

concluding
sentence

If the external powers stayed out of El Salvador, the Salvadoran people could settle the war among themselves.

support
needed
concluding
sentence

Another point of view of the government is that if the lower classes were allowed to take over the government, there would be absolute chaos because the people have no experience with government. However, with practice, the people could learn to rule themselves. _____
_____. Who is better to rule the people than the people?

explanation
needed

Also, some experts contend that war is always good for a sagging economy like that in El Salvador. It is true that El Salvador's economy is poor. _____
_____

support
needed

However, the great amount of money that has been spent on military equipment could have been spent in supporting the national economy, an economy which has in fact been destroyed by the civil war. _____
_____

support
needed

Still another opinion is that a war would thin out a population in an overpopulated country. While it is true that many people have been killed by the U.S.-backed military, the first law of human rights is the right to live. So any killing in El Salvador is unjustified. _____
_____

summary
recommendation

In conclusion, El Salvador would benefit by the U.S. military getting out of the country. It would be good to have financial aid given by the U.S. in some other areas: agriculture, education, medical facilities, and perhaps business. That would truly be investing in the future of El Salvador.

Carlos Muñoz
(Venezuela)

Study the student plan for an argumentative essay below. Then write a similar plan for your argumentative essay. Be sure to consider the audience *and the* purpose *of your essay as you write that plan. Then begin drafting your essay.*

Planning My Argumentative Essay

My audience: the Director of the Animal Health Program in Paraguay. This is a central institution in charge of performing investigations and making recommendations to farmers about the best ways to control certain diseases.

My purpose: to persuade the Director that using artificial insemination to control one disease is effective and not as expensive as the traditional methods.

Introduction: I explain the general situation that now exists and tell what the paper will discuss.

Body Paragraph #1: Background information. I mention the vaccine's effects on cattle and duration of immunity. I think the Director knows this, but I emphasize that the farmers now have to vaccinate twice a year, and that sometimes animals do not respond to the vaccine.

Body Paragraph #2: I introduce artificial insemination as an alternate way of eliminating the disease. My preference for artificial insemination becomes clear.

Body Paragraph #3: I demonstrate the differences between vaccination and artificial insemination. I lead to the conclusion that artificial insemination is less work and, in the long term, more lasting.

Body Paragraph #4: Counterargument paragraph. Opponents say that artificial insemination takes more work and more money. I demonstrate by the use of a chart that on the contrary, artificial insemination is only more expensive at the beginning. Within a short period of time, it will be cost-effective.

Conclusion: I summarize the problems with vaccination, and I state that artificial insemination can eliminate the disease in a short time. I stress that artificial insemination is economically feasible and recommend that its use be investigated further.

Cesar Prieto
(Paraguay)

Logical Fallacies

In argumentative essays, rational thought is a strong persuader. If the essay is based on emotions or feelings, or if the rational thought is flawed (and therefore not rational), the argument loses its strength. Below is a list of logical errors commonly made by students in argumentative essays.

HASTY GENERALIZATION: Jumping to conclusions.

> All required university courses are boring.
> Science fiction books are not worth the time it takes to read them.

Solution: Avoid words like "everybody," "all," and "nothing," and qualify statements.

STEREOTYPE: A form of hasty generalization, applied to people.

Happy families make happy children.
All English teachers have green eyes.
Women psychologists can't be trusted.

Solution: Qualify and specify your statements; prove with valid evidence.

OVERSIMPLIFICATION: Severe reduction of choices, sometimes limited to an either/or dilemma.

What's wrong with this country? Just *one* thing. There are 11.5 million women who started but never finished high school.
Love it or leave it. (Either love it or leave it.)

Solution: Qualify your statements; identify all causes and effects.

POST HOC ERGO PROPTER HOC: (After this, therefore because of this.) X happened before Y; therefore X caused Y.

He got straight As because he smoked a cigarette before every class.
The rooster crowed. The sun rose. Therefore the rooster made the sun rise.

Solution: Make sure that *time* is not the only thing linking cause and effect.

RED HERRING: A statement that has no direct relevance to the topic.

Crime, communism, and delinquency are on the rise. Therefore we had better abolish the federal income tax.

Solution: Be precise in distinguishing the relevant from the irrelevant.

FALSE AUTHORITY: Arguing that a person who is competent in one field will necessarily be competent in another.

James Johnson is a good congressman. Therefore he would be a good preacher/teacher/president/garbage collector.
Since Dr. Kissinger taught at Harvard, his ideas about foreign policy must be right.

Solution: Be certain that your sources are authorities in their fields.

STATISTICS: False use of numbers proves nothing.

Super-Slim Artificial Yogurt will help you lose weight because it has only 50 calories per ounce.

Solution: Ask yourself specific questions about statistics: Source? Applicability? Thorough study or mere speculation? Recent or dated? Local, national, international data?

VICE and VIRTUE WORDS: The use of words that connote bad or good emotional reactions in the reader.

Do you want your sons and daughters to fall victim to this Communist conspiracy? Or die at the hands of this menace?

The first choice of discriminating travelers is Holiday Inn, a prestige hotel for those who exect the best.

Solution: Use connotative words, but be sure that you have logical proof to support what you say.

FUNDAMENTALS FOR LOGICAL ANALYSIS

1. *Always* remember *never* to say *always* and *never* (and *all* and *none*, and *everyone* and *nobody*). Reasonable thinking should be reflected in reasonable language. All-inclusive statements can rarely be proved. Qualify and specify.
2. Even if you are sure that one thing is the cause of another, it may not be the *only* cause. Be careful not to oversimplify.
3. *Suspicious words* like "undoubtedly" and "obviously" are often followed by hasty generalizations and oversimplifications.
4. Any opinion you have must be qualified and specified, and must be supported completely with facts, examples, or personal experience.

___ EXERCISE 5H _____

Identify the logical fallacies in the following sentences. Some sentences may contain more than one fallacy.

1. Working conditions could be improved if women workers did not take so much time off for sick leave.
2. She couldn't sleep last night, so she failed the quiz this morning.
3. The United States, in formulating and applying its future foreign policy, must choose between a return to strict isolationism and total global commitment.
4. The Vietnamese cannot govern themselves.
5. Everyone who works for General Motors is rich; the median salary is $30,000 a year.
6. The law is a good one because Senator Byrd introduced it, and he is a good and honest man.
7. Of course Hawaii is about the healthiest spot in the world. Life expect-

ancy there for men is 70.1 years, as compared with 68.2 years for men on the mainland.

8. The airport is obviously unsafe. There have been three crashes there in as many years.

9. America is a land of easy-spending millionaires, sexy blondes, fabulous Park Avenue apartments, and easy morals. How do I know? Monsieur, I see your American movies!

10. Ban aerosol sprays or we'll all die of skin cancer!

—— Exercise 5I ——————————————————

Analyze the following passage in terms of logical fallacies. Do not merely agree or disagree with the statements, but analyze line by line the reasoning process involved. Do not substitute your ideas for Devlin's. Rather, objectively, logically, analyze the argument.

Seven months ago I was in South Vietnam under the auspices of the National Association for the Advancement of Underdeveloped Countries. Before arriving in South Vietnam, I had studied at length the causes of the political upheaval of impoverished countries and had concluded that the Buddhists were responsible for the situation in Vietnam because they refused to adjust their policies to the changing political factions.

Thus, when I arrived in South Vietnam and saw a Buddhist monk engulfed in flames, my opinion was confirmed: the Buddhists want to rule South Vietnam just as the United States tried, before the First World War, to maintain their political and economic isolationism while secretly trying to control the British government of Lloyd George. Therefore, the single question which must be asked is, "Should the U.S. forces in Vietnam eliminate the Buddhist faction in order to effect national unity?" The answer is obvious: everything else has failed; this is the only recourse.

Although this may seem a startling conclusion, the facts show that only after the Buddhists began to publicly burn themselves did the government of President Ky begin to crumble. Indeed, should the United States continue to subvert the ideals and principles of the South Vietnamese when the Buddhists are the source of the difficulty? Since Christianity teaches us that suicide is against the laws of God, we can see that the Buddhists' political actions are without any moral justification.

Therefore, the U.S. policy-makers should embark on a new course of action: minimize the efforts against the Viet Cong and devote their main force to a correction of this poisonous thorn in the side of the American lamb, a thorn which is dispersing and submerging the democratic way of life!

Dudley Erskine Devlin
Journal of Political Inequality (JPI),
December 4, 1970, pp. 181–82.

_____ EXERCISE 5J _____

Revise the rough draft of your argumentative essay. Look carefully at your opinions. Have you qualified them and used reasonable language? Have you supported each opinion? Use the Revision Guidelines on pp. 79–82, and use the Revision Processes on the inside back cover of this textbook to help with your revision.

Student Samples of Argumentative Essays

THE EFFECT OF THE U.S. FOREIGN POLICY IN VIETNAM

For Americans, April 30, 1975 was probably a breath of relief after carrying such a burden. Many Americans had awaited the collapse of South Vietnam for a long time, especially since the birth of the Paris Accords in January, 1973. In the eyes of these people who had stood against the draft or joined the antiwar movement, the unconditional surrender message of South Vietnam to the Communists was not only their own victory but also the victory of democracy: the Americans had used their supreme right to force their government to yield before their will. They considered the decision of abandoning South Vietnam as the

introductory material

(courageous) achievement of a civilized people. However, it is indisputable that the fall of (South Vietnam) was the direct and unavoidable result of the American withdrawal of support.

thesis: statement of opinion

paragraph hooks

Many (Vietnamese), of course, would not understand the (courage) and morality in the American

topic sentence

"withdrawal with honor." The day the Vietnamese ambassador left Washington, D.C., he bitterly lamented: "You Americans are too cruel." On the evening of April 4, 1975, in his last speech to the Southern Vietnamese people, Nguyen Van Thieu also accused the Americans of betraying one of their allies and selling out South Vietnam to the Communists. This opinion was repeated by many Vietnamese. Yet, people who deservedly spilled out their bitterness were not heard, perhaps because nobody wanted to pay attention to them. Those dead could not be revived from their graves, and within the re-education camps scattered in Vietnam, those former "anti-Communists" could only blame themselves for their naive faith in the "good will" of the American people and its government in helping (Vietnam) to repel Communist aggression and defend freedom and democracy.

America, because of ITS wrong policy and ITS numerous mistakes, contributed much to the fall of (Vietnam). The U.S. was right when IT wanted to become involved in the Vietnam issue after the Geneva agreements to prevent Vietnam from sliding under Communist control. *However,* American policy-makers made many mistakes in THEIR methods of intervention in Vietnam. *For example,* after the fall of the Ngo Dinh Diem regime, the U.S. government supported only the obedient generals whom they called "strong men." The Nguyen Van Thieu regime, which was rejected by the Vietnamese people, survived for several years under U.S. support. THIS support caused the Southern Vietnamese to become dissatisfied and *thus* weakened the war against the Communists. People didn't trust their own government; several meetings were held by the students who represented the people to request the resignation of thePresident. *Unfortunately,* HE did resign, but not because ofthe request from HIS people; *rather,* HE resigned because of the U.S. withdrawal of support. Later in the war, Americans made another big mistake. *First,* THEY mobilized all of their forces to destroy the Communist

Margin notes:

first argument

technique of support: *examples*

method of development: *cause-effect*

paragraph hook

pronouns used as coherence DEVICES

topic sentence

transitions

second argument

technique of support: *facts*

chronological organization

method of development: *cause-effect*

group attacking South Vietnam, yet *later* THEY negotiated with the Communists. *Finally,* Americans committed THEMSELVES to the "limited war" concept. THEIR troops in Vietnam did not seek victory on the battle field. THIS encouraged the stubborn Communists to continue the war *because* in a game, if a player knows that HE will win or at least tie, HE is not so stupid as to give up.

From the point of view of the South Vietnamese, the U.S. policies during the war contradicted previous U.S. actions during previous world conflicts. During World War I, for example, the U.S. persevered until the enemy was vanquished. The same was true during the second world war when the U.S. stopped the spread of **Communism** in Europe. And just thirty years before the fall of **Vietnam**, the U.S. had fought hard on an international level for the creation of Israel, then had brought millions of Israeli citizens from all over the world to their new country in the Middle East to become a strong and prosperous non-**Communist** nation. As a result of these conflicts, the worldwide reputation of being an adversary of communism and a protector of small countries had come with the U.S. into Vietnam. The betrayal of the trust of the **Vietnamese** people was symbolized by one man: Henry Kissinger, a man whose name still arouses anger and frustration among the South **Vietnamese**. Initially Mr. Kissinger's attitude towards the war was hawkish. However, in league with Le Duc Tho, Mr. Kissinger created the Paris Agreement that favored the unconditional withdrawal of the American troops from **Vietnam** and precipitated the tearful collapse of Saigon. His negotiations were directly responsible in creating a sea of tears for seventeen million **Vietnamese**. He cut the anchor and let the **Vietnamese** boat sink into the hands of the **Communists**.

Of course, **the Vietnamese** people understand that the business of politics is pragmatic and not always moral. Sometimes promises cannot be kept. However, the fact is that a small boy being undressed and thrown to an ant's nest would not be seen as a

[margin annotations: repetition of key words; chronological organization; paragraph hook; topic sentence; third argument; technique of support: example; counter-argument]

prediction

humanitarian action. We Vietnamese still remember that one day in the recent past, before Vietnam fell, some U.S. officials were quoted as saying: "South Vietnam is the outpost of the Free World; it should be protected at any costs." Then South Vietnam was suddenly tipped to the Communists. I wondered then why that "front line fortress" became unworthy. Where is the new outpost of the Free World now? And if an outpost is unworthy, will other areas be safe forever from the enemy?

rebuttal
and
conclusion

Van Tran
(South Viet Nam)

THE NECESSITY OF KOREAN FOREIGN LANGUAGE EDUCATION FOR KOREAN-AMERICAN CHILDREN

introduction

background information

Korean permanent residents in the U.S. face the problem of children who do not speak their native language. While the new immigrants feel relieved from their hard lives, the speed of their English proficiency is slow like a turtle's pace; on the other hand, that of their children is as fast as a rabbit. Here the necessity of Korean language education becomes an object of controversy. Some parents do not want their children to learn Korean; they want their children only to learn

thesis
statement
of intent

English. In my opinion, Korean language education not only promotes the development of children but also brings domestic peace, which is a common aim of immigrant homes; furthermore, Korean language education makes children understand the culture of their ancestors.

controlling
ideas

Con #1

Some parents insist that they need not teach the Korean language to their children. Their opinion is that if children learn two languages at the same time, they will have low language ability because they will divide their ability. However, [we have nothing to worry

topic
sentence

about on that point.] According to psychological research, children who learn two (or more) languages at the same time can improve their thinking faculties and creative abilities. For example, in Canada, children who spoke only English learned their school subjects in French in elementary school. The results were that these children not only could speak French proficiently after two or three years, but also had increased creative power, more sophisticated thinking faculties, and greater adaptability and intellectuality than other children who spoke only one language. Therefore, children who learn both (Korean) and English may be better, not worse, students .

Other parents refuse to teach (Korean) to their children because the children are unwilling to study and learn . Consequently, family problems occur when the parents insist that the children learn Korean. In contrast, however, **[Korean language education can be positively related to domestic peace.]** First, children tend to adapt themselves to American culture and to the English language quickly and easily, but their parents often have difficulty expressing their thoughts in English freely. If the parents cannot understand English well, and the children cannot understand Korean, a generation gap occurs. This gap can become wider and wider each day, and finally it will bring about family troubles. If the communication between parents and their children is poor because of the language, children will surely live in a world different from their parents. To prevent their (children) being lost from them, parents should teach the Korean (language) to their children .

Many Korean immigrant parents think that their (children) should become Americans as quickly as possible; therefore, they refuse to interfere with the assimilation process by teaching the children the (language) and culture of Korea. **[This is a serious mistake.]** Koreans are a minority in the U.S., and keeping in touch with their culture and ancestors is necessary in order to keep their pride and security. While assimilation of the new culture is good, keeping the old culture is just as important. Someday the children will ask themselves where they came from; they will have a need to

Margin notes (left):
Pro: technique = *incorrect*

concluding sentence

paragraph hooks

Pro: technique = insufficient

concluding sentence

Con #3

Pro: technique = insufficient

Margin notes (right):
method of development: comparison-contrast

supporting techniques: facts, example

transitions

method of development: cause-effect

topic sentence

transitions

paragraph hooks

topic sentence

method of development: cause-effect

know about their culture. To understand that culture, they must learn their native tongue <u>because</u> the language is the most important element that forms the spiritual value and racial consciousness.

concluding sentence

<u>In conclusion,</u> Korean language education is desirable for the children themselves and for domestic peace. What is most important is that the language is not only a means of communication but also a link to the mind and soul of the culture. Therefore, Korean language education in immigrant homes is important and should be required.

conclusion: summary

recommendation

techniques of support: facts, examples

transitions

Sung Sik Pak
(Korea)

___ EXERCISE 5K ___

As you prepare the final draft of your argumentative essay, consider the following checklist:

1. Have you communicated successfully with your audience?
2. How do you expect your audience to respond to your essay?
3. Is your essay authoritative? Credible? Valid?
4. Is the purpose of the essay clearly stated and explained?
5. Is your opinion presented with strong evidence?

Next, complete these special instructions:

1. Your essay must include an outline that shows which plan of organization you chose.
2. Circle and join the paragraph hooks between the body paragraphs in your essay.
3. In two body paragraphs, underline the transitional words and phrases.
4. At the end of your essay, provide the following information:
   A. the audience for your essay
   B. the purpose of your essay
   C. the number of words in your essay.

6

Summary and Analysis

Introduction

In academic writing assignments, you will frequently be asked to respond to written material. That is, you will be asked to read something (a journal article, a chapter in a book, a technical report) and to write a summary and an analysis of what you read. The assignments may have different titles:

A. a summary-analysis   E. a report on reference material
B. a book report   F. a response to a critical article
C. a critique   G. a research report
D. a literature review   H. a response to written material

While the assignments may differ somewhat, generally a response to written material consists of two basic parts:

A. a summary of the written material
B. an analysis of part or all of the material.

As with any writing assignment, you will need to be certain of the professor's expectations:

A. Is a summary required? If so, how brief or how detailed should it be?
B. Is *only* a summary required? A research report, for example, might require an extensive summary of several articles, and nothing more.

ysis required? If so, must you analyze the entire article or
ed parts?

condensation of the main ideas in an article. The length of a
ds on:

1. The assignment
2. The length and complexity of the article
3. The audience

The qualities of a summary are

1. **Objectivity:** No idea that is not the author's should be included in the summary, and *no opinion of the summary writer* should be in the summary. No judgments (i.e., whether the article was "good" or "interesting") are permitted in a summary.
2. **Completeness:** Depending on the assignment, the summary should contain every main idea in the article. Stating only the first main idea, or only one main idea and details to support it, will not give the reader a complete idea of what the article was about.
3. **Balance:** Giving equal attention to each main idea, and stressing ideas that the author stressed, will result in an accurate summary.

Questions to judge a valid summary:

1. Did you include all the important ideas?
2. Did you omit the unnecessary words and phrases?
3. Does the summary read smoothly?
   A. use of transitions: *also, thus, therefore, however*
   B. use of sentence combining
4. Would a reader of your summary who had *not* read the article have a clear idea about the article?

The goal of the summary is to give readers an objective, complete, accurate, balanced view of an article they have not read.

Process of summarizing material:

1. Read the article quickly, looking for main ideas.
2. Read it again carefully, absorbing the information.

3. Look for the thesis and topic sentences; they will give you the main ideas of the article that you will need for your summary.
4. Depending on the assignment, *select* the major ideas you will need to use in your summary.
5. *Arrange* these ideas carefully in order to achieve balance and completeness.
6. Begin the summary with a sentence that informs your reader of the title and author of the article:
   Examples:
   In the article "The Making of the Dutch Landscape," Audrey Lambert states that . . .
   Assignments in Exposition, a book by Louise E. Rorabacher, discusses . . .
7. Punctuation
   A. Underline the titles of books.
   B. Put the titles of articles in quotation marks.
   C. Ellipsis: Three dots indicate that something has been left out of a direct quotation.
      Examples:
      " . . . something has been left out of a direct quotation."
      "Three dots indicate that something has been left out. . . . " (**Note** that the sentence ends, so a period is added.)
   D. Brackets [ ] enclose information added to a direct quotation (for example, to replace a pronoun with a noun.)
      Examples:
      "[Cuomo's] philosophy is to share the burdens and benefits equally."
      "We are losing a war [in the Grand Canyon]."

___ EXERCISE 6A _____

Summarize a television program you have seen recently in
1. *approximately 25 words*
2. *25 to 50 words*
3. *50 to 75 words*
4. *approximately 100 words*
Notice that a simple statement of the main idea of the television program in #1 is expanded to a relatively complete description of the program in #4.

___ EXERCISE 6B _____

Write a summary of fifty words for the short article below. Use some of these structures in your summary:
1. *This article examines (discusses) . . .*
2. *X was investigated to determine whether . . .*

3. *This article addresses the question of whether . . .*
4. *In the article "_____," . . .*
Then think about how you might respond to the ideas in the article.

Wages for Housewives?

As working women continue to receive better and better wages, housewives still work at home without receiving paychecks. Should a woman who works at home, doing the housework and caring for children, be paid for her services? In a 1986 study at Cornell University, sociologists found that the value of the services of a housewife averaged $11,600 a year. This rate was based on a family composed of a husband, wife, and three young children. The $11,600 is what the husband would have to pay if he hired others to take over his wife's household chores. The researchers concluded that it would be fair for husbands to pay wives according to federal guidelines for minimum wages.

Another plan for rewarding women who work at home has been suggested by a former Secretary of Health and Human Services. He says that full-time housewives should be allowed to pay social security taxes, with their employers (that is, their husbands) contributing part of the payment. He feels that the present system is unfair. He said, "If you work as a clerk in a store you can qualify for Social Security, but if you stay at home and raise a family, nobody will give you credit for it."

___ EXERCISE 6C _____

Read the two short articles below. Then summarize each article in approximately one hundred words. Use some of the sentence structures in Exercise 5B in your summaries. Then think of how you might respond to the ideas in each article.

Transferring Western Technology to Developing Nations

During the 1980s, unemployment and underemployment in some countries has been as high as 90%. Some countries do not produce enough food; basic needs in housing and clothing are unmet. Many of these countries look to the industrial processes of the developed nations for solutions to these problems.

But the problems are not always solved this way. The industry of the developed nations is highly automated and very expensive. It provides fewer jobs than nonautomated industrial processes, and highly skilled workers are needed to maintain and repair the equipment. These workers must be trained, but many nations do not have the necessary training institutions. Thus, the cost of importing industry becomes higher. Students must be sent abroad to receive vocational and professional training. Often, just to begin training, the students must first learn English, French, German, or Japanese. The students then spend many years abroad, and some do not return home.

All nations agree that science and technology should be shared. However, countries adopting the industrial processes of the developed nations need to look carefully at the costs. Many of these costs are hidden. Students from these nations should study the problems of the industrialized countries closely. With care, they will take home not the problems of science and technology, but the benefits.

Foreign Students and the U.S. Student Shortage

In recent years, college and university administrators have faced a new challenge: a shortage of traditional, eighteen- to twenty-two-year-old full-time students. Trying to solve the problem, the 3,200 postsecondary institutions in the U.S. are offsetting the declining enrollment of traditional students by increasing the number of "nontraditional" students (those aged twenty-five and over).

Fortunately, while the American supply of full-time students is slipping, the worldwide supply is ever increasing. Bringing in more foreign students could help avert serious damage in U.S. postsecondary education while helping to educate young people of the developing world. Right now there are a record 342,000 foreign students in the United States, but they constitute only 3 percent of the total U.S. student population of 12 million.

Increasing that number would accomplish a number of desirable goals simultaneously: increasing the number of full-time students on U.S. campuses, internationalizing what has become a much too parochial American education system, and developing the potential of poor countries by educating and training their best and brightest students. It would also make friends for America throughout the world. Finally, and perhaps most important, it builds the foundations of a more peaceful world through improved mutual understanding across borders. Recruiting more international students, especially from developing countries, offers the U.S. an opportunity to address long-term problems at American campuses while spreading the bounty of higher education throughout a world thirsting for knowledge. That, after all, is the kind of positive force in world affairs that America can and should aspire to be.

___ EXERCISE 6D ___

Read one of the sample essays in this book. (See list of student essays at the end of the Table of Contents). *Summarize the article*
1. *in a single sentence that states the main idea of the essay.*
2. *in a summary of one paragraph (100 words) that gives a more complete (but just as objective) summary of the article.*

Planning an Analysis

As you read an article (or book, or report), you will respond to the material; you will form *opinions* about the ideas. *Analysis* requires more:

1. Why do you agree (or disagree) with the author?
2. What *support* do you have for your opinion?

To analyze means to observe carefully, to take an idea apart, and to discover how you think and feel about it. To communicate the results of your analysis to an audience, you must be able to *show* the audience why your opinion is worthwhile. You support your opinion with facts, examples, physical description, and/or personal experience.

The Process of Writing an Analysis of Written Material

1. Read the article (book, articles, reports).
2. Read it again, marking the points you would choose to discuss (respond to).
3. Decide on an overall thesis that agrees or disagrees (or perhaps agrees *and* disagrees) with the main points of the article.
4. Begin to generate support for your opinions; use one of the strategies demonstrated in Chapter 2.
5. Construct topic sentences for the body paragraphs of your essay; each topic sentence will *agree* or *disagree* with a single point in the article.
6. Gather support for the opinions you wrote in your topic sentences: use facts, examples, physical description, and/or personal experience.

General Form for Summary-Analysis of Written Material

For a response to written material that is approximately 500 words (2 double-spaced typewritten pages), the essay will probably have a total of 4–6 paragraphs. Below (Figure 6–1) is a diagram of the general form for summary-analysis essays.

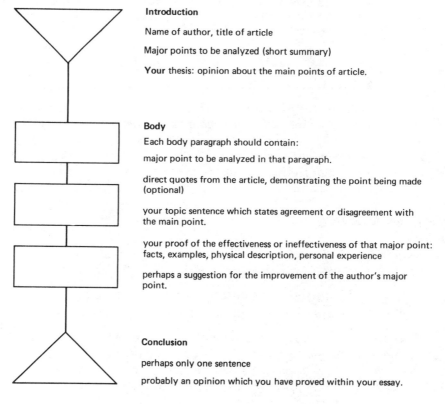

Introduction

Name of author, title of article

Major points to be analyzed (short summary)

Your thesis: opinion about the main points of article.

Body

Each body paragraph should contain:

major point to be analyzed in that paragraph.

direct quotes from the article, demonstrating the point being made (optional)

your topic sentence which states agreement or disagreement with the main point.

your proof of the effectiveness or ineffectiveness of that major point: facts, examples, physical description, personal experience

perhaps a suggestion for the improvement of the author's major point.

Conclusion

perhaps only one sentence

probably an opinion which you have proved within your essay.

FIG. 6-1

> **Note:** The structure of the summary-analysis of written material differs slightly from the structure of an expository essay:
>
> 1. The introduction begins with a specific sentence (title, author) and moves to a general sentence (the thesis).
> 2. Each body paragraph begins with a summary; the topic sentence is usually the second or even the third sentence.
> 3. The conclusion is often quite brief and contains a general response based on the opinions given in the body paragraphs.

Whatever the assignment, if both a summary and an analysis are required, the general format will remain the same:

I. First paragraph should include
   A. Name of the material read (book, article)
   B. Name of the author(s)
   C. Main ideas of the written material (brief summary)
   D. *Your* main idea (your *thesis statement of opinion,* your response to the material)

Example:

introduction { A recent article in the *Journal of Political Inequality,* "Underground Revolution," concerns the underground leftist organizations in Iran.

summary { Authors Swenta Bold, Geri Johnson, and Daniel Mroz discuss such information as the political beliefs, the demonstrations, and revolu-

thesis { tion in Iran. Probably because their news sources were incorrect or biased, most of the information in this article is biased or simply wrong.

II. General progression for body paragraphs
   A. First main point (second main point, etc.) to be analyzed is summarized briefly
   B. Quoted material to illustrate that summary (optional)
   C. Your response to that main point (the topic sentence): notice that your topic sentence is *not* the first sentence in the paragraph.
   D. Support for your topic sentence from your own experience or reading

Example:

summary ⎰   According to authors Bolt, Johnson, and Mroz, at least one of
    the major organizations is pro-Communist. "Perhaps the most dan-
    gerous guerilla force—the one, apparently, that led the attack against

quotation ⎰   the U.S. Embassy—is the pro-Moscow Fedayeen-Kalq, or People's
    Self-Sacrifice guerrilla." What is the meaning of "dangerous" here?

topic
sentence ⎰   This organization is not dangerous for Iranians or for Iran, but it is
    dangerous for Iran's enemy, for world imperialism; in fact, that was
    the reason for the organization: to revolt against the corrupt rule in
    Iran and against the imperialist force of the U.S. Second, the Feday-
    een denied the responsibility of the attack on the U.S. Embassy. And
    in fact, an official report from the government showed that a rightist
    group of Khomeini's supporters was responsible for attacking the
    embassy. After the attack, the leftist group called the Fedayeen pro-
    tected the embassy. Third and most important, the Fedayeen are not

support ⎰   pro-Moscow. In their political brochures it has been written many
    times that "We do not support any country and we are not supported
    by any country." As far as their policy has been shown to Iranians,
    what they say is true: they are not going to make Iran an independent
    country.

III. Conclusion
    A.   Statement of *your* conclusions after reading and thinking about
        the written material.
    B.   What points can you make? Where did the article lead you?

Example:

    Why did an important magazine like the *Journal of Political
Inequality* have these mistakes? Surely a worldwide magazine would
have better and more reliable news sources. A cynic might conclude
that this magazine is trying to influence people's minds about the
situation in Iran. Perhaps the *Journal of Political Inequality* wants
to frighten their readers away from communism. If it is true that the
news Americans get about Iran is controlled and biased, several questions arise: is other news, particularly about Communist countries
and revolutions in countries, also slanted? Is news generally controlled in the U.S.? If so, who is responsible for this control?

    One problem that student writers often have in summary-analysis essays
is keeping a clear distinction between the ideas in the article and the student
writer's opinions and ideas. To solve this problem:

1. Use the title of the article or the author's name in every paragraph, both to keep your reader aware of the topic and as a coherence device.
2. When using the author's name, use the *last*, not the first name (Bolt stated . . .).
3. Be certain that your topic sentence in each paragraph clearly agrees or disagrees with the main point of that paragraph.
4. Do not use examples or facts from the article to support your opinions. Use ideas that you generate yourself.

Additional suggestions:

1. In a critique or written response, agreeing totally with the article often leads to a repetitive essay; it is difficult to think up new examples of why an author is correct. It is easier to disagree with the author: disagreement is often easier to prove.
2. Perhaps the most balanced response to written material is some agreement and some disagreement. Keep that in mind as you plan your essay: if possible, agree first (the weaker paragraphs) and then disagree (the stronger paragraphs).

____ EXERCISE 6E _____

In recent years, a major political controversy in the U.S. has focused on the growing number of small handguns (sometimes called "Saturday night specials") in this country. The millions of members of the powerful National Rifle Association oppose government legislation of any kind of gun ownership; however, a number of people in the U.S. think that handguns should be made illegal.

Below are two letters representing opposite viewpoints. Read both letters. Select the letter with which you <u>disagree</u>. *In an organized* <u>essay</u>, *briefly summarize the main points of that letter; then discuss why you disagree with the letter, using facts and examples from your personal experience or your reading to support your opinion.*

Dear Sir:

    There are four reasons why the U.S. government must not outlaw handguns in this country. First, banning handguns is a violation of the rights of fifty million honest, law-abiding citizens. The U.S. Constitution gives all Americans "the right to bear arms," so any restriction of private ownership of guns is unconstitutional.

    Second, an armed citizenry is the only defense against crime and against a Communist takeover of the U.S.

Dear Sir:

    Handguns must be banned on a national level in order to reduce the rising crime rate in the U.S., a rate that is directly proportional to the number of available handguns. Today in the U.S., there are 50 million handguns; a handgun is sold in the U.S. every 13 seconds, adding 2 million handguns each year. By the year 2,000, there will be 100 million handguns in the U.S.—will we be any safer?

    Probably not. The statistics in-

Moreover, the right of self-defense is a fundamental one in this democratic country. If I know how to use a gun and feel I need one, no one should have the authority to deny me that right.

Third, don't confuse the owning of handguns with crime. Most of my law-abiding friends own handguns and use them for hunting, target practice, and self-defense. Instead of seizing our property, strengthen the criminal justice system so that criminals who use handguns in crimes are severely punished. Convict criminals—not guns.

Fourth, banning handguns would not work. If handguns were illegal, guns would still be sold despite the law; the people who bought them would be the real criminals, and the profits would go to organized crime. Those of us who obeyed the law would therefore be defenseless; we would be at the mercy of the armed muggers and thieves. Nobody in his right mind would turn in his gun and thereby become a willing victim.

Don't abuse our liberty and put our country in jeopardy by outlawing handguns. Handguns are an American culture symbol that cannot be eliminated. Remember: guns don't kill people. People kill people.

Harlan Mohr
Vice-President, National
    Sportsman's Association
Austin, Texas

volving murder with handguns in the U.S. are remarkable. During the Vietnam war, for example, more Americans were murdered with handguns in the U.S. than were killed in Vietnam. Recently the city of Los Angeles reported 32 murders with handguns in a single week. Today handguns are responsible for half the nation's murders. The fact is that people with handguns are far more likely to kill people than those armed with any other weapon.

Making handguns illegal will not affect hunting rifles and shotguns. But such a law will eliminate the small, easily concealed "Saturday night special" used so often by robbers or muggers. These handguns simply promote and perpetuate violence in society.

We live in a "gun culture" left over, perhaps, from our history of frontier justice, but the result of this culture has been that the U.S. statistically has more homicides than anywhere else in the world. The U.S. government needs to reverse the trend by banning the sale, import, and manufacture of handguns and by passing tough restrictions to keep handguns out of circulation.

Nelson T. Shield III
President, Handgun Control, Inc.
Washington, D.C.

Student Responses

Below is an essay about a controversial subject. Read it and then study the samples in which North American students responded to it.

THE DANGERS OF TELEVISION

When television was first introduced into American society thirty years ago, writers and social scientists thought that this new invention would better American life. "Television is going to bring American families closer together," predicted psychologist Joel Gold in 1949. Pictures which advertised television in the 1950s invariably showed a happy family gathered together in the living room, sharing the TV viewing experience. Who could have guessed that a quarter of a century later Mother would be in the kitchen watching a daytime drama, Dad would be in the living room watching a ball game, and the children would be watching cartoons in their bedroom?

Television has certainly changed American life, but not the way the first critics predicted. The first televisions were enormously expensive, so most families owned only one. By 1975, however, 60% of American families owned two televisions or more; some middle class families had as many as five television sets under one roof. Such multi-set families may keep family members in the same house, but that hardly brings them "together." In fact, family outings— hiking, going to the movies, going out to dinner—are often limited by TV because one or more family members don't want to go: "I'll miss my program," is the common complaint.

Perhaps more important than the lack of family outings is the destruction of family time together at home. Social scientists in the 1950s could not have realized how much television Americans would watch in the 1980s; the average American watches 6 hours of TV a day. That leaves little time for the special family characteristics and traditions that used to be formed during long evenings together. The time devoted to games, songs, and hobbies—all shared activities—in the years before TV is now dominated by "the tube." And especially damaging to family relationships is the elimination of the opportunities for talking; chatting, arguing, discussing. Without such communication, family life disintegrates.

Domination is the key word. Families in American today schedule their lives around the television. Children rush home from school to watch their programs while they do their homework. Mother shops between her special programs. The ski slopes are nearly empty on Superbowl Sunday; football on TV takes precedence. The family may even eat meals in front of the television. Moreover, television is used as a baby-sitter; small children nationwide spend countless hours in front of the TV, passively ingesting whatever flashes before their eyes. Addition of some sort inevitably follows; TV becomes a necessary part of life, and receiving a TV for his own room becomes the wish of every child. Moreover, parents use the television as a source of reward and punishment: "If you mow the lawn, you can watch TV an extra hour tonight," or "No TV for you. You didn't do your homework." Ultimately, life-styles revolve around a regular schedule of eating, sleeping, and watching television.

Isn't there a better family life than this dismal, mechanized arrangement? According to social scientist Mary Helen Thuente, "The quality of life is diminished as family ties grow weaker, as children's lives grow more and more separate from their parents, as the opportunities for living and sharing within a family are eliminated." Indeed, if the family does not accumulate shared experiences, it is not likely to survive. Consequently, if parents and children alike do not change their priorities, television will continue to exert its influence on American family life as baby-sitter, pacifier, teacher, role model, and supplier of mores and morals, thus supplanting the place of the family in society.

Harriet B. Fidler
(U.S.)

Below are paragraphs selected from several student responses to this article.

Note: There is no coherence between the paragraphs below because each paragraph was written by a different student.

Introduction #1

introduces article

summary

thesis (agreement)

"The Dangers of Television," an essay by Harriet B. Fidler, discusses the role television has played in changing American values. In the 1940s, television was predicted to bring families closer together. Its influence, however, has splintered family relations. The author indicates that children watch TV for hours; it has become a pacifier and a baby-sitter. Parents' roles as educators have been replaced by TV, preventing necessary interactions between family members. I agree with Harriet Fidler's idea that television weakens a family's ability to survive by taking away from the time they otherwise would spend relating to one another.

Introduction #2

introduces article

summary

direct quotation

thesis (agreement and disagreement)

In the essay, "The Dangers of Television," Harriet Fidler states that while a television in the home at one time served a purpose in bringing families closer together, it has recently become more and more detrimental to that very special relationship that exists between members of a family. She states that "if a family does not accumulate shared experiences, it is not likely to survive." I can speak only from personal experiences, but I agree with Ms. Fidler's basic assumption about the role of television in the American home. However, I believe that there are solutions to the problems she states.

***

Body Paragraph #1

summary and small quote

Ms. Fidler thinks that while television initially had a good effect on family life, it now "dominates" the family. I have seen

	the effects of television on my own family and agree with the au-
topic sentence	thor of this article. As a child, I can remember watching very little
	television. The majority of my time was spent outdoors with my
	family, gardening, playing, caring for livestock. Once a week my
	grandparents would come to visit and we'd all ride horses. How-
support:	ever, I did have a younger brother who preferred watching tele-
detail	vision to joining our family activities. At first we all wondered
personal	what was wrong with him. But as the years went by we began to
experience	join him in front of the TV; no longer were "Wild Kingdom" or
	"The World of Disney" the only programs I watched. Soon I too
	was watching situation comedies, game shows, sports events, and,
	eventually, anything that was on the tube.

Body Paragraph #2

summary and quote

topic sentence (agreement)

support: example, personal experience

In the article, Fidler stresses that in the beginning, televi- sion was "going to bring American families closer together." TV was not intended to become what modern day Americans have made it—a substitute for imagination. From my own experience, I readily agree with the author's statement. One situation exem- plifies her findings with striking clarity. When I first started baby- sitting for a family with a boy (10) and a girl (6), they owned no television. Our evenings would be spent playing Hide 'n Seek, Cha- rades and board games, and reading books, coloring and painting. Then came the big night: the first night of the new television set. No longer could I entice them with a game; now it was, "Please, just ONE more show?"

Body Paragraph #3

summary

direct quote

topic sentence disagreement

support: example, personal experience

Ms. Fidler states in her essay that instead of bringing fam- ilies together, television separates them by giving no time for con- versation or airing personal viewpoints. "Especially damaging to family relationships is the elimination of opportunities to talk. . . . " I disagree with this position. Maybe some families like the one mentioned in the article have problems communicating, but my family uses their leisure time more wisely. We play games, talk—often about television programs we have watched together— go camping and hiking as a family, and enjoy each other's com- pany. We watch TV frequently, but only programs we really want to see. Probably my brother's and my TV habits were formed by my mother, who controlled our TV watching when we were too young to know what was good or bad. For the American family used in the article, I think their TV viewing time should be or- ganized more wisely so the parents are able to spend more time with their children.

Body Paragraph #4

summary

direct
quotation

more
summary

topic sentence
(agreement)

support:
detail,
personal
experience

     The author makes a powerful point about family together-ness when she mentions the effect TV viewing has on simple fam-ily routine: "Life-styles revolve around a regular schedule of eating, sleeping, and watching TV." Practically, as well as traditionally, dinner is the single time when the family can finally come together. The opportunity is there for discussion, exchanging ideas, solving problems, and expressing concern and love. Sadly, however, TV has taken priority. Even in my family, although we are all required to sit at the dinner table together, there are times when the col-orful screen holds more interest than how our dog ate the room deodorizer or how Dad was run off the road on his moped. The point is that no matter how animated or boring the table discus-sion is, it should be a time cherished and not discarded for any TV program.

***
Conclusion #1

summary

response

     In summary, the philosophy stated in Harriet Fidler's "The Dangers of Television" and my personal beliefs about television viewing are almost alike. The senseless watching of countless hours of TV has left many families void of love and companionship. And, to top it off, we're perfecting the garbage to feed future genera-tions.

Conclusion #2

overall
personal
response

prediction

     Most people take television for granted and accept it as a necessary part of their everyday routine. Television has been used for so many years as a source of entertainment in America that most people wouldn't know what to do without it. Television, along with many other factors in our modern lives, is truly weakening family ties. If Harriet Fidler's predictions are true, there will prob-ably be a day when a family that does anything besides watch TV will be looked upon as strange and old-fashioned.

EXERCISE 6F

1. *Do the introductions follow the correct format? How could each of the introductions be improved?*

2. *Read the body paragraphs. Does each follow the format? Does each con-tain enough specific detail to prove the writer's topic sentence? How could you improve each of the paragraphs?*

3. Do the conclusions follow the format? Is one more effective
   How could each be improved?

Ratio of Summary to Analysis in Responses to Written Material

The percentage of summary and analysis in an essay depends on the assignment, the audience, and the available material.

1. An assignment that asks for a "brief summary" and a "thorough analysis" demands a different essay than an assignment that calls for "a complete summary with a brief overall opinion in the conclusion." The General Form for a Summary-Analysis of Written Material (p. 114), and the essay, "The Dangers of Television" assume that the audience has read the essay and expects a detailed response.

2. An audience that has read the article carefully needs only a brief summary; an audience that has never read the article needs a more complete summary. In fact, the first body paragraph of such an essay may be a lengthy, objective summary of the article (see Alternative Form A below).

3. If you are summarizing and analyzing a research article in your major field, the amount of supporting material available may be limited. Thus, your essay will have a greater percentage of summary and only a very limited analysis (see Alternative Form B on p. 124). In fact, your introduction may not contain a thesis statement of opinion. Rather, it may simply state the intent (purpose) of the research.

Alternative Summary-Analysis Forms

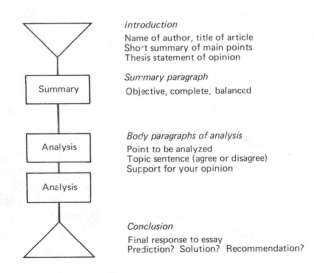

Alternate Form A

Introduction
Name of author, title of article
Short summary of main points
Thesis statement of opinion

Summary paragraph
Objective, complete, balanced

Body paragraphs of analysis
Point to be analyzed
Topic sentence (agree or disagree)
Support for your opinion

Conclusion
Final response to essay
Prediction? Solution? Recommendation?

Alternate Form B

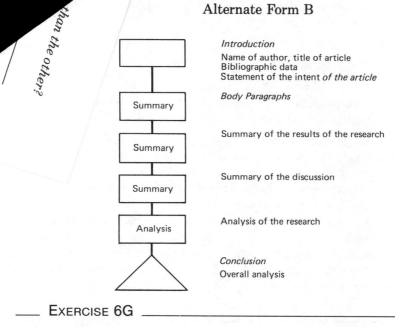

Introduction
Name of author, title of article
Bibliographic data
Statement of the intent *of the article*

Body Paragraphs

Summary of the results of the research

Summary of the discussion

Analysis of the research

Conclusion
Overall analysis

_____ EXERCISE 6G _____

*Read the following essay. Then, using the General Form for the response to
written material (pp. 114), plan a 500–700 word essay. Use one of the generating strategies demonstrated in Chapter 2 to develop supporting ideas for
your essay. Then, follow the process for planning summary-analysis essays
given in this chapter. Write the essay, following the form used by the students
who responded to "The Dangers of Television."*

SHOULD A WOMAN WORK OUTSIDE THE HOME?

In recent years, it has been observed that in those societies where women work
outside their homes in the company of men, there exist many serious social problems. Many studies have been conducted worldwide concerning the advantages
and disadvantages of having women work outside their homes. The basis for
each study was the following question: Is it helpful or harmful to women and to
their society to have women work outside their homes?

Some people consider that the work of a woman outside the home gives her
equal rights with men, social independence, and financial freedom. Perhaps each
of these results seems to be true on the surface, but this point of view is actually
very narrow and superficial. It certainly does not take into consideration the
serious social problems which are a direct result of women in the work fields who
constantly compete with, come in contact with, and keep company with men.
Consider just the religious view: all the heavenly books are quite clear about

woman's place in the world. The Bible and the Koran particularly state that women should stay at home and do the housework.

The basic fact is that women are not like men; both are different naturally in physical stature and emotional capabilities. God provided each with certain talents and features which help him or her in life. For example, there are certain jobs which are suitable for each sex simply because of physical abilities and limitations. Men can do work which needs great physical strength and endurance: bricklaying, working with heavy machinery, or other kinds of construction work. For women, these jobs are impossible because of their limited physical strength. On the other hand, there are some jobs most suitable for women: nursing, raising children, and housework. Women can do these jobs more efficiently because they are naturally fit for such work; they have patience and emotional endurance to do small tasks again and again without getting bored. Emotionally, men are better equipped to make strong decisions and to deal with problems that arise from making serious decisions about serious and critical problems. Women, on the contrary, are much better suited for the patience and kindness involved in raising children, and the children develop better as a result of the mother's kindness and understanding.

Moreover, God made man to take care of woman; in fact, God made woman from a part of man and gave man the woman to keep him company. Therefore, it is the duty of the man to provide a secure shelter for the woman, and he must also provide for her financially. He does his duty by working in the outside world, thereby giving her the opportunity to stay home and be both physically and financially secure. Woman, on the other hand, has as her duty to take care of the man—and his children—within the home. She does this by cooking, cleaning, and keeping the household at its best. This partnership between men and women is based on God's law and has survived for hundreds, perhaps thousands, of years.

However, today, as we see in the societies where the women go to work, there are many problems which may in the end destroy society as we know it. First, many people, especially men, do not find jobs because women have taken those jobs. Therefore, the men, with decreased job chances, and unemployment, are pushed to commit crimes. Children also take the wrong way because they have the feeling that their fathers and mothers ignore them; their parents push them off on the baby-sitters, and these parents have no time to direct and look after their children. The fathers do not even know what their childern do during the day since their mothers are also absent from the home, and so the fathers cannot discipline the children. This breaking apart of the family is the cause of the high rate of divorce; as the women become financially independent, they flee the responsibilities of being wives and mothers.

Not only do the crime rate and the divorce rate in such countries rise; the morals of such a society are lowered or completely lost. As women desert their natural jobs as the keepers of virtue and the teachers of culture, they too are assailed by the temptations of the world. For instance, in the past, when women stayed at home, it was rare that a woman committed a serious crime such as robbery or murder, but today it it not so unusual. As women become more and more a part of the men's world, their association with men results in immoral acts, the consequence being that many more women are becoming illegitimately pregnant. And at the present time, abortion for unmarried women is a common occurrence; sometimes it is even considered legal in these societies. This last example gives sufficient proof about the utter degradation and loss of morals in a society where women work outside their homes and bring themselves in contact with men.

In brief, having women work outside the home is morally wrong from a religious point of view. It is also a form of social injustice, for the consequences of having women in the work force cause great social problems. Finally, the long-term effects of allowing women to work outside their homes will be a change in the character of women, which will eventually destroy societies and indeed whole nations.

Mohammed Akade Osman
(Sudan)

___ EXERCISES 6H _____

Read an article from a major news magazine (Time, Newsweek) or read an editorial in a newspaper. Write a response to that article, using the processes and strategies explained in this chapter. Remember: because your audience has not read the article, the ratio of summary to analysis will change. Use the table below as a rough measure for your essay.

Ratio of Summary to Analysis in Response to Written Material Essays

	SUMMARY	ANALYSIS
General Form (audience has read the article and expects a detailed summary)	20%	80%
Alternate Form A (audience has not read the article)	30–40%	60–70%
Alternate Form B (audience is not familiar with the article; writer has limited supporting material)	60–70%	30–40%

This is a scientific/technical assignment. Select and analyze a recent research paper (one published after 1986). The objectives of the assignment are to (a) learn about a current area of research, and (b) critically examine the experimental methods and approaches used. Your analysis of the article should contain the following information:

Summary
1. *Title of the article and appropriate bibliographic information: volume number, page numbers, and date of publication*
2. *A description of the problem area studied*
3. *A statement of the questions that the author attempted to answer*
4. *The major findings and conclusions of the study*

Analysis
5. *The adequacy of the conclusions in studying the question asked*
6. *The practical significance of the study*
7. *Additional research needed on the problem*
8. *The value of the article in significantly advancing our understanding and solving of the problem studied*

Notice that the assignment calls for approximately 50% summary (#s 1–4) and 50% analysis (#s 5–8). Use Alternative Summary-Analysis Form B to organize your essay. Use the Revision Guidelines on the inside back cover of this book as you write the final draft of your essay.

7

Introduction to the Research Paper

You will spend the final part of this class writing a research paper, either in your major field or in an area in which you are interested. You will learn how to use research materials that are available in academic libraries, and you will investigate a topic of your choice, gathering materials and organizing them into a research paper. The process for writing this paper will be quite similar to the essays you have written previously in this class:

1. Select a subject and narrow it to a topic.
2. Use prewriting strategies to generate ideas and to ask questions about the topic.
3. List the information you have about the topic.
4. Organize the material:
   A. Write a thesis statement of intent and/or opinion.
   B. Construct topic sentences (and/or headings).
5. Write the rough draft, using
   A. techniques of support;
   B. methods of development;
   C. introductory and concluding techniques;
   D. coherence devices.
6. Revise the rough draft, and write the final draft.

In addition to the skills you have already developed, you will learn:

1. techniques of library research;
2. note-taking from library materials;
3. use of library materials in research papers;
4. organization of longer papers;
5. citation techniques.

_____ EXERCISE 7A _____

Do the necessary research and write a research paper of approximately 2,000 words on a topic of your choice. Use a minimum of eight sources (and a maximum of fifteen sources), some of which are books and some of which are periodicals (journals/magazines). At least two of your sources must come from articles (or books) published during the past three years. Write the research paper in the <u>form</u> required by your major field.

The order of your final draft should be:

1. *Title page*
2. *Outline of the research paper*
3. *Abstract (not more than 100 words)*
4. *Body of the paper*
5. *Footnotes or references*

Your final draft should be typed, double-spaced, without error; if typing is not possible, write your paper clearly and cleanly on one side of the paper only. No spiral-notebook edges, no wrinkled paper, no messiness is acceptable in the final draft. Put the research paper in a plastic folder or fasten it with a paper clip.

Selecting a Topic

Choose a subject that you

1. know something about; do not try to research a completely new area.
2. are interested in: you should want to know more about the subject.
3. want to communicate to a specific audience.

Choose your audience (e.g., your writing-course classmates? a major professor? classmates in your major field?)

1. What does your audience know about your subject?
2. What will the audience be interested in learning about the subject?

Narrow your subject to a topic.

Examples:

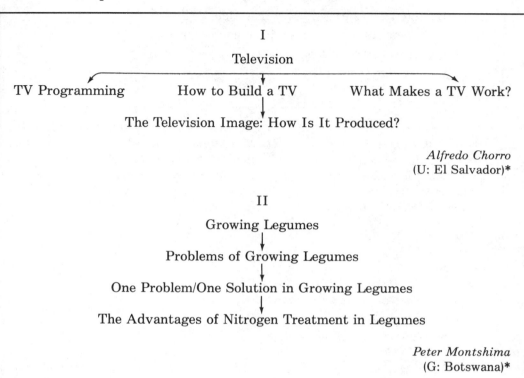

I

Television

TV Programming   How to Build a TV   What Makes a TV Work?

The Television Image: How Is It Produced?

Alfredo Chorro
(U: El Salvador)*

II

Growing Legumes

Problems of Growing Legumes

One Problem/One Solution in Growing Legumes

The Advantages of Nitrogen Treatment in Legumes

Peter Montshima
(G: Botswana)*

Student Samples

The following is a list of research paper topics from which successful research papers have been written by students in this course. These students included graduate students (G), undergraduate students (U), and high school students (H). In each case, the student chose a topic of interest, researched it in the library, and wrote an essay of approximately 2,000 words.

- Lead in Gasoline: A Significant Pollutant (U: Engineering)
- Classroom Activities that Increase Creativity in the Preschool Child (G: Child Development)
- The Process of Diamond Cutting (U: Business)
- The Causes and Effects of the 1973–75 Drought in Somalia (G: Range Science)
- Aeroflotation to Remove Grease and Oils from Water: Advantages and Disadvantages (G: Engineering)

---

*In the research paper chapters, U = undergraduate student, and G = graduate student.

- Injuries in Football: Can They Be Prevented? (H)
- Input and Output of the Tigris River: Control and Distribution of Water (G: Engineering)
- Marijuana: Its History and Uses (U: Humanities)
- Animals and Poisonous Plants: How Do the Animals Know? (U: Biology)
- Tryponosomiases: The Role of the Tsetse Fly in the Life Cycle of the Parasite (G: Parasitology)
- The Pituitary Gland (U: Anatomy)
- Problems of Undergraduate Foreign Students in the United States (U: Computer Science)
- Cellular Cofferdams (G: Engineering)
- How to Adapt an Engine for Racing (H)
- The Problem of G.I. Babies in Thailand (U: Sociology)
- UFOs: Fact or Fiction? (H)
- The Radiation Process Used to Mutate Barley (G: Agriculture)
- Carbon Monoxide and Health (U: Chemistry)
- The Bearing Capacity of Short-Bored Piles in Soft Silty Clay (G: Engineering)
- The Problems of Japanese Speakers of English (G: Linguistics)
- The Effect of Vestibular Stimulation on Autistic Children (G: Occupational Therapy)
- The Feminist Movement in Egypt (U: Engineering)
- Volleyball: Mind, Body, and Mental Toughness (U: Engineering)

Note: In the list above, notice that while the graduate students usually wrote about something concerning their major fields (see parentheses), the undergraduates often wrote about topics of interest that are not related to their major fields.

Asking Questions

As you narrow your subject to a topic, begin to ask questions for which your library research will provide answers:

1. Questions that require a single, factual answer: you will find the answers in general reference materials like encyclopedias and dictionaries. Ask a reference librarian for help in locating the appropriate source.
   Examples:
   A. What is the boiling point of carbon dioxide?
   B. What is nihilism?
   C. Who built the Statue of Liberty?
2. Questions concerning a process: you will find the answers in a book or a textbook about the subject. Locate these materials in the subject area of the card catalog.

Examples:
A. What is the Krebs Cycle?
B. How is sugar refined?
C. What is role playing?

3. Questions that need a broader discussion and current information: you will find the answers in books about the subject *plus* current information available in journals (also called magazines or periodicals). Use the card catalog to locate the books; in addition, use indexing journals to locate journals in the appropriate field.
Examples:
A. Are there alternative fuels for internal combustion engines?
B. What are the psychological effects of noise?
C. What is the role of chromium in human nutrition?

_____ EXERCISE 7B _____

Read the information sheet for the research paper below. Then construct a similar information sheet; use information about your research topic to answer each question.

INFORMATION SHEET

<u>Subject of Research Paper</u>: Mountaineering Equipment
<u>Topic of Research Paper</u>: The Best Footwear for Summer and Winter Mountaineering
<u>Audience for Research Paper</u>: Beginning Mountaineers
<u>Objective of the paper</u>: to conclude what kind of footwear is best for mountaineering in the summer and in the winter
<u>Questions to be answered in the research paper</u>:
1. Why is it important to choose good footwear?
2. What kind of footwear is the best for mountaineering in the summer? in the winter?
3. How can we choose the best footwear?
What I need to learn about in the library:
1. How to get information about mountaineering footwear
2. How to find books and journals
3. How to borrow and return books and journals
What I need to learn about writing a research paper:
1. How to use other people's words and ideas
2. How to do references

Yoko Fukada
(U: Japan)

General Format of the Research Paper

INTRODUCTION
1. Catches the reader's attention
2. Gives necessary background material
3. States the purpose of the paper
   A. thesis statement of opinion and/or
   B. thesis statement of intent

BODY: Each section of the research paper contains body paragraphs; each paragraph
1. contains a topic sentence and/or a heading that is directly related to the thesis statement.
2. contains supporting sentences and detail that explain, define, clarify, and illustrate the topic sentence of the paragraph.
3. shows complete thought development.
4. contains coherence devices; coherence between paragraphs consists of paragraph hooks and transitions.

CONCLUSION
1. Must be integrally related to the thesis statement
2. Should contain a summary of the main points
3. May contain a solution, a prediction, or a recommendation

Prewriting

Your research paper will combine information and ideas that you have about your topic with information and ideas that you find in library sources. Therefore, before you go to the library, you need to decide what you know about your topic. In the examples below, the students use prewriting strategies to focus their topics and to discover what information they need to search for in the library.

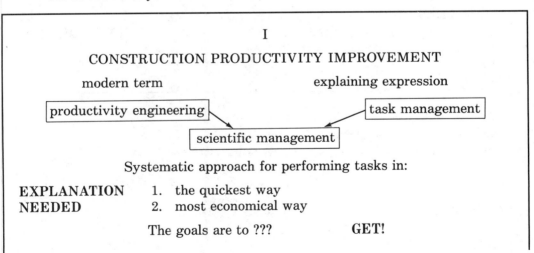

I

CONSTRUCTION PRODUCTIVITY IMPROVEMENT

modern term   explaining expression

productivity engineering   task management

scientific management

Systematic approach for performing tasks in:

EXPLANATION   1. the quickest way
NEEDED   2. most economical way

The goals are to ???   GET!

To apply the techniques of productivity engineering, we will face objections:

GET STATISTICS!

1. facilities vary for each project
2. product is different every time
3. work force is not permanent
4. operations are not repetitive
5. ????

EXAMPLES NEEDED

But similarities between construction and manufacturing are far greater than the differences.

GET:

1. Roundtable Reports
2. Statistics from top 400 companies
3. Tables and examples of productivity factors
4. Examples of successful communication

MORE INFORMATION NEEDED ABOUT:

1. major areas of task management
2. construction productivity improvement
3. hierarchical models

Kamalian Shaat
(G: United Arab Emirates)

II

SHOULD ROBOTS BE USED IN THE INDUSTRIALIZATION PROCESS IN INDONESIA?

I. Introduction: background of industrial conditions
background of employment and population conditions

GET INFORMATION

Pro (+)	Con (−)
—high productivity	—unemployment
—does not increase problems	—social problems
—strike for wages	—work monotonous
	—expensive (strongest
	—wages argument)

GET STATISTICS   **FIND EXAMPLES**

II. Explain that robots work monotonously   **ARE THERE**
     "   "   "   "   expensively   **OTHER ARGUMENTS?**

III. Creates unemployment (stronger argument)

IV. It does not create new jobs   **FIND MORE**
     (strongest argument)   **SUPPORT**

V. The opponents' arguments:
     cheapest, high productivity, no
     problems with workers' demands,   **HOW TO REFUTE?**
     can work 24-hours a day, and
     problems can be worked out over
     a period of time

VI. Refutation   **FIND SUPPORT**

VII. Conclusion: Recommendation? Prediction?

Joni Swastanto
(Indonesia)

_____ EXERCISE 7C _____

Think about your research topic. Using one or more of the prewriting strategies demonstrated earlier in this textbook, begin to generate ideas and information about your topic. What information do you know? What additional information should you look for in the library?

Going to the Library

Your first visit to the library should be primarily informational:
     At the General Information Desk, ask

1. how to get a library card; the card will permit you to borrow library materials.
2. for a list of basic information: library hours, book check-out rules, library fines, etc.

3. about library tours; find out when they are given and how you can join one of them.
4. for a "library locator" card; this will tell you where materials are located in the library.
5. whether or not there is additional free printed information about the library that you can have; such information will help you learn more about the library.

Note: the word *ask* is the most important word for the library. Remember that part of the librarian's job is to help the students in the library. Be courteous, but do not hesitate to ask for help.

In Other Parts of the Library, locate

1. the reference desk: where an experienced *Reference Librarian* will answer your questions.
2. the card catalog, where you will find listed almost all of the materials in the library.
3. the micro-text area, where you will learn to use microfilm and microfiche materials.
4. the general reference section, where you will find many kinds of encyclopedias and dictionaries.
5. the periodical display shelves, where recent magazines (called periodicals by librarians) are displayed.
6. other places of interest:
   A. the photocopy machines
   B. the foreign newspaper area
   C. the audio-tape storage areas
   D. the interlibrary loan department

Note: For more information concerning basic reference materials in the library (e.g., how to use the card catalog, how to find a book after you find the call number, how to use encyclopedias, and the Library of Congress classification system), see:

1. *The Process of Paragraph Writing*, by Joy Reid and Margaret Lindstrom (Prentice-Hall, 1985), Chapter 9.
2. *Your Library: A Reference Guide* by William Katz (Holt, Rinehart, and Winston, 1979).
3. *Guide to Academic Libraries in the U.S.* by Pat Byrd, Carol Drum, and Barbara Jean Wittkopf (Prentice-Hall, 1981).

Identifying Descriptors

Before your next visit to the library, you need to plan your research strategies. First, it is important to understand that library materials are arranged—cataloged—by librarians. For example, library materials in the card catalog are arranged alphabetically by subject "descriptors," words or phrases that identify the materials in each section. Therefore, in order to successfully find materials about your research topic, it is necessary to "think like a librarian," to identify various words under which materials about your topic could be cataloged.

As you plan your research strategies, begin by identifying words or phrases that *describe* your topic. If you have adequate, accurate "descriptors" of your topic, you will be able to locate information quickly. If you need assistance in identifying additional descriptors, ask a reference librarian for help.

Examples:

I

Topic: Relevant Elements in Playground Design

Possible Descriptors: playgrounds; children/play; parks; outdoor recreation; children/physical development; outdoor parks; playground equipment; playground design.

Aurora Valls de Novoa
(G: Venezuela)

II

Topic: Satellite Uses in Interncontinental Communication

Possible Descriptors: satellites; communication satellite; telecommunications; space satellites; microwaves; satellite communication.

Sami Lazghab
(U: Tunisia)

Consider your topic. Then, "think like a librarian." Identify possible descriptors for your topic.

Library Etiquette

Part of the job of the reference librarian is to help students with their library work. However, there are appropriate and inappropriate questions and behaviors that you should learn before you begin library research.

1. The most important ABC: A̲lways B̲e C̲ourteous. You will find the people in the library much happier about helping you if you *ask* rather than *demand* help, if you are patient and polite, and if you say "please" and "thank you."

2. Do not expect too much of the librarian.
    A. In most academic libraries, for example, an "open stack" policy prevails. Students must, therefore, locate and check out their materials themselves. Do not expect a librarian to perform these tasks for you.
    B. Most librarians have neither the time nor the desire to do your research for you. Here are some questions that would offend a librarian because they show that the student has not done enough of his/her own work:
        (1) I have to write a 10-page research paper on photosynthesis. What should I do?
        (2) My research paper is due tomorrow and the book I want is checked out. Can you get me another copy today?
        (3) Where do I get some stuff about skydiving?

3. There are, of course, many questions that a librarian would be happy to answer. Here are some examples that show the librarian that the student is working hard but has encountered a problem:
    A. I've look in the Serials Record for this journal, but I didn't find it. Could you check again with me to make sure I didn't miss it?
    B. I'm writing a paper about X. I've already found some books that are helpful. What indexing or abstracting journals should I use to find some journal articles about my topic?
    C. I've found a newspaper article about my topic, but I don't know how to find the microfilm. Could you please help me?

After you have become familiar with the library, you should begin to gather background information about your research topic:

To find information about your topic:

1. Look up your topic in the <u>subject</u> section of the card catalog. Use one or more of your descriptors to locate books about your topic.
2. Look up your topic in one of the following general encyclopedias; use your descriptors to locate information. Then read about your topic.
   A. *Encyclopedia Americana*
   B. *Encyclopedia Britannica*
   C. *Collier's Encyclopedia*
3. Ask a reference librarian which <u>subject encyclopedia</u> would have more background information about your topic. Look up your topic in a subject encyclopedia, and read about your topic. NOTE: There are many, many subject encyclopedias; three examples are *The Encyclopedia of Physics, The Encyclopedia of Educational Research,* and *The Encyclopedia of Criminology.*

_____ EXERCISE 7F _____

Ask a reference librarian where recent (current) periodicals (journals/magazines) about your general subject are "displayed." Go to those display shelves. The current periodicals (journals/magazines) are shelved alphabetically according to title.

Begin at the journals that have titles that begin with A. Look at each periodical for about two seconds. If the journal is not related to your subject, go on to the next journal. If the periodical might be related to your subject, pick it up. Look at the Table of Contents briefly:

1. Are the titles of the articles in your general subject area? If your answer is <u>no</u>, replace the journal and continue with the exercise.
2. Are the titles understandable, or is this journal too difficult/technical for your topic or your audience? If the titles are too difficult or too technical, replace the journal and continue with the exercise.
3. If the periodical (or perhaps another issue of that periodical, which you will find by lifting the slanted display shelf and looking underneath) <u>might</u> be helpful, write down the *title* of that journal and the *call number* of that journal. The call number tells you where older, "bound" volumes of the journal are located in the library.

Field-Specific Formats for Research Papers

The general form for most academic papers is the same: title page, abstract, outline; text of the paper (introduction, body, conclusion); footnote/reference page(s). But while the general form for research is similar for all major fields of study, each field differs in some small ways. For example, some fields of study use <u>headings</u> instead of (or in addition to) topic sentences; some fields use <u>footnotes</u> to document library material, while other fields use <u>references</u>.

Whether or not you are writing about a topic in your major field, you will construct your research paper in the *form* required by your major field. In this way, you will be learning the form you will use in your future academic work. Of course, using the form used in your major field may mean that your research paper may differ somewhat from your classmate's paper.

In order to learn the form required by your major field, you will need to see how students in your major field write their research papers. The exercise below will give you that opportunity.

___ EXERCISE 7G ___

Go to the library. Find a master's thesis in your major field of study that has been written by a graduate student at your institution. Ask a reference librarian for assistance in locating a master's thesis. NOTE: This thesis does <u>not</u> have to be about your subject.

Use your library card to check out the thesis. Do <u>not</u> read the thesis. Instead, look carefully at the <u>form</u> of the thesis. Study the information sheet below. Notice how one student has answered the questions. Then make your own information sheet, filling in the blanks with information from the master's thesis you are using from your major field.

Master's Thesis Exercise

Title: *Cost Benefit Analysis of a Computer-Controlled Irrigation System*
Author: Don Homan
Major Field: Agricultural and Natural Resource Economics
Call Number: HD1714 / H65 / 1984
Table of Contents: how is this thesis organized?
  1. Chapters? _X_ How many? _6_ Sub-Headings? _26_
  2. Sections? _____How many? _____Sub-Headings? _____
  3. Other? _____
General Formats of Thesis?
  1. Is there an abstract? _Yes_ How many words? _250_
  2. How many pages in the thesis? _65_ Typing double-spaced? _Yes_
  3. Overall organization: please list the chapter titles, divisions into sections, or whatever the basic organization the thesis uses; look at the *Table of Contents* for this information.
     I.   Introduction
     II. Review of Economics Literature
     III. Methodology
     IV. Review of Engineering Literature
     V.   Results
     VI. Conclusion

4. **Illustrations?** _____How many? _____
   Figures? <u>Yes</u> How many? <u>7</u>
   Tables <u>Yes</u> How many? <u>13</u>
Where are they located? Within the text? <u>Yes</u>
at the end of the text? <u>No</u> Both? _____
5. **Appendices?** <u>Yes</u> How many? <u>3</u>
   About what? <u>Computer programs</u>
6. **Citations**
   Footnotes? <u>Yes</u>   How are they indicated?
       A. _____ 1
       B. _____ 2
       C. Other? (Specify) <u>*</u>
   References? <u>Yes</u>   How are they indicated?
       A. _____ (1)
       B. _____ [3]
       C. <u>X</u> (Smith, 1987)
       D. Other? (Specify)_____
Where are the footnotes/references located?
       A. Within the text? <u>Yes</u>   (references)
       B. At the bottom of page? <u>Yes</u>   (footnotes)
       C. At end of text? _____
Is there a **Bibliography?** <u>Yes</u> Where? <u>at the end of the text</u>
   Reference page? _____Where? _____
   Literature Cited page? _____Where? _____
   Other? (specify) _____
How are the sources listed in the Bibliography/References/Literature Cited?
   Alphabetically by author's last name? <u>Yes</u>
   Alphabetically by title? _____
   By number? _____
   Other? (specify) _____
Are **direct quotations** ("_____") used in the text? <u>No</u>
   How are they indicated?
       A. quotation marks around the quotation? _____
       B. quotation indented and single-spaced? _____
       C. Other? (specify) _____
7. Is there anything else about the format of this thesis that you think will be important to you in writing your research paper? If so, please write that information below:
   <u>This thesis used an "Acknowledgments" page where the author</u>
   <u>thanked all the people who had helped him.</u>
   _____
   _____

Abdullah Muajel
(G: Saudi Arabia)

Choose one of the topics below. Write a paragraph about the topic, or give a two-to-four-minute oral report to your class about your library experience with the topic.

TOPICS:

the general information desk
the card catalog (subject section)
the card catalog (author section)
the card catalog (title section)
a terrible library experience
a successful library experience
how to get a library card
what I learned in the library
what I still must learn

general encyclopedias
the microtext room
how to thread a microfilm
    machine
the reference librarian
subject encyclopedias
checking out a book
strange periodicals
helpful periodicals

8

Library Research

For both the graduate student and the undergraduate, a knowledge of library skills is essential. The amount of material published each year in the United States is staggering; the Library of Congress, which receives a notice or copy of every book published in the United States, has over sixty million volumes, and adds over three million each year. Even a moderately small university library will contain a million volumes.

Because of the sheer bulk of this material, a successful student researcher must know how to look for appropriate materials; a researcher who does not plan library search strategies may grow old (and unsuccessful) in the library!

Note: Remember that the assignment for this research paper requires *only* 2,000 words, with a minimum of 8 sources and a maximum of 15 sources. While that assignment may sound enormous, you will soon find that it is very restricting. Therefore, you will not have the time or the space to read and report on *many* books and journal articles. Try to spend a relatively short amount of time accumulating sources. Find the necessary materials quickly; then concentrate on *writing* your research paper.

You have already completed several important steps in planning a research paper. You have:

1. narrowed a subject to a topic;
2. discovered what kinds of information you need from the library;
3. identified "descriptors" about your topic;
4. learned to use some basic reference materials in the library.

Now you need to decide where to find the materials necessary for your paper in the library. You will look for two basic kinds of information:

1. For general, background information, use encyclopedias and books from the card catalog.
2. For more specific, recent material, use recent books from the card catalog, and use current periodicals.

Four suggestions will make your research experience more pleasant and successful:

1. Be patient; plan to work for long periods of time in the library.
2. Be flexible about your topic; let the materials you find modify the topic.
3. Try to "think like a librarian."
4. Ask a reference librarian for help whenever you have a problem.

Using the Card Catalog

1. In the subject area of the card catalog, look up one or more of the descriptors you identified for your topic. If you cannot find those descriptors, identify a more general word to describe your topic.

Topic: Elementary School Teaching Methods in Iran

Descriptors: Iran/Elementary School; Iran/primary
    schools; Iran/teaching/teachers;
    Iran/teaching methods
            ↓
More general descriptors: Iran/education; Iran

Mahvash Hojjati
(U: Iran)

****
Topic: The Radiation Process Used to Mutate Barley

Descriptors: Radiation of barley; barley/radiation; barley; mutated barley

More general descriptors: radiation of vegetables; radiation processes in agriculture; agriculture/radiation; agriculture

Sylvia Estrada
(G: Nicaragua)

Of course, a more general descriptor will include more general source materials. You will have to judge by the titles whether or not those books *might* contain *some* information about your topic.

2. When you have identified titles of several books that may contain information about your topic, write the bibliographic data for each book:
   A. the call number
   B. the title
   C. the author

Note: be sure to recheck your information; it is easy to reverse call number letters, and a small mistake could prevent you from finding the book.

3. Use the library locator to find each book in the library stacks. You may discover that most of "your" call numbers begin with the same identifying letters (e.g., *HL*). These books will be located together in the same area of the library because they contain information about the same subject. Therefore, as you are looking for your books, look at other book titles on the shelves. They may also be helpful.

4. Do NOT read every book that you find. Instead, look in the *index* of each book for the descriptors of your topic.
   A. If your descriptors are not listed, do not spend further time with the book.
   B. If the descriptor(s) is/are listed, note the page number(s) of the pages devoted to those descriptors. Look briefly at those pages. If the information looks helpful, plan to check out the book.

> **NOTE:** Do not replace books on the library shelves. Leave the books that do not interest you on a table, on the floor, at the general information desk, or on special shelves designed for unwanted books. Workers in the library will reshelve the books.

___ EXERCISE 8A _____

Find four to eight books that might contain information about your topic. Write the necessary bibliographic information that will allow you to locate the books. Be sure to recheck your information, especially the call numbers, for accuracy. Then locate the books in the stacks of the library. Look in the index of each book for descriptors that concern your topic. Check out any books that might be helpful for your research paper.

Using Periodicals: Indexing and Abstracting Journals

Periodicals (also called journals or magazines) are the most widespread source of researchers. There are literally hundreds of thousands of periodicals published in English—150,000 in the sciences alone.

Although periodicals (journals/magazines) are listed in the card catalog (e.g., MECHANICAL ENGINEERING: PERIODICALS-INDEXES), a much more efficient and successful way to identify and locate journal articles in the library is by using indexing journals. An indexing journal is a list of articles, usually arranged alphabetically by subject. Each listed article contains the following bibliographic information that will allow you to find the article in the library:

1. title of the article
2. author of the article
3. title of the journal
4. volume number
5. page numbers of article
6. date of publication

The Readers' Guide to Periodical Literature

The most widely used and popularly based indexing journal is the *Readers' Guide to Periodical Literature*. It indexes (i.e., *lists*) articles from more than one hundred magazines of a general nature (e.g., *Time, Popular Science, House and Garden, Popular Mechanics*). If you learn to use the *Readers' Guide*, you will know how to use many of the other more specialized indexing journals in the library.

Each volume of the *Readers' Guide* covers a different period of time: two years for the thick, cloth-bound volumes, three months for the large paper-bound volumes, and two weeks for the thin paper-bound volumes. You must look in each volume of the set because each volume is arranged alphabetically for the period that it covers.

Most of the information in the *Readers' Guide* (and in other indexing journals) is abbreviated. There is a "Table of Abbreviations" in the front of each *Readers' Guide*. To use this indexing journal efficiently, you should become familiar with the common abbreviations: months, dates, volumes and page numbering. If you are uncertain about the complete name of an abbreviated magazine, look at the "List of Periodicals" in the front of the *Readers' Guide*.

Articles in the *Readers' Guide* are listed alphabetically under both the general subject of the article and each author of each article. And like most indexing journals, the *Readers' Guide* also contains subheadings, cross-referencing, and *see also* lists to help you locate materials more quickly.

The general form of the indexed articles in the *Readers' Guide* is:

Heading
    Subheading
        Last name of the author, first name. Title of the article. Title of the journal. Volume number:page number(s). Date of publication.

Below are several examples of entries in the *Readers' Guide;* notice the forms of the entries and the information about each article.

Sample: *Reader's Guide*

---

subject heading   **El Salvador**
         see also

      Guerillas—El Salvador   Other subject categories
      Military assistance, American—El Salvador

        Civil War, 1980

El Salvador's dim prospects. T.P. Anderson. bibl f   Sub-heading (citation)
Curr His 85:9-11+ Ja '86

[This article, "El Salvador's Dim Prospects," was written by T.P. Anderson. It has *bibl*iographical *f*ootnotes. It was published in the journal *Curr*ent *His*tory, volume 85, pages 9–11 (+ a little on page 12), in January, 1986.]

Inside guerrilla territory. R. Chavira. il map *Time* 123: 30   (citation)
Ja 20 '86

[The article, "Inside Guerrilla Territory," written by R. Chavira, is *il*lustrated with photographs or drawings; it also contains

---

a *map*. It was published in *Time* magazine, volume 127, page 30, on January 20, 1986.]

author heading   El Sayed, Refaat Phantom Ph.D.'s. por *Time* 127:62 Mr 3 '86   (citation)

[The article, "Phantom Ph.D.'s," written by Refaat El Sayed, is a *por*trait—that is, a story about someone. It was published in *Time* magazine, volume 127, page 62, on March 3, 1986.]

Other Indexing Journals

The periodicals indexed in the *Readers' Guide* are directed towards a mass audience; consequently, the *Readers' Guide* will be used primarily by undergraduate researchers. Graduate students, or researchers working in their major fields of study, will probably use indexing journals that are focused more clearly in their major fields.

Each major field has at least one indexing journal; there are over three hundred separate indexing journals available. Each indexing journal will list articles from a group of journals directly related to a specific interest. Student researchers will have to learn the indexing journal(s) in their major fields. Some will be arranged like the *Readers' Guide;* others will be arranged quite differently. Ask a reference librarian for help in deciding which indexing journals to use for your topic and in learning to use those indexing journals.

Below are a few examples of indexing journals with a specific focus:

1. *Applied Science and Technology Index:* Arranged like the *Readers' Guide,* it indexes about 225 English language periodicals in the fields of aeronautics and space engineering, automation, chemistry, construction, earth sciences, electricity and electronics, engineering, industrial and mechanical arts,, mathematics, metallurgy, physics, telecommunication, transportation, and related subjects. Easy to use; good for undergraduate researchers.

2. *Biological and Agricultural Index:* A cumulative subject index to periodicals in the fields of biology, agriculture, and related sciences.

3. *Business Periodicals Index:* Arranged like the *Readers' Guide,* it is a subject index to periodicals in the fields of accounting, banking and finance, general business, labor and management, marketing and purchasing, public administration, and related fields. Easy to use; good for undergraduate researchers.

4. *Engineering Index:* International in scope, it indexes and annotates selectively over 1,400 professional and trade journals; it lists publications of scientific and technical associations, laboratories and research insti-

tutes, government departments and agencies, and industrial organizations; also includes citations for papers of conferences, symposia, and selected books.

5. *Index Medicus:* A classified index of current medical literature of the world. About 2,300 periodicals are indexed completely or selectively in the medical and health sciences, biometry, botany, chemistry, entomology, physics, psychology, sociology, veterinary medicine, and zoology.

6. *Newspaper Indexes:* Compiled for major newspapers only; arranged alphabetically by subject; provide month, day, section of newspaper, page and column for each citation; published frequently—biweekly or monthly. Examples of newspapers indexed include the *New York Times Index,* the *London Times Index,* and the *Wall Street Journal Index.*

7. *Public Affairs Information (Service) Bulletin:* Covers materials in English concerning economic and social conditions as they relate to public administrations and international relations; published weekly and frequently annotated; indexes some government reports and books.

8. *Social Sciences Index:* Author and subject index arranged like the *Readers' Guide,* but covers periodicals in the fields of anthropology, economics, environmental sciences, geography, law, political science, psychology, and sociology.

9. *Humanities Index:* arranged like the *Readers' Guide;* subject fields indexed include archeology and classical studies, folklore, history, language and literature, performing arts, philosophy, religion and theology, and related subjects; author and subject entries; easy to use; recommended for undergraduate researchers.

Abstracting Journals

Abstracting journals contain the same basic information as indexing journals, but in addition they contain abstracts (short summaries) of the articles they index. An abstracting citation provides

1. Author of article
2. Title of article
3. Title of journal
4. Volume number, pages, dates

Below are examples of abstracting journals:

1. *Biological Abstracts:* Each issue contains abstracts from more than 5,000 periodicals; arranged by section and subsection, with subject, author, generic, and cross-indexes.

2. *Chemical Abstracts:* Over 14,000 scientific journals indexed and abstracted (over 95 percent of new worldwide basic chemistry literature

in more than fifty languages); a half million abstracts each year; arranged by subject categories; extensive indexing (for every ten words of abstracting, there are seven words of indexing).

3. *Child Development Abstracts and Bibliography:* Contains abstracts of articles from U.S. and foreign periodicals; arranged by subject; author and subject index; cumulated annually.

4. *Environmental Abstracts:* An indexing and abstracting service covering both published and nonprint (for example, radio and television programming, films) materials. Significant books, periodical articles from scientific, scholarly, technical and general publications, major conference proceedings, and other related entries are included; contains subject, industry, and author indexes.

5. *International Political Science Abstracts:* Abstracts are in English or French and are selected from a large number of periodicals published in various countries; classified by large groupings with cumulated annual author and subject indexes.

6. *Nutrition Abstracts and Reviews:* Published quarterly with an annual combined table of contents and author and subject indexes; titles are given in the original language and in English translation.

7. *Psychological Abstracts:* Considered one of the most complete abstracting journals; lists and abstracts new books, journal articles, technical reports; arranged in seventeen major classifications; full author and subject indexes to each volume.

8. *Selected Water Resources Abstracts:* Includes abstracts of books, journal articles, and reports that cover the water-related aspects of the physical and social sciences and engineering; included are the subjects of conservation, and the control, use, and management of water; arranged by topic, with several indexes.

Below is an example of an indexing journal:

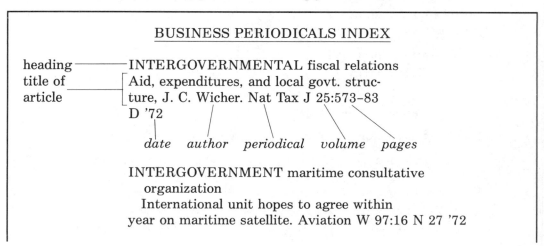

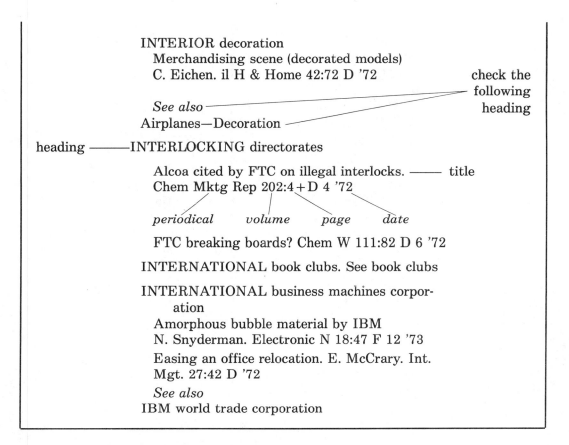

INTERIOR decoration
Merchandising scene (decorated models)
C. Eichen. il H & Home 42:72 D '72 ——— check the
following
heading

See also
Airplanes—Decoration

heading ———INTERLOCKING directorates

Alcoa cited by FTC on illegal interlocks. ——— title
Chem Mktg Rep 202:4+D 4 '72

periodical   volume   page   date

FTC breaking boards? Chem W 111:82 D 6 '72

INTERNATIONAL book clubs. See book clubs

INTERNATIONAL business machines corporation
Amorphous bubble material by IBM
N. Snyderman. Electronic N 18:47 F 12 '73
Easing an office relocation. E. McCrary. Int.
Mgt. 27:42 D '72
See also
IBM world trade corporation

Following is an example of an abstracting journal:

CHEMICAL ABSTRACTS

author   title

section ———————————18—Animal Nutrition
identifying ————89:4893d Importance of vitamins in
number   rabbit nutrition. Blazek, Stanislav (Vyzk.
                Ustav Biofaktoru Vt. Leciv, Prague, Czech.).
periodical———*Krmivarstvi Sluzby* 1977, 13(12), 265–7   place of work
                (Czech.).
language   A review with no refs. of rabbit require-   volume
                ments of vitamins A, D, E, K, B_5, B_6, B_{12},
year of   C, thiamin, riboflavin, niacin, folic acid, and   pages
publication   choline. A table of daily vitamin require-
                ments and tables of vitamin contents of 2
abstract   bioprepns are presented.

89:4895f Vitamin B_6 requirements of infants and children. McCoy, Ernest E. (Dep. Pediatr., Univ. Alberta Sch. Med., Edmonton, Alberta).

Hum Vitam B_6 Requir., Proc. Workshop 1976 (Pub. 1978) 257–71 (Eng). Edited by Sauberlich, Howerde E.; Brown, Myrtle L. NAS: Washington, D. C. A review with 27 refs. The basis for estg. *vitamin B_6* (8059–24–3) requirements in infants and children in relation to protein intake, exptl. studies on the vitamin B_6 requirements in infants and children, vitamin B_6 intake by breast- and formula-fed infants in relation to protein intake, plasma and erythrocyte pyridoxal phosphate levels in children and adults and erythrocyte amino-transferase activity in relation to vitamin B_6 intake are discussed.

title —————— 89:4896g The nutritional signficance of dietary fiber. Kimura, K. K. (Life Sc. Res. — author

periodical Off., Fed. Am. Soc. Exp. Biol., Bethesda, place of work
Md.) ————————————————— pages

U.S. NTIS, PB Rep. 1977, PB-275672, 74 pp.

date (Eng). Avail. NTIS. From Gov. Rep. An- government doc-
nounce. Index (U.S.) 1978, 78(7), 95. A re- ument location
view with 126 refs on the therapeutic value number
of dietary fiber in diverticular disease, aton-
ic constipation, and certain hemorrhoidal
conditions. Increased dietary fiber provides
bulk, gentle laxation, and ease of elimina-
abstract tion. The value of dietary fiber in suscepti-
bility to, prevention of, or therapy of other
disease and disorders remains to be established. There is little justification for increasing the fiber content of the American
diet, except in individual cases where medical considerations indicate addnl. dietary fiber may be beneficial.

Selected List of Indexing and Abstracting Journals

A. Field: Agriculture
  1. Abstracts
     a. *Abstracts of Tropical Agriculture*
     b. *Animal Breeding Abstracts*
     c. *Bibliography of Agriculture*
     d. *Forestry Abstracts*
     e. *Plant Breeding Abstracts*
     f. *World Agricultural Economics and Rural Sociology Abstracts*
  2. Index:
     a. *Biological and Agricultural Index**
B. Field: Biological Sciences
  1. Abstracts
     a. *Environmental Abstracts*
     b. *Food Science and Technology Abstracts*
     c. *Nutrition Abstracts and Reviews**
     d. *Biological Abstracts**
  2. Indexes
     a. *Index Medicus*
     b. *Zoological Record*
C. Field: Business
  1. Abstracts
     a. *Accounting Data Processing Abstracts*
     b. *Computer Abstracts*
     c. *Management Abstracts*
  2. Indexes:
     a. *Accountant's Index*
     b. *Business Periodicals Index**
     c. *Funk and Scott Index*
D. Field: Engineering
  1. Abstracts
     a. *Electrical Engineering Abstracts*
     b. *Pollution Abstracts*
     c. *Selected Water Resources Index**
     d. *Transportation Research Abstracts*
  2. Indexes
     a. *Applied Science and Technology Index**
     b. *Engineering Index**
     c. *Index of Mining Engineering Literature*
     d. *The Environment Index*

---

*Indexing and abstracting journals discussed in this text.

E. Field: Humanities
    1. Abstracts
        a. *Language Teaching and Linguistics Abstracts*
        b. *Religious and Theological Abstracts*
    2. Indexes
        a. *Art Index*
        b. *Essay and General Literature Index*
        c. *Humanities Index**
        d. *Music Index*
F. Field: Physical Sciences
    1. Abstracts
        a. *Chemical Abstracts**
        b. *Geophysical Abstracts*
        c. *Geoscience Abstracts*
        d. *Meteorological and Geoastrophysical Abstracts*
        e. *Physics Abstracts*
        f. *Statistical Theory and Method Abstracts*
        g. *Geotechnical Abstracts*
    2. Index
        a. *Bibliography and Index of Geology*
G. Field: Social Sciences
    1. Abstracts
        a. *International Political Science Abstracts*
        b. *Middle East Abstracts and Indexes*
        c. *Psychological Abstracts**
        d. *Sociological Abstracts*
        e. *Technical Education Abstracts*
    2. Indexes
        a. *Education Index*
        b. *Index to U.S. Government Periodicals*
        c. *Public Affairs Information Service Bulletin (PAIS)**
        d. *Social Sciences and Humanities Index**
        e. *United Nations Index* (UNDEX)
H. Others:
    1. Abstracts
        a. *Dissertation Abstracts**
        b. *Master's Abstracts*

Identifying and Locating Periodicals

1. Because the greatest advantage of periodicals is that they provide *current* information, you will probably want to begin searching the most

---

*Indexing and abstracting journals discussed in this text.

recent issues of the indexing journal(s) or the abstracting journal(s) that you are using for your research paper. Then work backward (in time) through the indexing/abstracting journal(s) until you have enough articles for your research paper.

2. Try to find more articles than you need, because:
   A. your library may not have that journal.
   B. the volume of the journal may not be available.
   C. the article you find may not be helpful.

3. When you find an article that might be helpful, write the necessary bibliographic data carefully and completely. In order to find a journal article in the library, you must have:
   A. Title of the article
   B. Name of the author
   C. Title of the journal
   D. Volume number of the journal
   E. Page numbers of the article
   F. Publication date of the article

be sure to check your information to avoid time-wasting errors!

4. When you have written the bibliographic data for a sufficient number of helpful articles, take that information to the <u>SERIALS RECORD</u>, a small card catalog just for periodicals. If you do not know where the Serials Record is located in your library, ask a reference librarian.
   A. Periodicals in the Serials Record are listed alphabetically by title. Look up the title name of the journal for your first article. If you find a card that lists the journal, the library has the journal that you want. Copy down the call number, just as you would a call number in the card catalog.
   B. Find the volume number of the journal that you are looking for on the Serials Record card. If the volume number is listed, the library has that volume.
   C. If the article is *very* recent, the issue may still be on the current periodical display shelves; go to those shelves and look
      (1) on the slanted shelf for the most recent issue
      (2) underneath the slanted shelf (lift up the shelf) for less recent issues
   D. If the article is a year or more old, the volume of the journal will be found by its call number. Locate the volume of the journal just as you would a book.
      NOTE: The call number for a journal will be the <u>same</u> for all volumes of that journal. Only the volume <u>number</u> will differ.
   E. Locate first the volume, then the publication date, then the correct page number of the article (in *that* order); then you will have found the article. Look briefly at the article. If it looks helpful, photocopy the title page and any other page that contains valuable information. You may want to photocopy the entire article, especially if it is not too long.

F. If the call number in the Serials Record says MICRO, the article you want is in the microtext area, probably on microfilm. Go to the microtext area of your library; locate the microfilm by its call number, and read the article on the microfilm machine. If the article is helpful, make a copy of it on the special microfilm copy machine.

G. If you have any difficulty locating an article, ask a reference librarian to help you.

___ EXERCISE 8B _____

Look up your topic in several current issues of an appropriate indexing journal. Use the process described above to find four to eight current articles about your topic. Photocopy those articles.

Other Research Sources

Government Documents

The U.S. government is the largest publisher in the world: 500,000 items are published annually by local, state, regional, and national government agencies. Many of these documents report research that has been funded by the government. If you have a topic that requires the use of government documents:

1. do not try to find the documents alone. Instead, consult with a reference librarian or a special government documents librarian.
2. remember that most government publications are not listed in the card catalog; the government documents section of your library has its own catalog.
3. there are four indexing journals that will help you locate government documents:
   A. Local government documents: Locate by using the *Index to Urban Documents*
   B. State government documents: Locate by using the *Monthly Checklist to State Publications.*
   C. National (federal) government documents: Locate by using the *Monthly Catalog of U.S. Government Publications.*
   D. United Nations documents: Locate by using UNDEX (United Nations Subject Index)

Master's Theses and Doctoral Dissertations

Most universities have copies of theses and dissertations written at that university. They will be listed in the card catalog. However, if you are looking for master's theses or doctoral dissertations written at other academic institutions (but not published elsewhere), you should:

1. look in *Master's Abstracts* or *Dissertation Abstracts;* these abstracting journals will help you identify relevant research and discover where the theses/dissertations are located. These abstracting journals include theses and dissertations written at more than 230 U.S. universities.
2. order copies of the theses or dissertations through the interlibrary loan department in your library:
   A. for a photocopy, you will probably have to pay for photocopying and mailing charges.
   B. for a microfilm copy, you will pay less.

COMPUTERIZED SEARCHING

Some academic libraries have computerized assistance for researchers. Such computers "search" one or more "data bases" (i.e., indexing or abstracting journals that are computerized) for the researcher. Below is a short printout from Info-Trac*, which has a computer program that searches the Readers' Guide, Business Periodicals Index, and the U.S. Government Index. Its data bases contain articles written only since 1982.

CULTURE	SUBJECT	InfoTrac Database InfoTrac 3:22a
		DATA DISPLAY

> CULTURE   *heading*
    see also
       ACCULTURATION
       BICULTURALISM
       CIVILIZATION
       CROSS-CULTURAL STUDIES
       CULTURAL LAG
       CULTURE DIFFUSION   *other*
       EDUCATIONAL ANTHROPOLOGY   *descriptors*
       HUMANISM   *(sub-headings)*
       INTELLECTUAL LIFE
       INTERCULTURAL COMMUNICATION
       LANGUAGE AND CULTURE
       LEARNING AND SCHOLARSHIP
       PERSONALITY AND CULTURE

Info-Trac is a product of Information Access Company, Division of Zitt Davis Publishing Company, Belmont, California 94002.

```
ACCULTURATION                              sub-heading

    >  ACCULTURATION
       see also
       ASSIMILATION (SOCIOLOGY)  ⎫
       DETRIBALIZATION            ⎪
       DIFFUSION OF INNOVATIONS   ⎬   other
       EAST AND WEST              ⎪   descriptors
       NORTH AND SOUTH            ⎪
       SOCIALIZATION              ⎭
    —AMERICAN SAMOA               ⎭     sub-sub heading
=       Samoa: a paradise lost? by Richard Bernstein il   ⎫
    New York Times Magazine v132–April 24 '83-p48(8) 1⎰   citation
       —BRAZIL
=       Beset by a golden curse: Brazil's Kayapo Indians.
    by Vanessa Lea il National Geographic v165-May '84-
    p. 16(2)
>    CULTURE SHOCK
=       Slim is in at British collections (men's wear).
    by Richard Buckley   Daily News Record-March 19 '86
    p1(2)
=       How To Offend a Mexican Businessman. by D.C.
    Anderson   Across the Board-June '85 p53–56.
```

There are several advantages of computer searching:

1. Time: the computer searches through all the volumes of an indexing journal quickly.
2. Accuracy: the computer selects *all* articles whose titles contain your descriptors, and the printout gives complete, correct bibliographic data.
3. Descriptor selection: some computer search systems offer a selection of descriptors if your initial descriptor is too general or is not in the computer's dictionary.

Of course, you still must locate the articles in your library; clearly, however, if your library has a computer search system, you should learn about it. You may not use a computerized search for your research paper in this class, but eventually you may have a need to do a search by computer.

Planning Computer Searches

Some computer search systems are free or low cost. Others are more expensive. Since you pay for computer time *by the second*, you should plan your searches carefully.

- A. Decide on a specific topic.
    - (1) Limit topic to an appropriate size: the time used by the computer to locate listings is the basis for the cost of the computer search.
    - (2) Be familiar with the current literature beforehand in order to use the computer most efficiently.
- B. Ask the programmer-librarian in your field whether or not a computer search would be useful: Does the computer have data bases in your subject area? Is your subject valid for a computer search?
- C. Discuss the topic with the programmer-librarian in your field; choose the most specific "descriptors" possible.
- D. Decide how definitive your search should be. Variables include
    - (1) time: estimate both your time and the amount of time your topic demands
    - (2) money: because the computer search is not a free service, you should ascertain the probable cost of your search before you begin.

Below is a small part of a computer search done on the *Dialog* system. This computer search service includes more than two hundred data bases (i.e., indexing and abstracting journals). Some of the data bases are complete (e.g., *Dissertation Abstracts:* 1861–present); others have only recent years of the journal on the computer (e.g., *Historical Abstracts:* 1973–present).

Notice in the computer search below that, in the case of the first citation, the librarian and the researcher were puzzled by the inclusion of that journal article. Therefore, at the end of the computer search, the librarian asked the computer for more information (see the last citation: *?), and the computer then gave more complete information.

Topic: OIL SHALE
Descriptors:
- A. oil shale
- B. shale oil
- C. shale
- D. kerogens
- E. oil shales
- F. oil shale (general)

File 4: CA CONDENS/CASIA77-Vol88(10)
(Copr. Am. Chem. Soc.)

*CA08800066483H   Journal:J. Chem. Eng.   Data   Publ: 78 Series: 28
Issue: 1 Pages 7–11
    Pressure-Temperature Relationship for Decomposition of Sodium
    Bicarbonate from 200 to 600 Degree F.

CA08810065143K Journal: Bull. Int. Assoc. Eng. Geol. Publ: 75
Series: 11   Pages: 77–82
    Relationships between Original Microstructure of Rocks and Soils and En-
    gineering Behavior

CA08810064441U   Journal: Preca   Res.   Publ: 77   Series: 4
Issue: 3   Pages: 221–7
    Irreversible Contamination of Precambrian Kerogen by 140-Labeled Or-
    ganic Compounds

CA08810064360S   Journal: Rend. Soc. Ital. Mineral. Petrol.   Publ: 77
Series: 33   Issue: 1   Pages: 109–23
    Anchizone Metamorphism in Sedimentary Sequences of the Northern Ap-
    penines (Preliminary Results)

CA08810064049X   Journal: S. African   Publ: 770621   Pages: 29 pp.
    In situ Recovery of Shale Oil   Patent No.: 76 04823

*? T6/5/1
CA08810066483H
    Pressure Temperature Relationship for Decomposition of Sodium
    Bicarbonate from 200 to 600 Degree F.
        Author: Templeton, Charles C.
        Location: Bellaire Res. Cent., Shell Dev. Co., Houston, Tex.
        Identifiers: Dissocn Pressure Sodium Bicarbonate, Carbonate
        Sodium Dissocn Pressure, SHALE OIL PRODN, Nahcolite Decompn

____ EXERCISE 8C _____

*List the bibliographic data for four to six books and four to six articles that
you have found about your topic in the library. List all of your references together; arrange the list alphabetically by the last name of each author. Be sure
that you have at least TWO current references (books or articles published
within the last three years) about your topic. Use the form below to write your
reference list.*

For books:

Last, First. Year. Title of Book. Place of Publication: Publisher.

For articles:

Last, First. Year. Title of article. Title of Journal. Volume: page number(s).

Example:

THE INFLUENCE OF THE COMMUNICATOR
AND THE PERSUASIVE MESSAGE

Bibliography

BETTINGHAUS, ERWIN. 1973. Persuasive Communication. New York: Holt, Rinehart, and Winston.

EMERY, MICHAEL C. and T. C. SMYTHE. 1972. Readings in Mass Communication. Dubuque, Iowa: Wm. C. Brown Company.

FORGAS, JOSEPH P. 1985. Language, goals, and situations. Journal of Language and Social Psychology. 24:126–138.

FULTON, BARRY R. 1970. The Measurement of Speaker Credibility. New York: John Wiley & Sons.

JURMA, W. E. 1983. Media mannequins: how they influence people. Vital Speech Day. 50:61–64. (MICROFILM)

McGUIRE, WILLIAM J. 1986. Cognitive consistence and attitude change. Journal of Abnormal and Social Psychology. 63: 345–353.

MILLER, GENERAL B. and MICHALE E. BOLOFF. 1980. Persuasion. New Directions in Theory and Research, Volume 8. Chicago: McGraw-Hill, Inc.

WINSTON, A. 1985. People together. Mass Media. 14:12–13.

Ligia Carolina Baland
(U: Colombia)

Using Library Materials

After you have collected the library materials you need for your research paper, you need to identify and extract the information that may be helpful for your paper. Researchers have different strategies for assembling information: making notecards, writing in notebooks, underlining photocopied articles, and/or cutting and taping sentences/ideas together. However, all researchers have two similar objectives:

1. to extract the most valuable information for their papers correctly and efficiently.
2. to give the exact reference for each piece of information.

Below are two examples of student note-taking from library sources. Although the strategies differ, notice that each student has clearly identified the source of each piece of information (including the necessary bibliographic data from each book/article and the page number from which the information came) so that he or she can correctly reference the material in a research paper.

I
VEGETATION AS AN ENVIRONMENTAL ELEMENT IN THE CITY

HT153
H65

Fran P. Hosken
Macmillan Co.
New York, 1981

The Language of Cities

*The purpose of the city is to increase the choices for personal satisfaction—the choices "for work and jobs, health and recreation, education and culture," and to fulfill our personal goals. (p. 21)

*Soon 75% of our population will live in urban areas of one kind or another. (p. 4)

HT151
D46

Thomas R. Detwiler
& Martin Mories
Univ. of Michigan
Press, 1986

Urbanization and Environment
*Environment (definition): "is an aggregate of external conditions that influence the life of an individual or population, specifically the life of man; environment ultimately determines the quality and survival of life." (p. 66)

*"An ecosystem is defined as the organisms of a locality together with their related environment, considered as a unit." (p. 69)

Patricia Alvarenga Flores
(U: El Salvador)

*****

Student Sample: Notebook

II
RURAL DEVELOPMENT IN PERU

4) Cotler, Julio. "The Mechanics of Internal Domination and Local Change in Peru," in Peruvian Nationalism, a Capitalist Revolution, ed. by David Chaplin. Tranaction Books, New Brunswick, N.J., 1979.

—internal colonialism (dual societies)
(p. 77)   —mestizo vs. Indian (explanation; lack of self-esteem)
—urban bias

1940: urban population, 25%
1961: urban population, 42%   (pp. 123–127)

5) Fitzgerald, E.V.R. "The State and Economic Development: Peru Since 1968,"
Cambridge University Press, London, 1986.

—Peruvian economy: (p. 98)
  modern sector
    export production
    large-scale industry and finance
    2/3 income generated
    1/3 employment

—traditional sector: (p. 99)
  containing the mass of peasants (producing for
    the domestic food market), artisans, small
    trades, and petty service workers
  2/3 unemployment (it generates)
  1/3 net income (it accounts for)

2) Alberti, Giorgio. Basic Needs in the Context of Social Change, The Case of
. Peru, Organization for Economic Cooperation and Development, Paris, 1981.

—Inca period: "one of the most highly developed civilizations dating
  prior to the Spanish conquest."   (p. 34)
—colonial heritage: hacienda institution   (p. 34)
—dual society in terms of economic system

Julio Alegria
(G: Peru)

Plagiarism

Serious problems can result from inaccurate or unidentified pieces of information. First, there can be frustration: the paper is due tomorrow, you have a valuable piece of information that you wish to include, but you cannot find the source of the information (or part of the source, e.g., a page number or an author's name). You *cannot* use the information if you cannot give the complete reference. Possible solutions: not using the information, or going to the library to search for the reference.

A second problem is more serious: plagiarism. The plagiarist is the student or scholar who leads readers to believe that what they are reading is the original work of the writer—when it is not.

There are several species of plagiarism:

1. *Word-for-Word Plagiarizing:* the writer copies exactly what is in the original text. IF the writer encloses that copied text in quotation marks and identifies the source in a footnote or reference, there can be no charge of plagiarism. However, a research paper cannot simply be a list of direct quotations. A reader might then justifiably feel that the writer's personal contribution to the paper was not significant.

2. *The Patch Job:* the writer takes phrases from the original text and "stitches" them together with his own words (e.g., "the," "and," "however"). The writer provides a few linking words and transitions, but the major part of each sentence is not the writer's words/ideas. Again, the writer can identify the source of the "patched" material, but a research paper should not be primarily a "patch job." Referenced material should not be the only material in a research paper.

3. *The Paraphrase:* the writer substitutes his/her own words for the author's words, but uses the author's ideas. While paraphrasing does not require quotation marks (it is not, after all, a direct quotation), it does require the identification of the source. Paraphrasing does *not* contain the student's ideas, so the ideas must be credited to the author. Therefore, a footnote or a reference is necessary. The purpose of a paraphrase should be to simplify or to throw significant light on a text. Paraphrasing requires much skill if it is to be done honestly.

The rule for footnoting/referencing is simple: ANY idea or copying of language that is *not* the student's should be referenced or footnoted. The reason: the people who write books and articles should be given credit for their writing and for their ideas.

Note: Some ideas are clearly drawn from an original source, but are ideas that are in "the public domain." That is, they are ideas that have been generally accepted and that many writers have used before. In this case, the student may use the ideas without footnotes/references. However, if there is any doubt about the source, the student should footnote/reference the idea.

EXERCISE 8D

Take notes on the books and articles you checked out of the library. Be sure to identify all your sources carefully and completely so that you can reference them successfully.

9

Writing the Research Paper

As you begin to draft your research paper, you will probably use some of the strategies that you have developed to write essays.

1. Begin wherever you think you have the best material (the beginning? the middle?)
2. Write *sections* of your paper as though they were small essays.
3. As you write, "weave" the library material into your paragraphs.
4. Carefully reference or footnote any idea that is not your own.

Documentation

One of the purposes of the research paper assignment is to give you the opportunity to use the library and to properly document information from relevant sources. For your research paper, a minimum of eight books and articles (and a maximum of fifteen) must be footnoted or referenced. These "citations" give credit to the authors of the library materials you will use in your paper.
You will document your sources in two ways:

1. Within the text of the paper, you will identify ideas that are not your own by using footnotes or references.
2. At the end of your paper, you will collect all of your sources into a list, called *References* or *Bibliography*. Usually these sources will be arranged alphabetically, according to the authors' last names.

General Rules for Documentation:

1. Any ideas that are not your own or any copied language must be referenced/footnoted.
2. Use the citation form used in your major field of study, even if your topic is not in your major field. Look at the master's thesis exercise you completed (in Chapter 7) for more specific information.
3. Be consistent in your citation format; the bibliographic data, the arrangement of that data, capitalization, and the system of punctuation should occur in exactly the same place in each reference/footnote.

Remember: failure to footnote/reference ideas that are not your own constitutes PLAGIARISM; the consequence for plagiarism is failure of the paper.

Techniques for Using Source Materials

Information from your library sources may be used *directly* or *indirectly*.

1. Direct use of sources are enclosed in quotation marks; quotations must be accurate, word-for-word transcription of a passage, which is then footnoted/referenced.
2. Indirect use of sources is usually in the form of a *summary* or a *paraphrase:* a summarizing or a retelling of an author's ideas in your own words. At the end of the paraphrase, you must put a reference/footnote.

Below are two paragraphs taken from library sources. Each paragraph is then paraphrased and referenced/footnoted. After that, sentences with direct quotations from the article are given. Notice that different methods of citation have been used in each example. Of course, *you* will use only one citation format in your research paper.

I

Original

Thailand's economy remains sound. GNP growth nearly reached 10% last year and should continue to be strong because of the many major projects in the pipeline. Although the balance-of-payment outlook for the next few years is clouded, the development of natural gas should begin to diminish Thailand's dependence on imported energy by 1992.

> —from "Thailand Overcomes Its Dislike of Borrowing" by Antoine W. van Agmael, *Economoney,* 65:135, September, 1983.

Paraphrase

The future of Thailand's economy seems healthy. If the GNP continues to grow at 19% per year, many important projects already planned can be implemented. In addition, Thailand's natural gas development will reduce her need to depend on foreign energy (van Agmael, 1983).

Direct Quotations

According to van Agmael, Thailand's "GNP growth nearly reached 10% last year. . . . " (1983:135).

Van Agmael believes that "the development of natural gas should begin to diminish Thailand's dependence on imported energy . . . " (1).

****

II

Original

There are many reasons why English is taught in nearly every country in the world: it has been, and still is, the vehicle of successful forms of imperialism, but it is the flexibility and wealth of the language that are most relevant to our present consideration. That English has thus become the most widely spread of the very few languages that can qualify as truly international is a fact that we have to live with—and take advantage of—since English has to be taught as such: to speak ELIC (English as a Language of International Communication) means that we no longer speak only of the nature of the language, but of its function as well.

—from "English as a Language of International Communication: A Few Implications from a National Point of View" by Gerard G. Hardin, *English Language Teaching Journal*, 21 (2):89, December, 1979.

Paraphrase

In addition to the role the English language has played in imperialism around the world, Hardin (1979) indicates that it has also been taught because it is a flexible and rich language. English heads the list of so-called "international languages," and if it is to become the language of international communication, as much attention needs to be given to its function as to its cultural content.

Direct Quotations

Hardin (1979) states that "English has thus become the most widely spread of the very few languages that can qualify as truly international . . . "

According to Gerard Hardin, English is "the vehicle of successful forms of imperialism . . . " [4].

Lead-In Techniques

Here are several suggestions for "lead-ins" to paraphrases and direct quotations:

According to X, . . .
A recent study by X shows that . . .
                       indicates that . . .
                       demonstrates that . . .
                       proves that . . .
                       provides information concerning . . .

X has suggested/suggests/suggested . . .
   states that/has stated that/stated that . . .
   believes that/believed that . . .
   writes that . . .

Recent research indicates that . . .

—— EXERCISE 9A ——————————————————————————

Read the paragraph below. Then write a pragraph that paraphrases the ideas in the paragraph. Give the necessary reference/footnote at the end of your paraphrase.

Then practice using sentences with direct quotations and footnotes/references by writing at least two sentences with direct quotations from the article. Use the citation format used in your major field of study.

Original

When danger threatens dolphins, they literally take to the air, in rapid leaps ten feet long. The action is so different from the dolphins' normal mode of travel— swimming just beneath the surface—that scientists have long wondered why they do it. Two maritime biologists have discovered the answer: at high speeds, leaping saves the dolphins' energy.

David Au and Daniel Weihs of Southwest Fisheries Center in La Jolla, California, calculated the energy that dolphins need to leap and swim. They measured water friction, the density of dolphins, and the amount of spray they kick up. As dolphins swim close to the surface in order to breathe, they waste energy by making waves. The faster they swim, the more they waste. Above ten knots, dolphins find it more economical to propel themselves through the air in leaps and bounds.

> —from "Why Dolphins Leap Away from Trouble," *Newsweek*, 182:77, July 21, 1980.

—— EXERCISE 9B ——————————————————————————

Use the citations from the three articles above to make a reference page or a footnote page. Use the format used in your major field. Arrange the citations alphabetically, according to the authors' last names.

More About Direct Quotations

1. Direct quotations of *less* than four typewritten lines are included in the text; direct quotations of *more* than four typewritten lines are indented on the left side and single-spaced WITHOUT quotation marks.

Example:

In his recent study on solar electricity, José Espinoza (Colombia), undergraduate electrical engineering major at Colorado State University, gave a brief historical summary of solar electricity:

> The phenomenon of solar electricity was first noticed at the end of the 19th century. It was known that an electrical current was produced when light was shone on an electrical cell. However, no one knew why this current was produced. Albert Einstein gave the answer in 1920. He explained the photoelectric effect, which paved the road for the discovery of the photovoltaic effect (12).

---

2. If you need to eliminate or add words to a direct quotation, follow the rules below:

Original: "Most authorities recommend that students take notes on 3×5 index cards rather than on notebook paper because the cards can be shuffled around easier."

(words eliminated from middle of sentence)
"Most authorities recommend that students take notes on 3×5 index cards . . . because the cards can be shuffled around easier."

(*ellipses:* 3 dots with spaces between them)

(words eliminated from end of sentence)
"Most authorities recommend that students take notes on 3×5 index cards. . . . "

(ellipsis + period)

(word added)
"Most authorities recommend that [university] students take notes on 3×5 cards. . . . "

[brackets]

More About Footnotes and References

FOOTNOTES

1. When you are paraphrasing or summarizing within a paragraph, and three or four sentences *in a row* come from the same source, do not footnote/reference each sentence individually. Instead:
   A. in the first sentence, refer to the author: According to X, . . .

B. use transitions to tie the following two or three sentences together.
C. footnote/reference at the end of the last sentence from that source.

> **Example:**
> According to Freeze, sea water intrusion is the migration of salt water into fresh water aquifiers. The flow or migration is due to the overdraft of the fresh water. If there is fresh water replenishment, the sea water is pushed back.[2]

2. Footnotes, which are generally used in the fields of Arts, Humanities, and Social Sciences, are generally indicated by a number typed 1/2 space above the line at the end of the source material.

> **Example:**
> According to George Jones, "lack of fiber in diets can cause carcinoma of the intestinal tract."[6]

3. Footnotes can be written either at the bottom of the page where the number occurs or on a separate "Footnote" page at the end of the paper. Notice that the first line of each footnote is indented, but the second line begins at the margin.

> **Example:**
>   FOOTNOTES (at the end of the paper)
>
> [1]John T. Elson, "Much Ado," *Time*, 282:71, January 19, 1985.
> [2]Ralph Gray, "How Do You Move the Mountain into the Classroom?" *National Education Association Journal*, 55 (3):35, June, 1966.
> [3]Richard Kluger, *Simple Justice* (New York: Knopf, 1975), p. 246.
> [4]Kluger, p. 27.*

4. Usually, footnotes are numbered chronologically, but sometimes the format is not chronological; rather, the source is identified by an alphabetically arranged numbered reference list at the end of the paper.

---

*When a footnoted source is repeated, do not use a complete citation. Instead, use the author's last name and the page number. Example: [12]Berry, p. 181.

Example:

BIBLIOGRAPHY (*or* REFERENCES)

1. Allard, R.W. (1960). *Principles of Plant Breeding.* New York: John Wiley & Sons, pp. 444–46.
2. Conger, B.J. (1973) "The Effects of Ascorbic Acid and Sodium Azide on Seedling Growth of Irradiated and Non-Irradiated Barley Seeds," *Radiation Botany,* 13:375–379.
3. Conger, B.J., D.D. Killion, and M.J. Constantin. (1983) "Effect of Fission Neutron, Beta and Gamma Radiation on Seedling Growth of Dormant and Germinating Seeds of Barley," *Radiation Botany,* 23:173–180.
4. Dick, W.E. (1957) *Atomic Energy in Agriculture.* London: Wellesley Publications, pp. 1–3.

References

1. References in the text of a research paper often consist of the author's last name and the year of publication in parentheses. If the author's last name is used in the sentence, only the year appears in parentheses.

Examples:

Lack of fiber can cause colitis and cancer of the large intestine (Jones, 1986).

Recent research by Jones (1986) indicates that lack of fiber can cause colitis and cancer of the large intestine.

2. If you are using the reference format, and you also use a direct quotation:
   A. introduce the quotation by identifying the author.
   B. put the year of publication and the page number of the quotation in parentheses.

Example:

As Nobel prize winner William Smith observed, "Nitrates produce malignant tumors in 100 percent of test animals within six months" (1987:59).

3. Most scientific and technical writing uses the reference format (X, 19_ _). However, occasionally an article will also contain an *in-*

formational footnote. Generally this footnote will be indicated with an asterisk (*), and the additional information will be given at the bottom of the page.

General Formats for References and Footnotes

There are some commonly used citation formats. Look at the examples below. Although the citation format in your major field of study may differ somewhat, studying the pieces of bibliographic data, the placement of that data, the capitalization and the punctuation of the general formats below will raise your awareness of reference and footnote formats.

In the examples below, notice:

1. which lines are indented;
2. which letters are capitalized;
3. what bibliographic data are included;
4. what sequence the data are presented in;
5. where each comma and period are.

REFERENCES or LITERATURE CITED (at the end of the paper)

Sample #1: (capitalization is underlined)
  Book reference

Last, First. Year. Title of Book. Place of Publication: Publisher.

   Article reference

Last, First. Year. Title of article. Title of Journal. Volume (section):page number(s).

BIBLIOGRAPHY OR REFERENCES (at the end of the paper)

Sample #2: (titles of books and journals are underlined)
  Book Reference

Last, First. Title of Book. Place of Publication: Publisher, year.

   Article Reference

Last, First. "Title of Article," Title of Journal, Volume (year), page number(s).

FOOTNOTES (bottom of page or end of paper)

Sample #3: (authors' names are reversed)
  Book Reference

[1]First Last, Title of Book. (Place of Publication: Publisher, year), pp. ⎯⎯⎯⎯.

Article Reference

[2]First Last. "Title of Article," Title of Journal, Volume, (year), pp. _____.

Below is a summary of the data from the students in one writing class who completed the master's thesis exercise in Chapter 7. Although your academic institution may have slightly different citation formats within its major fields, the information below demonstrates the similarities and differences of some major fields at one university.

Summary of Master's Thesis Exercise Data from One University

MAJOR FIELDS	ANIMAL SCIENCE	PLANT PATHOLOGY	RANGE SCIENCE
NUMBER OF:			
pages in thesis	70	43	60
words in abstract	250	205	237
chapters/sections	5 chap.	5 chap.	6 chap.
figures	0	0	4
tables	23	10	4
appendices	7 (tables)	10 (tables)	2
	***************		
references within the text	(X, 19_ _) *or* X (19_ _)	(X, 19_ _) *or* X (19_ _)	(X, 1986) *or* X (1986)
references at end of text	References	Literature Cited	Literature Cited
	Citation Form #1*	Citation Form #1*	Citation Form #1*

GEOLOGY	PHYSICS	CIVIL ENGINEERING	ELECTRICAL ENGINEERING
237	120	137	96
244	240	198	240
7 sect.	5 chap.	5 chap.	5 chap.
60	32	19	1
4	0	8	12
0	0	0	0
1 (glossary)	4 (computer programs)	6	5
	***************		
(X, 19__) *or* X (19__)	____(7)__ ____(3, 10).	(X, 19__) *or* X (19__)	____[10]__ _____[11].
information footnotes+ _____*	information footnotes+ _____*	information footnotes+ _____*	
References Citation Form #1*	Bibliography Citation Form #2**	References Citation Form #3***	References Citation Form #3***

(continued)

BUSINESS	PHYSICAL EDUCATION	SOCIOLOGY	PHILOSOPHY
95	50	282	164
293	248	362	300
5 chap.	5 chap.	5 chap.	6 chap.
7	3	2	0
10	3	46	6
0	0	0	0
0	1 (survey)	11	4 (tables)
		* * * * * * * * * * * * * * *	
footnotes:	(X, 19___)	(X, 19___)	footnotes:
	or	or	
_____(1)	X (19___)	X (19___)	_____1
_____. (2)			_____.2
		information footnotes: [+]	
		_____*	
Bibliography	References	References	Bibliography
Citation Form #3***	Citation Form #2**	Citation Format #3***	Citation Form #3***

*General Citation Format #1: **Last, First. Year. Title of article. Title of Journal. Volume: page number(s).**

General Citation Format #2: **Last, First, "Title of Article," Title of Journal, Volume, page number(s), year.

***General Citation Format #3: **Last, First. "Title of Article,"** *Title of Journal,* **Volume, No. ___, pp. _____, Month, Year.**

[+]Informational footnotes, with footnote (usually information) at bottom of page.

___ EXERCISE 9C ___

Look at the master's thesis exercise you completed in Chapter 7. What differences or similarities does the citation format in your major field have with the general formats above? Make a general format *for books and for articles that you can use as a guide for your footnotes/references in your research paper.*

Twelve Common Problems (and Solutions) Encountered by Student Researchers

1. My topic wasn't listed in the *Readers' Guide.*

Solution: Think of other words that describe your topic; if those words are not listed, try a more general term that describes your topic.

2. Some of the information I found was given in several of my sources.

Solution: Use the information from a source that does not have any other useful information; that way, you can use *that* source on your reference list.

3. My best sources were checked out of the library by someone else.

Solution: At the general information desk, explain that you want to "recall" a book and put it "on hold"; the librarian will give you a form to fill out and will tell you when the book will probably be returned. The book will be "held" for you at the information desk, and you will be notified.

4. I couldn't tell from the titles of the articles which would be related to my topic.

Solution: In an indexing journal with no abstracts, this is a guessing game. Try to guess well, and write down the necessary bibliographic data for more articles than you need. That way, some of them may be helpful, and you can abandon the others.

5. The library didn't have the journals I needed.

Solution: For this paper, there is no solution. You will have to work with other material (and/or modify your topic). For future papers, when you have more time to complete your research, use the interlibrary loan department in the library to order copies of the articles you need from other libraries.

6. When I narrowed my subject to a topic, I couldn't find many books.

Solution: First, you do not need "many" books for this assignment; too many books will make your job harder. Instead, look for four to eight books about your general subject; then look in the index of each book to find your topic.

7. Sometimes I found the right place in the stacks, but the book wasn't there.

Solution: First, check again: is the call number correct? are you in the right area of the library? are you on the right shelf? Then go to the information desk; ask the librarian to help you check:
   A. the list of books that have been checked out of the library; if your book is there, see Solution #3.
   B. the list of books in storage; if your book is there, ask the librarian to help you order it.
   C. the list of lost books; if your book is there, abandon the search.
Finally, if you have not located the book by this time, ask a reference librarian for help.

8. I need more library material for my topic.

Solution: If you have tried several descriptors, and you still have not found the minimum number of sources required by the assignment, ask the reference librarian for help. If that does not solve the problem, try modifying your topic to accommodate the material you have found. If all else fails, discuss changing your topic with your teacher.

9. The library material is better than my own ideas.

Solution: A research paper consists of your ideas PLUS material from the library. Even if you find ideas and language that you would rather just copy, remember that your ideas and language are a vital part of the paper. Try to "weave together" the ideas from the library and your own ideas for a successful research paper.

    10.   Most of the library material in my paper comes from one book.

Solution: This is a serious problem. Academic readers <u>expect</u> a breadth and depth of references. Using just one or two sources implies that you were too lazy or too stupid to do adequate research. Try to use library material in a balanced way in your paper, and see Solution #2.

    11.   My topic isn't written about in journals; all of my library material comes from old books or from encyclopedias.

Solution: Occasionally, especially with historical topics, this is true. However, ask a reference librarian to assist you in finding one or two current articles that contain a little information about your topic. Check the newspaper indexes and/or government documents if necessary.

    12.   I have some library material that I want to use in my paper, but I can't remember the reference.

Solution: Too bad. You cannot use the material unless you have the <u>complete</u> reference, including the correct page number. Go back to the library and search for the reference, or abandon the material.

Student Samples

On the following pages are student samples of parts of their research papers. Important features of each sample are indicated in the margins.

THE USES OF PASSIVE SOLAR ENERGY

Fauzi Zregan (Iran)
Writing Class
Intensive English Program
May 19___

Sample Abstract #1

PRE-SCHOOL CHILDREN AND PLAY

Abstract

introduction / topic / summary / conclusion

Play is the most important task for early childhood education and development. This research article is concerned with the areas of pre-school children's play. It analyzes in depth the meaning, the characteristics, and the value of play during children's growth. It also introduces the types and courses of play based on different age and development periods in the lives of pre-school children, and it stresses the importance of indoor and outdoor environments that affect children's play. Finally, successful ways to direct the play of pre-school children are suggested.

Kwang-Jim Chyu
(U: Taiwan, R.O.C.)

Sample Abstract #2

THE VOCATIONAL EDUCATION PROGRAM IN BOLIVIA

Abstract

focus of paper: argumentation

This paper deals with the recent system of Vocational Education implemented in Bolivia during the past five years. The experimental project, based on a similar foreign program, was a failure due to the fact that it was not adapted to the Bolivians' needs. This paper will show that the idea itself was good and may lead to a fine Vocational Educational system once a few major adaptations are realized.

Maria Teresa Teran
(G: Bolivia)

Sample Abstract #3

THE EFFECTS OF CARBON MONOXIDE

Abstract

introduction

In this paper, a general idea of carbon monoxide <u>is</u> presented, including the mechanism of carbon monoxide. Also present <u>is</u> the

Notice
use of
present
tense
passive
voice
chemistry of carbon monoxide. The most important aspect about carbon monoxide <u>is stressed</u>: its possible catastrophic effects on the global environment. Some specific examples of these effects <u>are discussed</u>: effects on the fetus, on the heart, on vegetation, and on experimental animals.

Marilia dos Santos
(U: São Tomé)

****

Sample Outline #1

HOW TO IMPROVE OLIVE HARVESTING IN LIBYA

<u>Outline</u>

I. Introduction
   A. General information about olive trees
   B. Thesis statement of intent
II. Traditional Methods of Olive Harvesting
   A. Hand picking
   B. Natural drop
   C. Beating
   D. Hand shaking
III. Mechanical Harvesting
   A. Combing
   B. Beating
   C. Mechanical shaking
      1. Stem shaking
      2. Main branches shaking
IV. Chemicals for helping in Mechanical Olive Harvesting
   A. Maleic hyrazide
   B. Ethylene releasing compounds
      1. Cyclohexamid
      2. Ethephon
      3. CGA 13586
V. Conclusion

Ali Darrot
(G: Libya)

Sample Outline #2

COUNTERTRADE:
THE NEW ALTERNATIVE IN LATIN AMERICA'S
FOREIGN TRADE

OUTLINE

I. INTRODUCTION
   A. General description of Latin America's problem of International Trade
   B. Countertrade as alternative

II. BALANCE OF PAYMENT DIFFICULTIES IN LATIN AMERICA
   A. Concept of Balance of Payment
   B. Deficits
   C. Situation in Latin America
   D. External debt

III. EXPORT AS THE PRINCIPAL INCOME IN LATIN AMERICAN ECONOMIES
   A. Few Commodities
   B. Export Instability
   C. Effects of World Market Price
   D. Payment Difficulties, Scarcity of Foreign Exchange

IV. ADOPTION OF NEW POLICIES AND STRATEGIES
   A. Bilateral Trade
   B. Countertrade

V. COUNTERTRADE
   A. Why Latin Americans are using countertrade
   B. Definition
   C. U.S. Companies' Interest in Countertrade with Latin America
   D. Countertrade Variables
   E. Forms of Countertrade
      1. Counterpurchase
      2. Compensation

Hernan Perez
(G: Colombia)

****

THE APPLICATION OF REMOTE SENSING IN ESTIMATING EVAPOTRANSPIRATION

Introduction

definition
of term

reference

Remote sensing is the science and art of obtaining information about an object, area, or phenomenon through the analysis of data acquired by a device that is not in contact with the object, area, or phenomenon under investigation (Lillesand and Kiefer, 1979). It offers us an excellent device to use in various fields: geology, forestry, water resources, engineering, and land use. Evapotranspiration is water lost from this earth's surface that man tries to study to control in order that we can use it. It is quite difficult to study and estimate the quantity of evapotranspiration from the very large earth's surface, but now

thesis
statement
of intent
and opinion

we have found a new tool: remote sensing. This paper will discuss the advantages of remote sensing and will propose the use of remote sensing by the Ministry of Forestry in Thailand.

Arthorn Boonsaner
(Thailand)

Sample Introduction #2 (with footnote)

THE CAUSES, EFFECTS, AND PREVENTION OF AUTOMOBILE ACCIDENTS IN THE UNITED STATES

heading

Introduction

information
about
general
topic:
"accidents"

background
statistics

Nowadays in the United States, accidents are an important cause of death, injury, and property damage. An accident is "something that happens without a cause that can be seen at once, usually something unfortunate and undesirable."[1] There are many kinds of accidents, such as work accidents, home accidents, and public accidents. The statistics of the National Safety Council estimate that at least $87.4 billion was the cost of all the accidents in the U.S. in 1985, and $40.6

footnote
(bottom of
page)

[1]A.S. Hornby, *Oxford Advanced Learner's Dictionary of Current English* (Great Britain: Oxford University Press, 1978), p. 5.

billion was the cost of motor vehicle accidents. Moreover, the death total—99,000 people died accidentally in 1985—includes about 50,800 who died in motor vehicle accidents. From the number of deaths and the cost of damage, motor vehicle accidents are a cause of more deaths, injuries, and property damage than all other types of accidents.

<small>narrows discussion to "motor vehicle accidents"</small>

This paper deals with motor vehicle accidents, which are a major problem in the United States. It discusses the categories of such accidents, and the ways to prevent alcohol-related traffic accidents.

<small>thesis statement of intent</small>

Piyanut Suwanchinda
(U: Thailand)

Sample Introduction #3

THREE CHESS GRAND MASTERS

Introduction

<small>general statement</small>

Chess, the game of kings and the king of games, is a game that intelligent people play, and the more intelligent person wins. The story of chess is a long one; we should look at its first appearance, and how it spread. We should also discuss its rule development and describe its chess championships and champions. In this paper, I'm going to give a short background about chess's first appearance, and how it spread to the rest of the world. Then I will describe three famous chess players: Theophilus Thompson, Alexander Alekhine, and Bobby Fischer.

<small>thesis statement of intent</small>

Esmaeel Al-Hammad
(U: United Arab Emirates)

****

Sample Body Paragraph #1 (with references)

THE HISTORY OF ZAIRE'S INDEPENDENCE

<small>topic sentence</small>

After independence, the Congolese changed their country's name from "Belgian Congo" to "Democratic Republic of Congo." However,

<small>direct quote</small>

"the country was ill-prepared for independence, though Patrice Lumumba tried hard to maintain cooperation between the various [po-

reference litical] parties" (Growther, 1983:510). Each province formed its party, trying to be free from the central government when Lumumba was Prime Minister. Lumumba called for help from the United Nations, and they responded, but not in the way he wanted. So Lumumba asked the Soviet Union to cooperate. His failure was due to his relations with Soviet Union's leaders because the other parties were against Communism (Snell, 1960).

REFERENCES (at end of the paper)

Bureau for the Belgian Congo & Ruanda-Urundi. *Traveller's Guide to the Belgian Congo and to Ruanda-Urundi.* Brussels: Putterie, 1956.

Growther, Geoff. *Africa on a Shoestring.* Australia: Lonely Planet, 1983.

Lumumba, Patrice. *Congo, My Country.* New York: Praeger, 1962.

Merriam, Alan P. *Congo: Background of Conflict.* Chicago: Northwestern University Press, 1961.

Snell, David. "Independence Dance in Congo," *Life,* 45:21, July 11, 1960.

Thorton, John H. *The Kingdom of Kongo.* Madison, Wisconsin: University of Wisconsin Press, 1985.

NOTE: citation form:

book

article

Mbembo (Ben) Bongutu-E-Kuma
(U: Zaire)

Sample Body Paragraph #2: Humanities and Social Sciences

DEVELOPING CREATIVITY IN THE PRE-SCHOOL CHILD

topic sentence

transitions

Through the class activities, the teacher can develop creativity in the preschool child by giving importance and value to what the child has made and by encouraging him to develop his own ideas and thoughts. *For example,* when the child paints a boat on the sea, the teacher could ask him what he had painted, what colors he had used, and why he had painted it. *In this way,* not only the teacher but also the child is evaluating and describing the product. *Furthermore,* if the teacher ascertains that a child is not happy with the task he has accomplished, the teacher should show him the value of the task. This will give the child security in his work and will allow him to further develop his creativity. *Finally,* the dual evaluation of the task by teacher and child will be constructive; the teacher can suggest new ideas by asking the child if there is another way he can accomplish the task and by making the child aware of various alternatives available to him.

Ana Paez
(Venezuela)

Sample Body Paragraph #3 (with Table)

THE IMPORTANCE OF ARTIFICIAL LIGHTING IN INTERIOR DESIGN

A. Color

Color is, in fact, a quality of light reflected from an object by the human eye. When light falls upon an object, some of it is absorbed. That which is not absorbed is reflected, and the color of an object depends upon the wavelength that it reflects. So light causes the different color cones, and the visible color phenomenon depends upon lighting (7). The most masterful color scheme can be ruined simply by leaving it in dullness or by washing it out with glare. On the contrary, artificial lighting can create new colors by softening or intensifying those colors the decorator used or by blending them harmoniously.
The repetition of colors and light reflection are shown in Table 1. It indicates the effects of light on color.

TABLE 1

The Relation of Colors and Light

COLOR	REFLECTION
White	85%
Ivory	75%
Light Gray	65%
Yellow	60%
Tan	60%
Dark Gray	15%
Olive Green	10%
Dark Brown	10%
Dark Blue	5%
Black	5%

Bradford, B.T. *Easy Steps to Successful Decoration.* New York: Simon & Schuster, 1976, p. 206.

Jee S. Han
(U: Korea)

Sample Body Paragraph #4 (with references)

SOME SOCCER PROBLEMS AND INJURIES

heading   II.   Common Soccer Injuries

sub-heading   A.   Sprains

definition
cause-
effect
development

solution

double
reference

The first common soccer injury is the sprain, a tissue injury that happens only in a joint (where two bones connect). The players can sprain their wrists, knees, and elbows, but the most common sprain that soccer players face is the ankle sprain. This happens because of the forced starts and stops or the quick changes of direction that occur in the game; sprains occur frequently if the player wears cleated shoes. (5) When a player hurts his ankle, twists or sprains it, the first thing that helps the injury is to put ice on the injured part for 30–40 minutes so that the ice will constrict the blood vessels. After 48 hours, heat is used to increase blood flow to the injured area. (5,8) To prevent many sprains, the soccer player should stretch well before playing. (2)

WORKS CITED (at the end of the paper)

NOTE
citation
format:
(non-
chronological
numbers
in text)

(1)   Alen, Glen. "The deadly reality of a soccer game." *McCleans*, 2:27. June 10, 1985.

(2)   Ford, George. Basic Soccer. Boston: Alen and Bacon, 1982, 1–3.

(3)   Gammon, Clive. A day of horror and shame. *Sports Illustrated*, 12:20. March 8, 1985.

(4)   Lejeune, Anthony. Soccer madness. National Review, 3:31. July 12, 1986.

(5)   McEvoy, Marie-Victoire. First aid for common soccer injuries. Soccer World, 60:38–41. January, 1980.

(6)   _____. Conversation with the Arabic Pele: Al-Mujalla. The International News Magazine of Arabia, 31:80. Spring, 1986.

no author
cited in
article

(7)   _____. Sprain first aid. Soccer World, 63:70. March, 1983.

(8)   _____. Sprain: Prompt treatment. Soccer World, 66: 72. June, 1986.

Sultan Al-Hajri
(U: United Arab Emirates)

Sample Body Paragraph #5: Scientific and Technical Writing

LABORATORY AND FIELD EXPERIMENTS ON THE CONTROL OF THE WHITEFLY

heading:
no topic
sentence

Materials and Methods

Tomatoes were grown as host plants in 12.5 cm diameter pots containing methyl bromide-fumigated soil mixed with organic manure prior to experiments and maintained under favorable greenhouse conditions. Cultures of tobacco whiteflies were maintained in separate insect-proof cages in the greenhouse, usually on tomatoes, for use in establishing infestations, or as a source of eggs and immature whiteflies of known age.

support:
facts,
physical
description

Whitefly eggs and juvenile stages of know age were obtained every two to three days by successfully exposing groups of French beans in the secondary leaf stage for twenty-four hours to caged, ovipositing adults. Adults were then removed from the plants, without affecting the eggs, by gentle plowing. Then the plants were placed in a cage in a greenhouse free of adults, and the eggs and immature whiteflies were allowed to develop until they were ready to be used.

Thabet Allawi
(G: Jordon)

Sample Body Paragraph #6 (with references)

THE CAUSES AND EFFECTS OF THE 1973–75 DROUGHT IN SOMALIA

sub-heading
(substitutes
for topic
sentence)

B.   Effects on Livestock

reference

The life of the livestock in Somalia depends completely on the rainfall because rainfall is essential for the growth of forage, and it is the only source of water for the livestock (Elmi, 1985). When the rainfall ceased in the 1973–75 drought period, the livestock faced great problems. Movement was the first effect. The livestock moved from place to place to search for water and forage. But everywhere was barren land with no vegetation. Starvation and malnutrition followed; the animals died in great numbers. It was reported in the Sanaag region that deaths of livestock were more than 100,000 per day (Ministry of Livestock and Veterinary Medicine, 1983). Diseases erupted everywhere. Riderpest and anthrax were the most common diseases that killed a lot of animals (Herbane, 1980). According to Barre (1976), the number of livestock that died in the 1973–75 drought was estimated

development:
effects

references

support:
facts,
statistics

at five to six million. Even the surviving animals, very few in number, were skinny, unable to move, and useless in market terms.

REFERENCES (end of paper)

government document   Barre, Hassan B. 1976. "Death of Animals in the Drought of 1973–75," _Journal of East African Ecology_. 12:65.

Elmi, Yousef O. 1985. "Western Needs of Livestock," International Livestock Center for Africa, Bulletin No. 14:52. Addis Ababa, Ethiopia.

conference proceedings   Elmi, Yousef O. 1977. "Nomads After Drought," Proceedings of the 1977 International Rangeland Development Symposium, Columbia, Missouri.

Habane, Obsiye M. "Livestock for Africa," International Livestock Center for Africa, Bulletin No. 10:33. Addis Ababa, Ethiopia.

article   Lewis, I.M. 1975. "Deliberate Fire," _Journal of Ecology_. 35:88.

Jama, Abdulkadir, J. 1972. "Livestock Concentration," Proceedings of the 1972 International Rangeland Symposium, Boise, Idaho.

collective author   Ministry of Livestock and Veterinary Medicine. Bulletin No. 123:45–47. Mogadishu, Somalia.

Warfa, Ahmed W. 1982. "Population in the Drought," _Journal of Somali Ecological Society_. 6:12–13.

Jamal A. Bahdon
(G: Somalia)

Sample Body Paragraph #7 (footnotes within the text)

Decision Making in Small Businesses

heading   Pricing Policies

topic sentence   There are two principal factors, cost and competition, which influence the pricing policies of many small businesses. The knowledge of costs is very important to pricing decisions. Before a price can be established for a given product or service, the cost of producing the product, rendering the service, or buying the new materials must be calculated. "A variable cost information such as the purchasing charges, labor costs, and handling fees is usually found in the com-

footnote   pany's accounting records."[8] Most small businesses rely heavily upon

---

[8]Nicols, Gerflad E. "On the Nature of Management Information." In _The Management Accounting_. April 1969, pp. 9–13.

the pricing policies of their close competitors. However, one must keep in mind that the successful businessman should be aware that too low prices will reduce profits, and too high prices can cause a decline in sales or customers. Therefore, a price is agreed upon which assures everyone an adequate profit. In addition to these, one should not fail to notice the fact that the area which is often the most critical between firms is non-price competition. While managers in small business must still take an active role in pricing, and competitor's prices must still be considered, nonprice competition attempts to increase sales by emphasizing product differences, promotional activities and customer services. "Generally, nonprice competition can take the following forms: (1) liberal credit terms, (2) free delivery to customers, (3) increased production warranties, (4) convenience of location, and (5) longer store hours."[9]

direct
quotation +
footnote

footnotes
at bottom
of page

[9]Santon, William E. *Fundamentals of Marketing.* 2nd ed. (New York: McGraw-Hill Book Company, 1972), p. 210.

Jooh Lee
(G: Korea)

Sample Body Paragraph #8 of Technical Research

ANALYSES IN BASINS WITHOUT SUFFICIENT DATA

topic
sentence

Many studies have been made in order to develop empirical formulas expressing precipitation for various durations as a function of frequency. The formulas have the form:

$$i = \frac{KTp^x}{t^n} \tag{6}$$

formulas

$$tp = C_t \,(LLc)^{0.3} \tag{7}$$

reference
to equation

where L is the length of the main stream, Lc is the length between the mass center of the basin and the main stream, and C is a coefficient that varies between 1.35 and 1.65. For rains with a duration tr = tp/5.5, Snyder found that the peak of the unit-graph was given by the equation:

$$Qp = \frac{CpA}{tp} \tag{8}$$

where A is the drainage area, Cp a coefficient that varies between 0.56 and 0.69. For the base time Snyder adopts the following equation:

$$T = 3 + 3\,\frac{tp}{24}$$

(9)

formula references where tp was defined in equation (7).

  With the unit-graph of a basin the maximum discharge that can be expected for any rain of any frequency can be found. The accuracy of the method depends on the accuracy in the evaluation of the constants.

Eduardo Lopera
(G: Venezuela)

Sample Body Paragraph #9 of Figures in Research

MEMORY MANAGEMENT TECHNIQUES

II. Techniques
 A. Single Contiguous Allocation

  This technique consists of assigning that part of the memory that is not occupied by the operating system to one job, if the space available is big enough for the job; otherwise, it will be assigned to another one. Using this scheme, only one job can be processed at one time so, as we can observe, multiprogramming is not permitted. Figure 9-1 shows a flow chart of the technique.

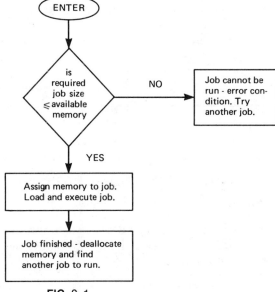

FIG. 9-1

However, if the job that is being processed is smaller than the memory available, then the rest of the memory remains allocated but unused. If, for example, there are 256 k bytes of memory, and a job requires 64 k bytes, and the operating system requires 32 k bytes, then 256 k bytes − 32 k bytes = 224 k bytes allocated plus the 224 k bytes − 64 k bytes unused, which represents over 50% of all memory.

Marysabel Alarcon
(G: Venezuela)

****

Sample Conclusion #1

VITAMIN C

Conclusion

summary   In 1932, Charles Glen King and W. A. Waught isolated vitamin C. Many scientists were very interested in this discovery and did research on it. We now clearly know the chemical properties of vitamin C, the metabolic processes of vitamin C in our bodies, the functions of vitamin C for humans, the optimum amount of the vitamin for human needs, and the distribution of vitamin C in foods. Also, we know that vitamin C can prevent us from getting some diseases and may be helpful in preventing other diseases.

We understand that vitamin C is an important and necessary nutrient for humans. The intake of a megadose of vitamin C is very good recommend-ation in curing some diseases, but it may have side effects for some people. for future research To determine the effect of vitamin C on some diseases such as cancer, further study is required.

An Tsai
(U:Taiwan, R.O.C.)

Sample Conclusion #2

NUTRITION AND AGING

heading   VI. **Conclusion**

Humans will grow older and die. Although many hypotheses of the causes of aging are proposed, the biological mechanisms responsible for them are unknown.

Research has shown that as man ages, a reduction in caloric intake and most nutrients occurs. This appears to be due to a decrease in basal metabolic rate and a marked reduction in physical activity. Furthermore, there is no direct relationship between income and nutritional deficiencies. However, as income decreases, especially to or below poverty levels, nutritional deficiencies become more frequent and more severe. The dietary intake of protein, niacin, thiamine, and iron, particularly of calcium, vitamin A, and vitamin C, is most likely to be low.

summary

Aging, a period in the life span, is not a disease or a sickness. But, as man ages, disease often follows. The elderly therefore need others' help. The increased number of older persons in the population has produced many medical, social, and economic problems. How we provide better medicare and medicaid for the elderly and how we make a good, complete planning and an evaluation in nutrition programs for the aging are two important problems which we have to solve in the near future.

*recommend-
ation*

Cheun-Cheng Wu
(G: Taiwan, R.O.C.)

Sample Conclusion #3

INCREASE IN THE PRODUCTIVITY OF CROPS IN THE SUDAN THROUGH AGROECONOMIC RESEARCH AND NITROGENOUS FERTILIZER

Conclusion

*topic
sentence*

The research work in the Sudan is of greatest importance to technology. It is used to improve the per capita income of the farmer and to expand the national economy by increasing the productivity of the food as well as the cash crops grown in the Sudan. Moreover, the research is not confined to the previous mentioned crops, but is continuing on other various crops with a view to finding strains adapted to environmental conditions and response to other uses of technology. It is continuing at a maximum pace and is geared toward optimum utilization of resources, such as water, land, labor, and capital stock. This implies continuous improvement in managerial standards and crop culture methods. Further research is continuing on the introduction of new food crops, including soybean, safflower, sunflower, legumes, and various fodder crops for livestock, with the view to integrating

summary

animal production with crop production. Research is also continuing on the introduction of water economizing techniques, considering that the crop yields are unaffected by the reduced water intake.

paragraph hook

On the other hand, nitrogenous fertilizer has been shown to result in substantial increases in the yield of crops. Even when there is a cost for using nitrogenous fertilizer to increase the yield of all crops, the net revenue is sufficient to raise the income of the tenant farmer, to improve his standard of living, and to improve the national income. With all these methods and experiments, research work, coupled with the use of nitrogenous fertilizers, has done the lion's share of increasing the productivity of all crops by improving the seed quality and the soil fertility, and they have been essentially responsible for the economic boom periods in my beloved country, the Sudan.

solution

Hashim Elobeid
(G: Sudan)

****

Sample References #1 (Bibliography)

THE PROCESS OF DIAMOND CUTTING

Bibliography

recent publication

Bauner, M. *Precious Stones.* New York: Dover Publications, Inc., 1986.

article

Claycomb, A. "Polishing Diamonds: A Lost Art?" *Journal of Gemology,* 22:34–36 (April, 1984).

Fichser, J. Daniel. *The Science of Gems.* New York: Charles Scribner & Sons, 1966.

older book: background information

Kraus, E.H. and E.F. Holden. *Gems and Gem Materials,* New York and London: McGraw Book Company, Inc., 1931.

Schiller, John. "Preparing Gems for Fashioning," *Journal of Gemology,* 20:44–45 (June, 1982).

Sinkankas, J. *Gem Cutting,* New York: D. Van Nostrand Company, Inc., 1979.

Willems, J. Daniel. *Gem Cutting.* Chicago: Chas. A. Bennet Company, Inc., 1948.

Yasuji Ishigami
(U: Japan)

Sample References #2 (Works Cited)

THE FEMINIST MOVEMENT IN EGYPT

Works Cited

Recent Article — Botje, H. "Egyptian Women Advance." *World Press Review.* 54:30–57 (December, 1986).

Busha, Hanaa. "Women Under Arab Legislation." *Women of the Whole World.* 15:46–48 (1985).

Dornemann, Luise. "Hoda Charoui." *Women of the Whole World.* 1:41 (1960).

recent book — El Saadawi, Nawal. "Arab Pioneers of Women's Liberation." *The Hidden Face of Eve.* London: Wellesley, 1985, pp. 169–83.

Malani, Indira and Urmilla Phadnus. *Women of the World.* New York: Chas. Scribner & Sons, 1982, pp. 159–74.

Matson, Rosemary. "Women Reborn: A Humanistic Revolution." *Humanist.* 42:33 (May–June, 1982).

newspaper article — Silk, Mark. "Is God a Feminist?" *New York Times Book Review.* 87:11 (April 11, 1982).

newspaper article (microfilm) — Tolchin, S. and M. Tolchin. "The Feminist Revolution of Jihan Sadat." *New York Times Magazine.* 85:20–21 (March 16, 1980).

Hana Al-Qemlas
(U: Kuwait)

Sample References #3

The Relationship between Meterology and Oceanography

References

notice different punctuation — Booth, R. N., 1969: Sea-surface temperature patterns in the North-East Atlantic. *World Meteorological Organization,* 103, 77–85.

Donn, William, 1986: *Meteorology with Marine Applications.* 2d ed. New York, McGraw-Hill.

Flittner, Glenn A., 1973: Sea temperature structure and its relation to the United States tuna fisheries in the Eastern Pacific. *World Meteorological Organization,* 103, 37–54.

Gupia, S. K., 1982: Estimation of surface temperature in remote pollution measurement experiment. *J. Appl. Meteorology.* Vol. 17, No. 10, 1450–57.

Hela, Umo., 1961: Fisheries hydrography. *London Fishing News.*

Imai, Iehiro, 1979: Collection and dissemination of sea-surface temperature data for the North-West Pacific and their utilization for fisheries. *World Meteorological Organization*, No. 103, 19–25.

Namius, Jerome, 1982: Use of sea-surface temperature in long-range prediction. *World Meteorological Organization*, No. 103, 1–10.

article in French

Romer, J., 1981. Variation de la temperature de la mer au voisinage de la surface. *World Meteorological Organization*, No. 103, 97–104.

Jean-Blaise Ngamini
(U: Nigeria)

10

Grammatical Explanations and Exercises

This section will present the most practical rules you will need when you write essays. It is not a complete grammar review. Rather, it is concerned with those problems encountered by most writers. Each explanation of a rule is followed by a brief exercise. If you need more practice with that particular problem, consult a handbook of grammar such as *Mastering American English: A Handbook-Workbook of Essentials* by Hayden, Pilgrim, and Haggard (Prentice-Hall, 1956), *Guide to Language and Study Skills* by Martin *et al.* (Prentice-Hall, 1977), or Understanding English Grammar by Azar (Prentice-Hall, 1982).

Verb Problems

Verb Tense

Verb tenses and verb tense agreement are often problems for ESL writers. Rules for the use of verb tenses are so various and often so complex that frequently second language errors occur. For the university professor, verb tense errors are serious; they often interfere with communication. Therefore, the second language student should make every effort to correct verb tense errors. To minimize verb tense errors

1. Try to write as often as possible in the simple past tense.
2. Read your writing *aloud* after you finish, and *listen* as well as *look* for errors.

Below are several exercises concerning verb tense use and verb tense agreement. By completing the exercises, you should be able to determine whether or not you are having significant problems with verb tenses. If you need a thorough review, use one of the handbooks mentioned above. Another source of verb review that stresses two-word verbs is *Idiom Workbook* by Berman and Kirstein (Institute of Modern Languages, 1979).

—— EXERCISE 10A ————————————————————————

Since I _____ this writing course, I _____
        (take)   *(feel)*
that I _____ less each day. Every night I _____
        (know)   *(try)*
_____, but I _____ adverse feelings against this
  (study)   *(have)*
subject. In fact, I _____ not _____ to study, even
                      (do)   *(like)*
in my native language. Also, my major, electrical engineering,
_____ not _____ it necessary for me to _____
  (have)   *(make)*   *(write)*
very much, so I _____ not _____ much practice.
                  (have)   *(have)*
Even so, I still _____ to class optimistic each day, and I
                   (come)
_____ "Alfredo, you _____ learn to _____
  (think)   *(may)*   *(write)*
English. Your government _____ for you to _____."
                            (pay)   *(learn)*
Then the teacher _____ the assignment on the blackboard,
                   (put)
and my mind _____ to _____ it immediately. I
              (begin)   *(reject)*
_____ myself at night _____ to _____
  (imagine)   *(try)*   *(write)*
something, and when the class _____, I _____,
                                (finish)   *(think)*
"What in the world _____ I _____ about this
                      (do)   *(know)*

terrible subject, writing? What _____ I write? My vocabu-
(can)

lary _____ so limited, and I _____ not
(be)   (can)

_____ my ideas well."
(express)

Alfred Chorro
(El Salvador)

___ EXERCISE 10B ___

In the paragraphs below, many of the verbs have been changed to an incorrect tense. Identify the verbs and correct the incorrect usage.

In my country many customs still existing about the choice of a woman for me to married. Despite the influence of other cultures, especially American, the Latin American woman has always submit to the man; she has working in the home and take care of the children. The counsel which parents generally give their sons state that the chosen girl must to be pretty (if that are possible), kind, intelligent, and faithful, and that she must to came from a good family. Virginity was one of the most important requirements for her to being considered a good woman. She must also has obedience and possesses a certain level of culture if she is to be a successful wife and mother. Although some of these requirements are began to disappear, the traditional woman in Latin America was still thought to be the best choice for a wife.

Ramon Vega
(Colombia)

Teachers of foreign languages should to be extremely well-qualified in order to carried out their duties properly. In fact, a teacher may be possess a minimum of a graduate degree from a certified educational school or institute if he to teach high school or below. Besides the academic degree, teachers shall not considered teaching only as an occupation for earn money; they should also be interests in teaching. It was not only necessary that teachers to be knowledgeable in their major fields, but they should also been skillful as well. For example, the language teacher must knowed the target language well enough to be imitating by his students. Proficiency in the target language include four skills: understanding, speaking, reading, and writing. A teacher may also knew the linguistic facts of the language of the students in order understand the problems they will to learn in the target language. Furthermore, the teacher must have familiar with the audio-lingual techniques. Knewing all these will helped the students to learn correctly and quickly.

Abbas Al-Ballal
(Saudi Arabia)

Passive Voice

The use of the passive voice in expository prose *slows down* the sentence structure and causes the reader to tire easily. However, most scientific prose uses the passive voice in the interest of objectivity, and in some cases the passive voice is useful.

Academic prose uses passive voice

1. when the agent is unknown or unimportant:
   Turkish coffeehouses, called "Kahuehane," were founded centuries ago.

2. to describe technical processes and to report research procedures and reports:
   Choline and Vitamin B complex were administered to the rabbits; the effects of the elements on the animals were then observed.

3. when the agent is a victim: speakers of English often use passive voice to describe disaster. Listen to a news broadcast: in any event in which a person suffers violence or catastrophe, passive voice conveys the sense of real accident, of the victim's helplessness.
   She was hit by a car.
   The man was shot by the firing squad.   by someone
   The woman was trapped in the burning building. or something
   The child was kidnapped.

   In each instance the passive voice makes it brutally clear that the subject was not acting but was acted upon. That, of course, is the point: it carries a sense of shock, of helplessness, in the face of calamity.*

---

*The Lively Art of Writing, by Lucille Vaughn Payne (New York: Mentor, 1965).

The general rule is to write in the passive voice only when you make the decision that it will be useful. The test for passive voice is: Can you add "by someone" at the end of the sentence?

The garden was planted.
Dinner was cooked.   (by someone or something)

If you choose not to use the passive voice, make the subject *perform*. Make it *do something*. In the sentences below, the first sentence of each pair is written in the passive voice; the second sentence changes the verb to active voice.

1. Thunder was heard in the mountains.
   Thunder growled/grumbled/rumbled/crashed/snarled in the mountains.
2. The results of the experiment were analyzed.
   The results of the experiment showed that the snow carried radio-activity.
3. The car was driven down Main Street.
   The car careened/lurched/rattled/purred down Main Street.

___ EXERCISE 10C _____

Change the passive voice in the paragraph below to the active voice, rearranging the sentences in any way you like to create a coherent paragraph.

The prison had been escaped from by a man who had murdered six people without reason. Even though the prison had been judged to be the most secure in the country, the escape had succeeded because it had been carefully planned. While a prison guard was distracted, his gun was taken and he was hit on the head with a gun. Then the guard's uniform was put on. Next the heavy fence around the prison was climbed and the barbed wire on the top of the fence was cut with a metal cutter that had been stolen from the prison repair shop. The river which surrounded the island was swum despite the frigid water, so the escape was completed. In the town near the prison, precautions were taken: doors were bolted, windows were locked, and children were called inside. Policemen from nearby towns were ordered to the area, and roadblocks were set up; every car was searched thoroughly. Fortunately, the murderer was recaptured later that day by the same policeman who had been knocked unconscious. The capture was performed when the murderer's gun was not able to be fired because it had become wet in the water.

Sentence Structure and Punctuation Problems

For the second language student, the difference between an English sentence that is correct and comprehensible and one that is incorrect is often a matter of recognizing that English sentences are generally shorter and are punctuated differently than sentences in other languages.

―― EXERCISE 10D ――――――――――――――――――――

Below is a paragraph without adequate punctuation and capitalization. Please identify the sentences (the independent clauses) and put in the necessary punctuation and capitalization.

About half a year ago in Nagasaki prefecture an american protector cut the nets and let dolphins which the fishermen had caught escape the fishermen were very angry and they brought a law suit against the american but at the trial the american said that the act he did was moral and legal because dolphins are very clever animals and so we must protect them. What he said about dolphins is true but the american should have thought about the fishermen's lives the sea around Nagasaki prefecture is a good fishing ground and many fishermen make a living by catching the fish also there are a lot of dolphins in that area and dolphins eat the fish which are the source of the fishermen's livelihood so the fishermen try to catch the dolphins in order to protect their business the american however only had a single thought the protection of the dolphins he didn't know how important fishing is for the japanese.

Keio Maeda
(Japan)

Following are sets of rules and exercises that show ways of varying the length of sentence structures in English and of avoiding incorrect sentence structures.

Semicolons

Semicolons are used to vary sentence length within a paragraph and to join related short thoughts. The rules for semicolons are as follows:

1. A semicolon can be used *only* if two *independent* clauses exist. An independent clause is a complete sentence: a subject-predicate group that can function independently.

   I like painting
   I am quite ignorant about the history of art ⎱ independent clauses

2. A semicolon may be used to join two independent clauses [b̲̲] related:

   I like painting; I am quite ignorant about the history of art.

3. In some cases, using a conjunctive adverb will make the sentence more coherent. Conjunctive adverbs can be considered **long** words:

however	moreover	consequently
therefore	nevertheless	

   I like painting; **however,** *I am quite ignorant about the history of art.*
   A. These **long** words are *not* grammatically necessary, but they often make the sentence sound better.
   B. These **long** words usually come *after,* not before, the semicolon.
   C. A comma usually follows these **long** words.

4. A semicolon may *not* be used to join an independent clause to a dependent clause:

   Because it is fun Fragment (incomplete sentence)
   I like painting

   In this case, a comma should be used;

   Because it is fun, I like painting.

___ EXERCISE 10E _____

Decide which of the following groups of words can be joined by a semicolon. In the sentences where you use a semicolon, indicate which word might help the coherence of the sentence.

1. The class laughed out loud   I didn't think it was funny.
2. Matthew helped   Michele refused.
3. The wedding ring was beautiful   she decided to buy it.
4. Her music lesson was this afternoon   on the east side of town.
5. Lino had an unpleasant meeting with his professor   he continued to like him.

_____

Summary: The basic rules for semicolons include

A. A semicolon can join *only* two *complete* sentences.
B. The two sentences must be related in content.
C. Conjunctive adverbs (the **long** words) can be used, usually *after* the semicolon, to make the sentence more coherent.

Coordinate conjunctions (which may be considered *short* words)—*and, or,* , *yet*—*cannot* be used with semicolons.

painting; but *I am quite ignorant about the history of art.* (incorrect)

is case, a common should be used:

e painting, but *I am quite ignorant about the history of art.*

Commas and Coordinate Conjunctions

Another way to join two independent clauses (complete sentences) is to use a comma plus a coordinate conjunction.

1. Coordinate conjunctions are the **short** words:
   and   for   yet
   but   or   so
2. Two complete sentences that are related in content may be joined by a comma plus **short** word:

   He was lazy, **so** he failed the class.
   He was lazy, **but** he passed the class.
   He was lazy, **and** he failed the class.

Note: When joining two complete sentences with a comma, you *must* use a comma *plus* a *short* word.

---

3. With one complete sentence and one incomplete sentence, you will use *only* a **short** word.

   He was lazy **and** *enjoyed sleeping until noon.*
   He was lazy **but** *worked when he needed money.*
4. When joining two complete sentences with a comma, you may *not* use a *long* word (a conjunctive adverb): however, nevertheless, therefore, consequently, moreover.

   He was lazy, however he passed the class. (incorrect: run-on sentence)

   If you use a comma plus a *long* word, you will have written an R.O. (run-on) sentence or a *comma splice,* which is considered a serious grammatical error.

   Correct: *He was lazy; however, he passed the class.*

*Join the independent clauses below with a comma and a **short** word.*

1. To apply for this job you must have a degree in chemical engineering you must have two years' experience.
2. Air fares have increased most people still prefer to travel by air.
3. Unemployment and the cost of living have risen the country is in trouble.
4. The wind began to blow the sky remained clear.
5. All of the people at the conference are teachers not even one teaches mathematics.
6. It was raining when Tony came home from school he watched television instead of going to football practice.
7. Gilbert was hit by a car yesterday he was not seriously injured.

_____ EXERCISE 11G _____

In the following groups of sentences, join the independent clauses either *with a semicolon (and a* long *word, if you wish) or* with a comma and a short *word.*

1. A twenty-nine–year-old woman had been taking fertility pills
   she gave birth to quintuplets.
2. Two men robbed the First National Bank
   they fled with an undetermined amount of cash.
3. Hospital rates will increase 12% this year
   a 9.67% salary increase and inflation are responsible for the rise in rates.
4. A surprise thunderstorm dumped more than two inches of rain in the city last night.
   the rainwater caused some flooding and a long power outage.
5. The police found a marijuana patch growing in the back yard of a residence near City Park
   they removed 300 to 350 plants.
6. The city of Chicago has filed a suit in district court against the architect of the new City Hall
   the suit is seeking $750,000 in damages as well as attorney fees and court costs.
7. In many hospitals, doctors routinely prescribe antibiotics for patients before surgery
   there is no proof that these drugs are necessary to prevent infections.
8. American Express deceives the audience in its television commercials
   they imply that American Express is the only company that offers a refund for lost traveler's checks.
9. The governor has ordered all state agencies to reduce mileage by a minimum of 5%

institutions can either limit parking spaces or require employees to drive only three days a week.

10. Tom Watson has won four golf tournaments and finished second in four others this year

he thinks he can play better golf than he has this season.

Subordinating Words

Some words can change a complete sentence (an independent clause) into an incomplete sentence (a dependent clause). These subordinating words include

although	when	after	until
because	while	if	unless
which	before	since	

We missed our flight to Missouri.	complete sentence
When we missed our flight to Missouri . . .	fragment
He played tennis exceptionally well.	complete sentence
If he played tennis exceptionally well . . .	fragment
He watched too much television.	complete sentence
Because he watched too much television . . .	fragment

When you use a subordinating word, you must add a complete sentence to the information. This complete sentence may be added either before the dependent clause (incomplete sentence) or after it:

We were furious when we missed our flight to Missouri.
If he played tennis exceptionally well, *I would enjoy playing with him.*
His wife divorced him because he watched too much television.
Because he watched too much television, *his wife divorced him.*

Note: If the *complete sentence* is added before the dependent clause, no additional punctuation will be used. But a comma must be used if the complete sentence is added *after* the dependent clause.

—— EXERCISE 10H ————————————————————————

Join the following sets of words together by using a subordinating word either at the beginning of the sentence or before the second part of the sentence.

1. He never gives up _____ he has become an enormous success.

2. We were certain we would not survive _____ we were lost in the mountains.

3. A turtle differs from other reptiles _____ its body is encased in a shell.

4. The people have spoken _____ manufacturers are now producing smaller cars.

5. The doctor diagnosed her disease _____ he has still not found the right medicine to treat her.

6. There were more than 1,000 fans at the football game _____ it was raining.

7. The students went to the library last week _____ they had learned to use research materials.

8. Most Americans drink milk _____ most Chinese do not.

9. There are twenty species of daffodils in my garden _____ I ordered them from all over the world.

10. Infection can cause both fever and pain _____ take his temperature to be sure of the problem.

Sentence Structure Review

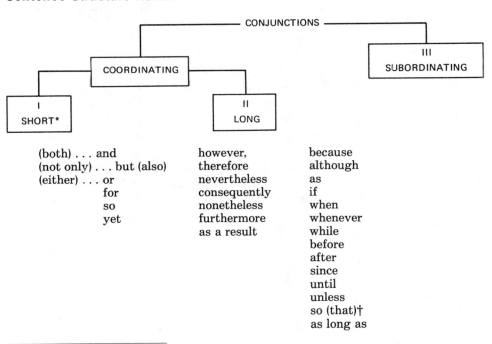

SHORT*	LONG	SUBORDINATING
(both) . . . and	however,	because
(not only) . . . but (also)	therefore	although
(either) . . . or	nevertheless	as
for	consequently	if
so	nonetheless	when
yet	furthermore	whenever
	as a result	while
		before
		after
		since
		until
		unless
		so (that)†
		as long as

---

*Called correlative conjunctions when they include the words in parentheses.

†The meaning is different from *so* in List I.

SENTENCE PATTERNS

1. _____ .   (Just one main or independent clause)

(I)

2. _____ , and _____ .   (Two main clauses joined by *any* word from List I.)

(Two main clauses joined by a semicolon and no conjunction. Should be used only if clauses make a related pair of ideas.)

3. _____ ; _____ .

(II)

4. _____ ; however, _____ .   (Two main clauses joined by a semicolon and *any* word from List II.)

(Two clauses joined by *any* word from List III. In this case the clause after the conjunction is no longer a main clause; it is dependent, and so it must not be preceded by a comma.)

(III)

5. _____ because _____ .

(Same as Pattern 5 except that it has been written inversely, and must therefore have a comma.)

(III)

6. Because _____ , _____ .

_____ EXERCISE 101 _____

Each of the sets of sentences below can be joined in several ways:
    A. *A semicolon (optional: + a* long *word)*
    B. *A comma + a* short *word*
    C. *A subordinating word: because, although, while, when, if, etc.*
Choose two *ways for each sentence. Rewrite the sentence if necessary.*

1. Conditions in the small country have grown severe _____ refugees have risked death to escape.
2. The house was not quite finished _____ we moved in.
3. I enjoy visiting with Americans in their homes _____ talking with them helps my English.
4. The soccer game was ready to begin _____ one of the team members fell and broke his arm.
5. The statement will be spoken only once _____ listen carefully.
6. Most people cannot afford to buy houses _____ prices have increased 75% in the last year.
7. Mankind must limit population growth _____ overpopulation will result in famine.
8. You may ride your bicycle on this street _____ do not go out in the busy highway.

9. His face was wrinkled _____ he looked older than I remembered him.

10. The girls put away their winter clothes _____ their closets were nearly empty.

Colons

Generally a colon means "as follows." Colons are often used for emphasis in a paragraph. Rules for colons include

1. Use a colon to introduce and emphasize a series (three or more words or phrases) at the end of a sentence:

    I like three nutritious sandwiches: peanut butter and jelly, turkey and cranberry sauce, and egg salad.

Note: If the series comes in the middle of a sentence, punctuate with dashes.

The three instruments she plays—piano, clarinet, and drums—could make beautiful music together.

---

2. Use a colon to emphasize a point:

    He has one disability: a broken arm.

Note: Use a colon only if what precedes is a complete sentence. However, the phrase following a colon does *not* have to be a complete sentence.

---

3. Do *not* use a colon unless what follows the colon *directly modifies what comes before it:*

    I am impressed by one virtue: compassion.   (correct)
    I am impressed by one virtue: others, however, are worth mentioning.
        (incorrect)

Note: In the sentence above, use a comma + a *short* word, or a semicolon, as in

I am impressed by one virtue, but others are worth mentioning.
I am impressed by one virtue; others, however, are worth mentioning.

Insert colons where they will fit below. Use dashes when they are necessary.

1. He was a mess _____ dirty, unshaven, and bloody.
2. Dr. Schweitzer's great talents _____ surgery, diagnosis, and innovative medicating _____ made him famous.
3. It was no accident _____ he hit me on purpose.
4. There is a basic difference between graduates and undergraduates _____ the former are dedicated to study, and the latter are dedicated to socializing.
5. Shelley has a favorite teacher _____ Mr. Claus.

Quotation Marks

1. Use quotation marks to indicate direct speech. Within a sentence, quotation marks surround a direct quote, and the first word is capitalized. Usually the final punctuation comes before the final quotation marks.

   Example: She said, "Love is like a flower."

   > **Note:** A comma is used after the introductory phrase.

2. Titles of articles and chapters in books are enclosed in quotation marks.

   Examples: Stephen Frazier, in his article "The Masculine Mystique," states that women want "the swagger but not the sweat" of the masculine world.
   The author of *The Women's Room*, Marilyn French, has written a compendium of many previously published women's books.

   > **Note:** Titles of books and periodicals are usually underlined; in print they are italicized.

3. If you are only using part of a quotation, use ellipsis points to indicate that some of the words have been omitted.

Example: In the article "What It Will Be Like If Women Win," Gloria Steinem looks toward the feminist Utopia, and agrees that " . . . men might well feel freer and live longer."

Note: The period comes <u>before</u> the quotation mark.

---

4. Quotation marks can indicate a special word or a special phrase.

   Example: "Disinterested" and "uninterested" can mean quite different things.

5. A different quotation that is interrupted in the middle is punctuated in the following way:

   Example: "Women," Riophe states, "have recently arrived at a new pride of ownership" (p. 77).

6. A quotation within a quotation is surrounded by single quotation marks.

   Example: Camille asked, "Have you read Chapter 8, 'Library Research'?"

___ EXERCISE 10K _____

Punctuate the following sentences with quotation marks, commas, periods, underlining, and capitalization.

1. Leslie asked what makes a person feel lonely?
2. The article titled islam: yesterday and today appeared in time magazine.
3. Marysabel she called come in the living room.
4. Please look up the meaning of lagniappe.
5. One hundred years of solitude is a famous colombian novel.
6. John Wayne received his only oscar for his performance in true grit.
7. Farrage said Fawzi if you don't study for the TOEFL you will not improve your score.
8. Sports illustrated is a magazine which my husband receives every week.
9. The chapter titled photosynthesis in sawyer's book introduction to horticulture has finally arrived in the bookstore.
10. Shannon Sayer's newest romantic novel is entitled summer of pearls.
11. The new john f kennedy library has been built on the columbia point peninsula in dorchester, six miles from cambridge massachusetts.
12. On her t-shirt was written migrant education, harvest of hope.
13. The new york times reported that cholesterol in the blood does not come from foods directly but is produced by the body.

14. The encampment of tel al malach—the hill of salt—is a huddled cluster of tents on the northeastern negev, the barren desert that adjoins the sinai.
15. In a recent issue of time magazine, Sarah Weddington, 34, states: my purpose is to put women into the mainstream of life.

Parallel Structure

Parallelism is the repetition, not of thoughts, but of grammatical structures. These structures can be simple (a repetition of single nouns), or complex (a repetition of complete sentence structures). Whenever a sentence contains two or more similar elements, these elements must be kept parallel.

Balance is always inherent in parallelism: word balances with word, phrase with phrase, sentence with sentence. The result is rhythm within a paragraph that strengthens the coherence and emphasizes the ideas.

Parallelism is only one of several ways of achieving rhythm and coherence in a paragraph, and should therefore be used sparingly.

Examples:

1. She was a woman **who** underst**ood** children, **who** enjoy**ed** housework, and **who** worshipp**ed** her husband.
2. Michael wanted **to catch** a snake, **to put** it in a cage, and **to take** it to school.
3. During spring break the students went **to Oregon**, **to California**, and **to Utah**.
4. In order to pass the TOEFL examination, he had barricad**ed himself** in his room, chain**ed himself** to his desk, and buri**ed himself** in his books.
5. **If we are to finish** this textbook, **if we are to have** a chance of finishing, we must meet each day for at least two hours.

___ EXERCISE 10L _____

Below are several sentences that contain errors in parallelism. Correct these sentences by strengthening the parallel structures.

1. Fertilizer is used to enrich the soil, to improve crops, and for making more food.
2. She took a shower, got dressed, smiled at the mirror, and her lipstick was checked.
3. Rodney Stephens was the editor of the largest newspaper in the city, a diplomatic representative to Kuwait, and he invented many useful devices.

4. It can be dangerous for one's health to diet continually, to sleep all day, and not doing any exercise.
5. I enjoy reading, swimming, jogging, gardening, and going on hikes.

EXERCISE 10M

Complete the unfinished sentences below with at least three parallel structures.

1. He was a criminal. He was a person who . . .
2. To win the spelling bee, she thought, she needed only to . . .
3. On Peggy's trip through Europe, she traveled to . . .
4. Raise your right hand . . .
5. Dr. Lindstrom has contributed a great deal to this community: lecturing, . . .
6. Before you leave, please close the door . . .
7. If your car will not start, try checking the battery, . . .
8. Since they moved into the house, they have painted all the rooms, . . .
9. The sports facilities are beautifully designed: modern, . . .
10. Those students are so lazy; all they do is watch television, . . .

Sentence Combining

The unity and coherence of a paragraph depends primarily on organization and the use of rational thought. Unity and coherence can be strengthened in a paragraph by varying sentence structure:

1. Short sentences are used for emphasis.
2. Longer sentences are used for smoothness.
3. Parallel structures are used for rhythm.

Too many short sentences can result in choppiness. To avoid this break in the coherence of a paragraph, combining several short sentences into longer, more smoothly flowing sentences can improve the paragraph.

Sentence combining is not simply an exercise to be accomplished. It is a skill to be learned and integrated with your writing style.

EXERCISE 10N

Below are series of sentences that can be combined in several ways. Combine them in at least two ways. Use whatever punctuation is necessary—commas, semicolons, colons, or periods—and use whatever connectors are necessary: coordinate conjunctions, subordinate words, or conjunctive adverbs.

1. Shelley had a birthday party.
2. The party was in the basement.
3. Several girls came to the party.
4. They talked all night.

1. The lilacs bloomed.
2. The blooms were on the bushes.
3. The bushes were in the back yard.
4. The blooms were lavender.
5. The blooms smelled delicious.

___

_____ EXERCISE 100 _____

Combine the following sets of sentences in at least one way.

1. Trips take Joseph Cancellare to Australia and India.
2. The trips are to the field.
3. Cancellare is a marine geologist.
4. He studies characteristics in the field.
5. The characteristics are chemical.
6. The characteristics are physical.
7. The characteristics are of marine aerosols.
8. He studies their distribution.
9. The distribution is over the ocean.
10. He studies their impact.
11. The impact is on conditions.
12. The conditions are meteorological.
13. The conditions are climactical.

*****

1. Crickets chirp.
2. The chirp is soft.
3. The crickets are in the grass.
4. The grass is in clumps.
5. The whippoorwills sing.
6. They sing in the trees.
7. The sound of owls can be heard.
8. The owls are screech owls.
9. The sound is eerie.
10. The sound is in the distance.

The following paragraphs are written in short, choppy sentences. Combine some of the sentences to increase the unity and coherence of the paragraphs. It may be necessary to rewrite some of the sentences; use coherence devices, and perhaps even rearrange the sentences.

It's snowing outside. I feel a kind of loneliness. Everything looks lonely outside. No one is on the streets. All I see are empty cars and snow. The trees are bare. They look cold. They look lonely, too.

*****

My house is big. It is comfortable. It has a lot of rooms. It has a big backyard. The backyard is as big as the house. There you can find flowers. You can also find trees with all kinds and sizes of fruit. Little animals live there too. You feel as if you are in Eden. You hear the sounds of many bird songs. Everything is relaxed and happy.

*****

This is not my first time away from home. It is the longest. Maybe it is the most helpful. I have to learn to be independent. I have to solve my own problems. That will make me more responsible. I have to keep track of my money. I have to be careful how much I spend. If my decisions are wrong, it's my own fault. It's no one else's fault. Being alone is the best way to learn responsibility.

*****

When I was in high school I had many friends. I could divide my friends into two groups. One group was friends who worried. They worried about the future. They worried all the time. They were good students. They were responsible. They were loyal friends. They didn't have too much time for friendship. The second group didn't worry about anything. They were poor students. They were often in trouble. They lived in the present. They lived for the present. They had time to spend with everyone. They had a lot of fun. They were very friendly.

*****

Nicaragua is a country. It is one of the countries of Central America. Central America is located on the isthmus. There are five countries in Central America. Nicaragua is in the middle of the isthmus. It is the largest of the countries in Central America. It is about 81,249 square miles. It is not as big as the United States. In comparison it is much smaller. But size is not so important. Nicaragua is beautiful.

Diction

Being able to use the English language effectively will be very helpful for your writing. The use of a good dictionary and a thesaurus (a dictionary of synonyms) is essential for expanding your vocabulary and learning to use that new vocabulary correctly. However, other diction (word) problems such as incorrect spelling or a limited vocabulary will also hinder your writing. If you have difficulty with spelling, please review the rules in *Spelling by Principles*, by Genevieve Smith (Prentice-Hall, 1966). You might also wish to use *The Bad Speller's Dictionary*, by Krevisky and Linfield (Random House, 1967). If you need to broaden your vocabulary, consulting a book like *Words, Words, Words*, by Marvin S. Zackerman (Collier Macmillan, Second Edition, 1980) will be very helpful.

Precision in Diction

In English, brevity, precision, and accuracy are the marks of a good writer. In order to make your writing more precise, observe the following rules:

1.   Try not to use *there is* or *there are* too frequently. These phrases are often useless in the sentence and only lengthen without strengthening the sentence structure.

___ EXERCISE 10Q _____

Omit the words there is *and* there are *from the sentences below. Rewrite the sentences if necessary.*

A.   There are fifty men who are trying out for the football team.
B.   There is a great difficulty in understanding English.
C.   There is a girl in physics class who has a mind like a computer.
D.   There was too much noise where I was sitting.
E.   There was a crowd of happy students in the hall.

2.   Try not to use the word *thing*. It is a vague referent that often confuses the reader. In this humorous selection, notice the confusion of the description because of the frequent use of *thing*.

The man stands by the horses, on each side of the *thing* that projects from the front end of the wagon, and then throws a tangled mess of gear on top of the horses and passes a *thing* that goes forward through a ring and hauls it out, and passes the other *thing* through the other ring and hauls it out on the other side of the other horse, opposite to the first one, after crossing them and bringing the loose ends back, and then buckles the other *thing* underneath the horse and takes another *thing* and wraps it around the *thing* I spoke of before and puts another *thing* over each horse's head with broad flappers to it that keeps the dust out of his eyes, and puts the iron *thing* in his mouth, and brings the end of these *things* aft over his back after buckling another one around his neck to hold his head up, and hitching another *thing* on a *thing* that goes over his shoulders, and then takes the slack of the *thing* which I mentioned a moment ago and fetches it aft and makes it fast to the *thing* that pulls the wagon and hands the other *things* up to the driver to steer with.

4. Try not to begin a sentence with the same phrase with which you ended the previous sentence. This "echo" effect is unnecessary and slows down the paragraph.

A student should maintain a grade point average of "B" *in his major field. In his major field* a high GPA will assist him in getting a job.

Better: A student should maintain a grade point average of "B" in his major field *because* a high GPA will assist him in getting a job.

5. Try not to use unnecessary words. Wordiness slows down the paragraph.

In my opinion I think that an author when he is writing shouldn't get into the habit of making use of too many unnecessary words that he does not really need in order to put his message across.

Better: An author should not use unnecessary words.

___ EXERCISE 10R _____

The sentences below are poor because they are imprecise. Eliminate the passive voice and any unnecessary words. Make each sentence as brief and precise as you can. Rewrite the sentences if necessary.

1. After removal of the old finish is completed the next step is preparation for the new finish. Preparation for the new finish is perhaps the most painstaking step.
2. Those big pointed things in Egypt were all built by slaves.
3. There are several girls that I date.
4. One factor we should consider is how important a thing good water is to public health.
5. The radio he built was a beautiful thing.
6. The terrain can be seen by obtaining a topographical map of the area one intends to cover. The area to be covered having been studied, the task is now what to carry within the pack.

7. The best time to have a garage sale is on the weekends. Weekends are preferable because people are home more and have more time to spend at garage sales.

8. It was Senator Hart who proposed the bill.

9. I would like to point out a case where the views of the church and the views of science are similar. The case in point is original sin.

10. I will use the Department of Education at CSU for an example. In this department there are two full-time secretaries, one part-time secretary, two students aides, and one full-time audiovisual aide.

11. The thing we should consider is our budget.

12. It was Mr. Eastman who convinced me that education was a necessary step.

13. The kind of rat that is brown in color is as supple in its ability to change its shape as a piece of rubber is.

14. There was a number of gate-crashers who managed to get in.

15. Since Shanna wished to converse while she was in Sweden, she decided to study it.

16. A sentence ought not to have any words that are not entirely necessary, and for that matter, there should be no unnecessary sentences contained within a paragraph. This is true for the very same reason that a drawing, if it is to be a good drawing, should have no lines that are not completely necessary.

17. If the disturbance is discovered to be a real frog, the heart is filled with excitement, the body become a tense ball of anxiety, and the case is about to begin.

18. By September 23, pitchers should be ready to go into full practices. Practices are organized so that all baseball players can better themselves as individuals through the process of perfecting fundamentals. Fundamentals to work on as a pitcher are: wind-ups, throwing drills, and good follow-throughs.

Confusing Words

Below are three sets of words that second-language writers often confuse. The rules are not complete; however, they should provide you with enough information to use them correctly in your writing:

1. **Another:** An adjective or pronoun used with a single *referent* (*an other*); never used with "the."
   Example: One reason Matthew passed the exam was that he studied very hard; *another* was that he had plenty of time to write his essay.

   Other: An adjective or pronoun used with either single or plural referents; often used with "the."

Examples: Rafia could only taste the cinnamon in the cake, but Maha said *the other spices* were allspice and cloves.

Rafia could only taste one spice in the cake, cinnamon, but Maha said *the others* were allspice and cloves.

Today the mailman delivered a lot of mail. Some envelopes contained bills, but *other* envelopes held letters from my family.

Today the mailman develivered many envelopes. Some contained bills, but *others* held letters from my family.

2. **Especially:** Adverb (-ly)

Example: Stephen was *especially* talented as a left wing in soccer.

Special: Adjective

Example: Elisabeth gave us a *special* gift: a bowl that she had made in pottery class.

3. **Afterward:** An adverb meaning subsequently or thereafter; often *then* can be substituted for *afterward*.

Example: We went to the picnic; *afterward* we went to my favorite disco.

After: A preposition or a subordinating conjunction that is followed by a dependent phrase or clause; *then* cannot be substituted for *after*.

Example: After we went to the picnic, we went to my favorite disco.

---- EXERCISE 10S ────────────────────────────

Below are sentences that use one or more of the six words above. Fill in the blanks with the correct word.

1. _____ inventing "dry plates," George Eastman, the founder of Eastman Kodak, made photography a portable pastime by creating flexible film that could be rolled up and fitted into a _____ camera.

2. Researchers at the University of Pennsylvania have demonstrated that a dieter should drink a cup of hot soup before a meal; _____ his eating pace will be slower.

3. One goal of the agricultural experiment is to determine the best fertilizer for wheat; the _____ is to decide the amount of water necessary for proper growth.

4. It is impossible to learn statistical analysis, _____ f you have never learned how to add or subtract numbers.

5. _____ I saw the movie I wanted to read the book.
6. Alfalfa is _____ sensitive to pollution by ozone and sulfur dioxide. _____ ozone lowers the resistance of the plant, the alfalfa dies of a fungus.
7. Dermatologists say that sunlight is _____ hard on the skin because it kills some cells and damages others.
8. A new dairy farmer in Latin America has two _____ problems. _____ he has found the land he wants, he must choose a good herd of cattle. Then he must solve the _____ problem: getting the necessary financial help to operate his farm.
9. Whether you go to the beach, to the mountains, or to _____ place, you will rest, see friendly people, or engage in _____ amusements.
10. _____ we left the movie theater, we went to _____ place where we could order dinner.
11. Just before dawn we sneaked to nearby trees; _____ we proceeded to _____ bushes that were only a few yards from the fence.
12. Although Turkish coffeehouses are very simply decorated, they have a _____ atmosphere.
13. In Argentina it is necessary to test canned beans with _____ litmus paper to measure the hydrogen content; this test is _____ necessary if the container has been damaged.
14. We swam from one side of the lake to the _____.
15. The idea of escape depends on different conditions that vary from one culture to _____.

Prepositions

One form of word choice that second language students often have difficulty with is prepositions. Below are some exercises involving the use of prepositions. If you have considerable difficulty in choosing appropriate prepositions, consult a review of preposition usage, such as the *Dyad Learning Program: Prepositions* by Alice C. Pack (Newbury House, 1977).

___ EXERCISE 10T _____

Fill in the following blanks with appropriate prepositions.

Natural selection can favor certain mutations and provide them with an advantage _____ survival. A trait _____ humans called sickle cell anemia offers an excellent example _____ how natural selection operates _____ favor a genetic mutant. Sickle cell anemia is a condition caused _____ sickle-shaped red blood cells that _____ normal individuals are round. The outward manifestation _____ this anomalous condition is a reduced ability _____ carry oxygen _____ the muscles _____ the body. Because oxygen is essential _____ the proper functioning _____ muscles, individuals _____ sickle cell anemia become easily exhausted and sometimes delirious _____ exercise. However, one who is born _____ the sickle cell anemia trait is immune _____ malaria. _____ regions _____ Africa where malaria seriously threatens survival, up _____ forty percent _____ the population exhibits the sickle cell trait. What ordinarily would be an undesirable mutation becomes a selective advantage _____ areas where malaria jeopardizes the viability _____ normal individuals.

Kurt Bucholz
(U.S.)

The road soon narrowed and followed close _____ the base _____ the purple-green mountains. Hilary saw the beauty _____ the mountains, the colorful flowers and vines growing _____ the road's edge. Every tree and bush seemed alive _____ blossoms, a riot _____ color pressed _____ the shadowed backdrop. River water lapped _____ grassy banks, and a statue _____ the Christ figure stood quietly _____ a rose arbor.

White walls stretched away _____ the entrance to *Quinta Christina,* and the narrow lane was paved _____ cobblestone. The

house, built _____ white stucco _____ a red-tiled roof, reflected its colonial architecture _____ an intricately carved facade.
The cobblestone drive would _____ a well-tended garden, wet
_____ mist _____ a fountain that sent slender spires
_____ water _____ the late afternoon air. _____
one side of the house a pebble-strewn path led _____ the stables,
barely visible _____ the background. Overhead the sky was clear, a
brilliant blue fringed _____ clouds that pressed _____
the mountains.

Shannon Sayer
(U.S.)

Editing

Being able to correct errors in your writing will improve it; however, identifying your own errors may not be easy. Usually you will be able to see errors
in the writing of others more easily than in your own writing.

—— EXERCISE 10U ————————————————————————

*Below are sentences taken from student papers that contain many errors.
Identify each error and correct it; you may have to change the spelling, the
sentence structure, the diction, the verb tenses, or the punctuation in the sentences. You should try to make each sentence as clear, as correct, and as precise
as you can. Some sentences have more than one error. Do not rewrite the sentences; simply revise the errors.*

1. It is possible to solve your problems with only to have a little bit of
   peace, and a little meditation, and mental relaxation.

   Correction: It is possible to solve your problems with a little peace, a
   little meditation, and a little relaxation.

2. Escape is getting away from something harmful to oneself; for example,
   to run away from a treacherous dog.
3. I asked the taxi driver how long would it take to the airport, he said that
   about half and hour.
4. Working outside the home help women to be sociable; so it would be help-
   full as an educational process.

5. When the student woke up he found the note, when he had read it he run to school to appologize for his mistake.
6. Realizing how important the writing class; I attend it this semester.
7. For example; young people don't have enough attention from his parents, the father is busy in his businesses meetings.
8. With most American food you don't loose time to prepared a dinner, because, you only put the food in the oven for 20 minutes at 400 degree F. and your dinner it is ready so you can use the time to study.
9. I am entitled to rights like self-satisfaction and a career; But now I don't want it because the responsibility take too much effort.
10. Each course usually have a large amount of material to be study and understood; that it seemes imposible to learned them in a week only.
11. I took Guilherme and put on him some warm dress, I don't need asked to him why he had ran away.
12. I doesn't need explain my behavior to nobody, I can understand if I am no do my assignment I will hurt only myself.
13. For some women is hard to combine efficiently the house work with a job, because many of they are pressure for time.
14. Because the TOEFL test you ability to listen, read, and to answer questions about what you listen and read about.
15. The Bong Lhang snake attacks the light of an automobile so you can see many of them are run over by automobile died on the streets.
16. Lacking calcium; for instance, the blood took the calcium from the tooths and bones.
17. In the evening Kuta Beach is very beautiful, I never missed the sunset, I just sat on the beach, listen to the soft breeze whispering a nice melody, enjoying the illumination of the sun.
18. For example, using a tractor to plow the land.
19. Often the powerful country help the repressed people to escape from a dictatorship however it dictates to them which system they must elect.
20. I was completely surprised when my roommate took off his clothes; and he stretched out on his bed.

___ EXERCISE 10V _____

The paragraphs below have been changed so that they have a variety of errors in spelling, sentence structure, and punctuation. Correct the errors, changing sentences to improve the clarity and precision if necessary.

Fourty year ago in Saudi Arabia there are no regularly school but there are a rings in the mosques and people learn in this ring some lesons about the Koran, Islam, read, and writting by the sheiks. Consequently now there is much regular school for example there are seven University. The student in those school learned by the educational technology, and by the best teachers who from Saudi Arabia or from another countries. Those student learned science as chamistry biology physic but also to literature, and history and also mathematic and engineer and agriculture. In fact there is a very big defferent between past and present.

Abdullah Husain
(Saudi Arabia)

*****

When you enter to my apartament in the north you will saw to front of you the siting room which have a confortable rugs, TV., the lamps, stereo and much picture. On your left hand (just the north East) you see the dinning room which has a table about sex chairs and besides they you will saw to kichen which is a refrigerator, dishwasher, and the pots. In the south East I had a bedrooms for me husband and I which have queen bed. In the south West you will see a room to me childrens which have two bed and toys for me son. Among the dinning room and the first room you will find the restroom. In fact my apartament was very confortable.

Yolet Goitia
(Mexico)

*****

There are much differences between American food and Persian food. The most of American foods contains meat, potatoes, and some time vegetables. Steak, hamburgers, and hot dogs is the favorite American meats. The American food is almost sweet, but not usually. Even tomato sauce has sugar. And also crackers have sugar adding. Also American added salt to food for example butter contain salt and vegetable oil. These kind of foods are making fast and takes less time to cook it. In the another hand the most Persian food consisting to rice mixed by many vegetable or meat for example Kabab and Cotelet. We doesn't put to sugar or very salt to the food. Instead we adding spices as cumin and thyme. Finally Persian food are make lower than American foods and take more times to cook.

Nahid Azadi
(Iran)

*****

Color and temperature effect the soil productivity as the darker soil in colored, more absorption of temperature then the lightest color. When soil temperature be high that cause raise of water and hot temperatures which increase the water movement and the activity of the roots in order to absorb the water and the nutrition and the minerals from the soil. On the otherwise, the dark color soil means the high contains of organic matter and developed soil but the light colors soil like the sand of soil means not contains organic matter and under-developed soil. However, the dark soil be more productive soil than light color soil due to the dark soil has high number of organic matter and minerals. Also the absorption temperachure increase the soil reaction and decomposition of the organic matter which produce simple forms of minerals available for the plant absorption.

Mohamed Yacoub
(Libya)

Appendix

The Resume

The resume is a formal summary of your background written in a clear and precise format. You may be asked to submit a resume with a university application for admission, and you will certainly enclose a resume as part of an application for employment in the United States.

Resumes generally contain the following information:

A. **Personal:** Name, address, age, marital status, and so forth
B. **Academic:** Information about schooling, from high school through graduate and postgraduate work
C. **Employment:** Jobs you have held, either part time or full time

Rules for resumes include:

A. Resumes should be typed, without error, in the clearest possible form. The person who reads your resume is being introduced to you through a single piece of paper, so the initial impression that person gets will come from the appearance of the resume.
B. Arrange the resume according to its purpose: for example, if you are applying for university admission, the resume might show your previous academic background first, and you might include a section

showing academic honors or publications that would impress an admissions officer.

C. The statement of employment on a resume should begin with the *most recent position* you have held, and go backward. In that way, a personnel manager can see immediately what you are doing at the present, and can then look at employment during previous years.

D. Other sections in the resume are individual: Have you had nonacademic education the might show the reader that you are special? Have you done volunteer work that gives you valuable experience in a specific field? Do you have hobbies or interests that might set you apart from the rest of the applicants? Have you done military service? What other events in your life could you include that would indicate your special talents?

E. In some cases you may wish to elaborate about your employment, particularly if you accomplished something that would enhance your initial impression if you included it on your resume.

Format for resumes:

A resume is a summary of your life in outline form. You will choose the headings and then list the subheadings. The organization of the resume will depend on the material you select and the purpose of the resume.

On the following pages are examples of student resumes and a letter that might accompany a resume if you were applying to graduate school. The formats of the resumes differ, but the general organization and information are the same.

____ EXERCISE _____

Choose the format that suits your needs best, and then write a resume for yourself.

Sample of Student Resume

Tanasak Wahawisan
905 W. Laurel, Apt. 301
Houston, Tx. 77079

EDUCATION: | 5/74–3/76 | Suankularb High School, Bangkok, Thailand
| 5/76–9/79 | Chulalongkorn University, Bangkok, Thailand

Degree: B.A. Major—International Relations

Minor—Business Administration

EXPERIENCE: | 8/72–11/79 | Self-Defense Training Course—Judo—Brown Belt Certificate.

3/74–5/75 | Student Representative—member in the student parliament.

5/75–3/76 | Student Representative—member in the student parliament.

7/76–8/79 | Research Assistant—working the Southeast Asian Relationship Research, Department of International Relations, Faculty of Political Science, Chulalongkorn University, Bangkok, Thailand.

5/76–3/77 | Social Work—working in the Social Helping Association for Orphans, Bangkok, Thailand.

6/76–3/77 | Freshman Head Boy. Faculty of Political Science, Chulalongkorn University, Bangkok, Thailand.

8/76–3/79 | University Athlete—member on University sport team: rugby-football, volleyball, fencing, and shooting. Certificate for Excellent Rugby-Football Player, 1978

5/79–9/79 | Teaching Volunteer—teaching the young children in the slums, Bangkok, Thailand

PERSONAL:
Born: 6/23/58 Nan, Thailand
Appearance: Height: 5'11" Weight: 175 lbs.
Health: Excellent, no physical limitation
Marital Status: Single, free to relocate

Sample of Student Resume

CHEN, CHIIN-PIN
Palmer House, Apt. 3
Ames, Iowa 50010

EDUCATION

9/71–6/75	Tamkang College of Arts and Sciences Taiwan, R.O.C. B.E., Hydraulic Engineering Degree
1/80–present	Iowa State University Ames, Iowa 50010 Major: Civil Engineering (M.S.)

MISCELLANEOUS EDUCATION

9/79–11/79	FORTRAN Programming Course—phase II National Taiwan University Taiwan, R.O.C.; Degree: programmer

EMPLOYMENT

4/79–12/79	Moh and Associate Consulting Engineers Taipei, Taiwan, R.O.C. Position: Assistant Hydraulic Engineer
6/77–3/79	Taiwan Hydro. Engineering Consultant Co. Ltd. Taipei, Taiwan, R.O.C. Position: Assistant Engineer

MILITARY SERVICE

7/75–5/77	Army Corps of Engineers Position: Engineer, Second Lieutenant

PERSONAL

Born: 6/16/53, Taipei, Taiwan, R.O.C.
Appearance: Height: 5'10" Weight: 145 lbs.
Health: Excellent, no physical limitations
Marital Status: Married
Hobbies: Photography, badminton, swimming, table tennis

Sample of Student Resume

Mohammad Saeed
1220 E. Stuart St. #26
St. Louis, Mo. 63124
Telephone: (313)493-5266

Birth: March 21, 1952
Marital Status: Single
Nationality: Iranian

EDUCATION

1975   B.S. Economics, Tehran University, Iran
1976   Certificate, Industrial Management, Manchester University, England

PROFESSIONAL EXPERIENCE

For the past five years, I have been involved in the pipe-making industry: gas, water, and waste disposal pipelines. The companies for which I have worked have supplied equipment, chemicals, and pipes for irrigation and sewage purification. I have both the necessary education in industrial management and practical experience to carry out successful projects. I have specialized in setting up a company, marketing research, managing the staff, economic analysis, and negotiations in all phases. The following lists the more significant industrial and service transactions that illustrate my experience:

1975–1978   Managing Director of A & S Overseas Development Company, which manufactures a variety of pipes and waste disposal equipment. Hale, Altrincham, Sheshire, England

1977–present   Managing Director of Haji-Firouz Public Company, which supplies drinking water and mineral water, and produces irrigation pipes. Zardoust Avenue 4th St. #4, Tehran, Iran.

1973–1978   Chairman and Marketing Director of Amir-Akram Insurance Agency Company. Pasargad Building, Mosadegh Avenue, Tehran, Iran

GOALS

I am interested in management and motivation to achieve high productivity regardless of the age of the organization. I enjoy the study of human behavior and relationships and am interested in accurate decision-making techniques.

HOBBIES

I have valuable experience in horse breeding and horse jumping, and I am also a pilot and parachutist. I have done military service for two years in the air force.

Jerome (Jerry) G. Rueth
18 W. Mulberry
Ft. Collins, Colorado 80521

OBJECTIVES

My objectives are to work as a structural engineer, utilizing my knowledge and experience in reinforced concrete and steel design, construction management, soil mechanics, and solar energy design. I am also very much interested in a position involving work in a foreign country, where I might use my skills in the French language.

EDUCATION

1973–1978   Purdue University, W. Lafayette, Indiana
Bachelors degree in Civil Engineering with a major area of study in structural analysis and minor areas of study in construction management and soil mechanics.

1982–Present   Colorado State University, Ft. Collins, Colorado
In the process of completing a doctoral program in Mechanical Engineering, specifically, solar energy design. Thesis topic: deriving a more accurate Solar Load Ratio correlation for cylindrical water walls.

QUALIFICATIONS

—proven ability to work and function well in a foreign country.

—ability to communicate in French in any office or social situation.

—excellent verbal and written communication skills along with a good ability to gather and analyze data.

—outgoing personality, accepting of others, good leadership qualities.

EMPLOYMENT

5/81–8/84
Assisted in research on the ARKLA absorption chiller.

8/81–12/81
Taught accounting and business math at Bishop Noll Institute in Hammond, Indiana.

3/80–7/80
Worked with the head of Peace Corps' vocational education program to develop an extension of the program to develop an extension of the program in the direction of alternative technologies. Wrote a successful project proposal for funding.

6/78–3/80
Civil engineer in Peace Corps for the province of El-Kelaa-des-Sraghna, Morocco, attached to the Ministry of the Interior. Surveyed potential sites for schools and government buildings, monitored the quality of public

construction, designed the reinforced concrete for a mosque and public housing projects, and wrote the specifications for public housing projects.

Summers 1973–78
Carpentry and manual labor for Rueth Development Company, a residential builder in the Calumet region of northwestern Indiana.

PERSONAL DATA
—excellent health.
—interests include jazz, classical, and ragtime music; theater; basketball; martial arts; politics.
—single, willing to relocate.
Recommendations provided on request.
Office/Home Phone: 415-221-3759

Business Letter Writing

Sample of Business Letter

Below is a business letter that accompanied a resume. It is written in correct letter form and contains detailed information not available in the resume.

Raul Almaguer-Tapia
25-B Aggie Village South
Fort Collins, Colorado 80526
June 28, 1986

Graduate School
Colorado State University
Fort Collins, Colorado 80523

Dear Sir:

This is a summary of the activities in which I have been engaged since I graduated from San Luis Potosi University.

I became a Geological Engineer in June, 1980 at at San Luis Potosi University, San Luis Potosi, Mexico.

Afterward I worked for Compañia Minera Las Torres S.A. engaged in the following project:

From June 1980 to September 1985 I was in charge of the geologic works at the Cebada, Bolañitos, and Peregrina mines, Guanajuato District,

Mexico. Also my bachelor's thesis work was developed on the basis of an Economic Geology evaluation of the Peregrina Mine. Most of my work was related to the mining operation of the former mines, and also the exploration of new areas nearby.

From October, 1985 to January, 1986 I worked for Consejo de Recursos Minerales, searching for silver vein deposits in the El Maguey Project, Guanajuato District, Mexico. My work consisted of a systematic sampling of the entire mine, and diamond drill exploration.

In January, 1986 the Banco de Mexico sponsored me to study English at Colorado State University and afterward to take graduate courses in economic geology.

I plan to finish my Intensive English courses in August, and I would like to continue my studies in Economic Geology pursuing a degree of Master of Science. I would also appreciate advice as to what preparatory courses I may need before beginning work on the Master's.

Thank you very much,

Raul Almaguer-Tapia (Mexico)

Sample of Business Letter

Alvin Ludwick
1706 Durant
Berkeley, CA 94007
Phone: 415-221-3759
May 26, 1987

Mr. Gus Brest van Kempen
Skidmore, Owens, Merrill
33 W. Monroe
Chicago, Illinois 60603

Dear Sir,

I understand that you may be interested in finding a structural engineer who has a background in construction management to work in the Blida, Algeria office to assist in the supervision of the university and hospital construction. Steve Grassi, who is presently working on the project, informed me of the possibility of an opening. Steve is a good friend from our Peace Corps service in Morocco.

Two of my qualifications that may be of particular interest are my ability to speak French well and my previous work experience in Morocco. Some of my other qualifications may be found in the enclosed resume. I would also like to add that since I have been pursuing a masters program here at the University of California, Berkeley, I have taken advantage of the facilities to keep up with my language skills. I find overseas work very desirable, and I believe that I would really enjoy this project.

I am extremely interested in interviewing at your earliest convenience for this or a similar position. My present schedule is flexible, so I am amenable to any date or time you desire. For your convenience I have enclosed a self-addressed, stamped envelope. Thank you very much for your attention.

Sincerely,

Alvin J. Ludwick

Index

A

Abstract and concrete topics, 44
Abstracting journals, 149
  examples of, 149–51
  selected list of, 153–54
Although–because thesis, 92
Argumentative essay, 91
  alternative forms, 94
  generating materials for, 95–99
  logic in (*see* Logical fallacies)
  planning, 91–93
  possible structures, 93–95
  student samples, 103–08
Audience:
  expectations of, 2
  focus on, revision, 80

B

Bibliographic data, 160–61
  examples, 171–72
  and note-taking, 162–63
Body paragraphs:
  in the essay, 59
  outlining of, 56
Brainstorming, 19, 47–48
Business letters, 230–33

C

Card catalog:
  use of, 144–46
Cause-effect development, 38–40
Citation (*see* Documentation)
Classification development, 37–38
Clustering, 20
Coherence devices, 69
  paragraph hooks, 75–79
  pronouns, use of, 69
  repetition of key words, 69
  transitions, 70–72
Colons, use of, 207–08
Commas, use of, 202
Comparison-contrast development, 33–36
Computerized searching:
  advantages, 158
  examples, 157–60
  planning, 159
Conclusions, 59–61
Confusing words, 216–18
Contrast (*see* Comparison-contrast)
Controlling ideas, 10

D

Definition (*see* Extended definition)
Descriptors, 137
Developing ideas, 17
Diction, 214–16

Dissertation Abstracts, 157
Drafting the essay, 68
  (*see also* Revision)
Documentation:
  bibliography, 171–72
  footnotes, 169–70
  general formats, 72
  paraphrasing, 166–68
  quoting, 166–69
  references, 171–72
  uses, 165–68

E

Editing, 82–83, 220–23
Essay, the, 42
  body paragraphs in, 59
  conclusion to, 59–61
  drafting, 68
  introduction to, 57–59
  outlining, 52–56
  planning argumentation, 113–14
  schematic representation, 43
  selecting a topic, 43–44
  title, 45
Examples (for support), 24–25
Extended definition, 32–33

F

Facts (for support), 24–25
False authority (fallacy), 100
Flow charting, 23
Footnotes (*see also* Documentation)
Formats:
  argumentative-essay alternatives, 94
  field specific, research, 139–40
  general, for research paper, 133
  summary-analysis, alternatives, 123
  summary-analysis, general, 114–15
Fundamentals for logical analysis, 101

G

General and specific, 6
  (*see also* Subject and topic)
Generating strategies:
  for the argumentative essay, 95–97
  brainstorming, 19, 47–48
  clustering, 20
  flow charting, 23
  listing, 18
  outlining, 20–21
  questions, 45–47
  for the research paper, 133–35
  treeing, 21–22
Government documents, 156

H

Hasty generalization (fallacy), 99

I

Indexing journals, 148, 150–51
  examples of, 148–52
  Readers' Guide, the 146–48
  selected list of, 153–54
Intent (*see* Thesis Statement)
Introductions, 57–59

J

Journals (*see* Periodicals)

K

Key words and phrases in coherence, 69

L

Library:
  etiquette, 138
  going to, 135–36
Library exercises, 135–37, 140–41
Locating research materials, 145–46
Logical fallacies, 99–101
  false authority, 100
  hasty generalization, 99
  oversimplification, 100
  post hoc, 100
  red herring, 100
  statistics, 100–01
  stereotype, 100
  vice/virtue words, 101

M

Magazines (*see* Periodicals)
Master's Abstracts, 157
Methods of development, 30
  cause-effect, 38–40
  classification, 37–38
  comparison-contrast, 33–36
  extended definition, 32–33
  process, 30–31

N

Note-taking, notecards, 162–63

O

Opinion (*see* Thesis Statement)
Outlining:

complete body paragraph, 56
of the essay, 52–56
generating strategy, 20–21
point paragraph, 12
Oversimplification (fallacy), 100

P

Paragraph, the, 8
point paragraph, 12
process of writing, 14–15
Paragraph development (*see* Methods of development)
Paragraph hooks, 75–79
Paragraph organization (*see* Point paragraph)
Paragraph relationships, 51
Passive voice, 196–97
Peer evaluation exercise, 64–65
Peer revision checklist, 82
Periodicals:
    identifying and locating, 154–56
    Readers' Guide, the, 146–48
    using, 146
Personal experience (for support), 29
Persuasion, 88
    goals of, 89–90
Physical description (for support), 25–27
Plagiarism, 163–64
Point paragraph, 12
Post hoc fallacy, 100
Prepositions, 218–19
Prewriting (*see also* Generating strategies):
    for essays, 45–48
    for the research paper, 133–35
    strategies, 18–23
Process development, 30–31
Process of writing a paragraph, 14–15
Pronouns (in coherence), 69
Punctuation:
    colons, 202
    commas, 202
    quotation marks, 208–09
    semi-colons, 200–02

Q

Questions, generating strategy, 45–47
Quotation marks, 208–09

R

Readers' Guide, the, 146–48
Red herring (fallacy), 100
References (*see* Documentation)
Reliability of the writer, 90–91
Research materials:
    books, 144–46
    government documents, 156

periodicals, 154–56
Research paper, the, 128–29
    documentation, 165–72
    general format, 133
    generating strategies, 131–35
    going to the library, 135–36
    identifying descriptors, 137
    note-taking, 162–63
    prewriting, 133–35
    problems and solutions, 174–76
    sample pages, 177–92
    sample references, 192–94
    selecting a topic, 129–31
Résumés, 224–25
    samples, 226–30
Revision, 79
    process, 79–82
    peer revision checklist, 82
Revision checklist, 16

S

Sentence combining, 211–13
Sentence structure problems, 200–11
    coordinate conjunctions, 202–04
    dependent clauses, 204–05
    independent clauses, 200–01
    parallel structures, 210–11
    review, 205–06
    subordinating words, 204–06
Showing and telling, 3
Statement of intent, 49
Statement of opinion, 49
Statistics (fallacy), 100–01
Stereotype (fallacy), 100
Subject and topic, 8
Summary, 110–13
Summary-analysis essay, 109
    alternative forms for, 123
    general form for, 114–15
    planning, 113–14
    ratio of summary to analysis, 123–24, 126
Supporting techniques, 23
    examples, 28
    facts, 24–25
    personal experience, 29
    physical description, 29

T

Thesis statement, 48–49
    of intent, 50
    of opinion, 50
Titles, 45
Treeing, 21–22
Topic:
    abstract/concrete, 44
    organizing, 45
    for research, 129–30

selecting for the essay, 43–44
Topic sentence, 9
  writing a, 11
Transitions, 70–72
  cause-effect, 71
  chronological, 70
  comparison, 71
  concession, 72
  conclusion, 72

contrast, 71
middle paragraph, 71–72
spatial, 71

V

Verb problems, 195–99
Vice-virtue words, 101